MIAMI ROAD

A SON'S MEMOIR

JERRY KIRSHENBAUM

GLENDALE HOUSE BOOKS

Miami Road: A Son's Memoir

Published by Glendale House Books
New York, NY

Copyright ©2025 by Jerry Kirshenbaum. All rights reserved.

No part of this book may be reproduced in any form or by any mechanical means, including information storage and retrieval systems without permission in writing from the publisher/author, except by a reviewer who may quote passages in a review.

All images, logos, quotes, and trademarks included in this book are subject to use according to trademark and copyright laws of the United States of America.

ISBN: 979-8-9987579-0-7 (paperback)
ISBN: 979-8-9987579-2-1 (ebook)

BIOGRAPHY & AUTOBIOGRAPHY / Memoirs
BIOGRAPHY & AUTOBIOGRAPHY / Jewish
BIOGRAPHY & AUTOBIOGRAPHY / Cultural & Regional

Cover by Lisa Schwebke.
Interior design by Bryan Canter.

All rights reserved by Jerry Kirshenbaum and Glendale House Books.

Contents

1. Mook — 1
2. Wyatt Earpszki — 13
3. "It Was All Funny" — 24
4. Milton Kramer — 38
5. Roosevelt Road — 50
6. Relathieves — 64
7. Peeling Onions — 75
8. Goo-Goo Eyes — 86
9. Sleeping With Cats — 100
10. Educated Fools — 114
11. Laryngitis — 131
12. Beware Of The Yarmulkes — 142
13. Three Boutonnieres — 157
14. Master Class — 178
15. Two Bobbies — 198
16. Loose Lips — 211
17. Molotovs and Von Ribbentrops — 238
18. Taphephobia — 251
19. Punchlines — 265
20. "I Get No Complaints" — 277
    Epilogue — 295

    Acknowledgments — 301

Chapter 1

Mook

WE WERE TALKING MEANDERINGLY ABOUT other things, my father and I, when he asked, out of the blue and beyond strangely, "What's a headache feel like?" Tossed off in that oh-by-the-way manner of his, the question sounded like the start of another of his jokes, but you couldn't be sure. Many decades past young and still sharp of mind and tongue, Dad was a kidder, but a sly kidder, nothing like those laugh riots who tug at your elbow and assault you with, "Have you heard the one about....?" He was too cagey and laid-back for that sort of thing. His humor was of the dry-wit variety, and he picked his spots. He slayed you softly, his quips rays of sunlight peeking through the dark clouds of his life.

Some of his witticisms were of his devising, others were poached. He wasn't above borrowing *shtick* from one or another of the great Jewish comedians he admired — if not Shecky, Rodney; if not Rodney, Henny; if not Henny, Myron; so forth and so on — but the similarities between the jests of those esteemed philosophers of our ancient people and his own funny business made it hard to assign ownership. In the most conspicuous blurring of the lines, the battle of the sexes was a laugh-getting staple for the professional jokesters, and it was for my father too.

"My wife and I have gone 34 rounds, and I keep waiting for my corner to throw in the towel," he liked to say, adjusting the figure for the number of years — there would be a knee-buckling 60 in all — that he and Mom had been exchanging haymakers. "The missus and I don't gee and haw," he also declared, invoking the commands for making a team of draft horses turn right (gee) or left (haw) in unison. Of the business demands that got him out of the house in the mornings and away from Mother, he pleaded, "My days are fine. I just need a night job."

Even when he clearly was disinterring a rib-tickler from the Jewish joke graveyard, it was understood that the all too real difficulties in his marriage left him no choice. "Everywhere my wife and I go, we hold hands. If we ever let go, we'd kill each other," went one such exhumation, dead-panned by him as original truth.

But there were moments, and this revealed itself to be one of them, when you thought my father had a joke up his sleeve, and his sleeves were empty. His face, on inspection, wore the furrowed-brow look of dilemma. Lately more than ever, he seemed to be hearing people complain of migraines and other head throbs, and he was uncertain if he'd ever experienced such discomfort in his own noggin. What, he truly was asking, did one of those afflictions feel like?

And strange to say, I can't rule out the possibility that my father had made it into his 80s headache-free. He was, after all, a medical anomaly. When he entered a drugstore, it was usually only to pick up something for Mother. Steering a path through the over-the-counter aisles where the analgesics, vitamins and cough suppressants were shelved, he was the picture of spousal dutifulness, puzzling over the list in his hand of the curatives his wife required. He seldom visited those precincts for himself, or the pharmacy counter either. Other oldsters deposited pills in packets arranged by the days of the week and subdivided into morning and night, but my father was neither pill counter nor pill swallower.

Come to think of it, I can't remember his ever taking an aspirin. I mention this because of the possible relevance to the matter under consideration: his question about headaches.

He had a trove of pet sayings. "Life is sweet as long as you have your health," was one of them. That of course isn't always true. One can be fit as a Stradivarius, but any number of unwelcome occurrences — financial ruin, loss of a loved one, the horrors of war — can take away life's sweetness. Be that as it may, until not long before he died — officially at 94, although he may have been two or three years older — Milton Kirshenbaum had his health.

You had only to look at him to tell. His skin was impossibly smooth, and his hair, even when it turned gray and then white, both more or less on schedule, remained forever full. He never looked his age except at bedtime, when he removed his dentures, which glowered shark-like in a glass of Polident-treated water on the nightstand. At such moments, cheeks hollow and gums bare, he was almost unrecognizable. Once, in my presence, somebody made bold to ask him if he had his own teeth. "I paid for them, if that's what you mean," he replied.

What few health issues he had were structural. He underwent two surgeries, one for a hernia, the other a late-in-life hip replacement when his purposeful gait began to falter. One of his shoulders was said to be slightly lower than the other, a defect discernible only to tailors measuring him for suits. The adjustment must have been easy to make because he looked snappy in suits, although he wore them only when the occasion demanded. "My Sunday-go-to-meetin' clothes," he called those get-ups, as distinct from "glad rags," his term for women's finery.

Most of the time, though, he dressed down. He toiled in a dusty, gritty business — the buying and selling of used burlap and cotton bags — and his principal recreation was poker, which he played two, three, even four nights a week in rooms thick with cigar and cigarette smoke. One venue was the basement of one of the regulars, a sanctum known as The Pit. My father was reputed to be a killer poker player. As a child, I imagined him emerging from the depths of The Pit weighed down by his winnings and wearing the Dale Earnhardt cap somebody gave him. The cap was black, with an image of NASCAR champ Earnhardt, arms raised in triumph, against the backdrop of a checkered flag. Dad wasn't into stock car racing, but he thought the cap went smartly with his workday and poker-night ensembles, and he wore it for years.

Before me is a batch of black-and-white photos I took of my father time-stamped APR 73. In the first of them, he's standing outside a brick building, a cigar clenched in his mouth. His pants are baggy. Three ballpoint pens nose out of the pocket of a checkered woolen shirt. Over the shirt is an unzipped windbreaker. He has luxuriant sideburns, which will soon disappear because at this moment in the history of men's tonsorial fashion, the Elvis influence is growing tiresome. The front end of a truck is visible. At any time, my father owned two or three trucks — not 18-wheeler rigs but "straight jobs," smaller vehicles consisting of cabs with fixed cargo containers. The sides of each of his trucks bore the names, in red block letters with white shadow accents, of his company and the cherished Lake Michigan metropolis in which I was born and raised.

HARBOR BAG CO.
BENTON HARBOR, MICHIGAN

It also says Harbor Bag Co. above the entrance to the building, at 226 Riford Street in an industrial section of Benton Harbor. Other photos take us inside the building. As a print journalist *(Minneapolis Tribune, Time, Sports Illustrated)* dating to the Neolithic pre-Internet age, I'd be derelict if I didn't undertake to describe the scene. My father is in his office, leaning back in his desk chair, looking unfazed by the disarray around him. Scraps of paper are strewn on the floor, and sequoia-size rolls of white paper of unknown purpose are heaped on a couch, rendering it unavailable for taking a nap or even for sitting. A huge black safe occupies a corner of the room, and scores of flattened cartons, a commodity Dad trafficked in as a sideline to his bag business (he also dabbled in bushel baskets, making him a triple-threat container merchant), are bunched every which way along the walls. A chest of drawers is buried under more cartons. From the top drawer a grayish gunnysack dangles to the floor, looking like a backwoodsman's beard.

On the desk are two rumpled men's hats, a phone book, a roll of tape, note pads, scattered slips of paper, a black rotary phone and four ashtrays, two begging to be emptied, the other two at the ready. Windows allow dust-refracted light to seep into the room through Venetian blinds. A sewing machine stool is overturned on the floor behind the desk, and a broken chair blocks a door to what may be a closet. Another door, this one to the office bathroom, is ajar, but we can't see inside, sparing us a frightful sight. Several times Mom, armed with her arsenal of soap powders, brushes and bleaches, came to clean the sink and toilet, but it was a Sisyphean task, too much even for her heroic efforts.

Some items are missing. Gone are the unread copies of *The Wall Street Journal* that once piled high on the desk. My father subscribed to the *Journal* because as a businessman he thought he should, and even after he realized the paper wasn't for him, he took forever to cancel his subscription. Absent, too, is the calendar on the wall with the Marilyn Monroe nude photo that was the centerfold of the first issue of Hugh Hefner's *Playboy*. My father had a supply of these calendars made up with Harbor Bag Co. imprinted on them to give out. When I was little, I sneaked glances at the one on the wall, but I knew better than to rely on it either as representative of what the average woman looked like or as an accurate indication of the date. The calendar remained in place for the better part of a decade, stuck on the same month and year, Marilyn never aging or catching cold.

As the office untidiness suggests, my father wasn't an inside man. He made his living on the road. He dipped a toe in the financial markets — I regularly checked the stock listings to see how his Campbell Soup and International Telephone and Telegraph shares were doing — but with modest success. "I made money the hard way," he said with a mixture of pride and resignation. Other than to sign the paychecks for his employees — the longest-serving were three men, Slow, Shorty and Brownie, and a woman, Willie, all African Americans — he used the office mainly to make phone calls and shoot the breeze with visitors.

I was there, age nine or 10, one day after school when Allen

Denn, who was in the business of distributing seafood to area restaurants, entered, preceded, as the joke goes, by his stomach. Mr. Denn was shaped like a globe that was mostly equator. Dad was happy to see him. "Allen," he said, "pull up a couple of chairs and sit down."

Next thing I knew, they were deep into gin rummy, another card game my father played. Making room for the deck of cards and a pad for keeping score, he cleared a corner of the desk with a sweep of a forearm, sending scraps of paper floating to the floor. To occupy my time in such contingencies, I usually had with me a paperback novel or magazine — in autumn, say, Street & Smith's college basketball preview issue. But I must have been growing restless and Dad would be a while because when the last hand was played, it was arranged that Mr. Denn would give me a lift home.

Like Dad's trucks, the van waiting outside had words printed on it, in this case CAPTAIN DAN'S FISH MARKET, UNION PIER, MICHIGAN. Seated next to Captain Dan, I saw that the bottom half of the steering wheel had been sawed off to allow it to clear his stomach. He had me home in no time, but the odor of fish lingered. And to think this was only the five Great Lakes. I couldn't imagine what the Seven Seas smelled like.

MY FATHER ARRIVED in the U.S. from the Old Country as a toddler. His birth name of Schmul was discarded, and he was fleetingly called Samuel, the Anglicized version of Schmul, before being given the name for keeps of a slightly older cousin: Milton. He also received the cousin's nickname: Mook. The namesake boys were separated by a single letter in their surnames. The other Mook's wing of the family was Kirschenbaum. Our branch was Kirshenbaum, absent the "c." Looseness with nomenclature is common in immigrant families like ours. In Europe, our forebears sometimes spelled the name Kirszhenbaum, Kerszenbaum and other variations, but the "z's" fell overboard during the Atlantic crossing.

I don't know the meaning of Mook, and my father didn't know either. To his pals, he was Mook or Mookie. To Mom, he was Milt. Some women playfully called him Milty. One of my girl cousins called him Uncle Milky, which gave everybody a laugh. To me, he was Daddy, then Dad, sometimes Pop or Pops. When I was making fancy, I addressed him as Father.

This is a father-son story in which the son has by far the easier row to hoe. At times I cut away to tell of goings-on in my life, with its manifold pleasures and manageable missteps, and of happenings in Benton Harbor, which in its glory years was more fun than a mid-sized Midwestern town had any right to be, but my father is central to the narrative. He's either present or just around the corner and soon to reappear, his influence felt all the while.

The arc of his life is familiar in the Jewish memoir genre — begins life in an Eastern European *shtetl*, suffers severe privations, makes a go of it in the New World — but he differentiated himself from the up-by-the-bootstraps herd by the steeliness, good humor and equanimity with which he contended with family sorrow and upheaval that would have toppled the less sure-footed. He was a role model for me and would have been even more of one if his example of calm and fortitude had been humanly possible to emulate.

Yet his indomitability occupies only one side of the balance scale on which he is to be measured. On the other side are his devilish, contrarian nature and the rough edges he never completely smoothed over. Not to forget, as if one could, the yarns, pearls of wisdom and wisecracks with which he entertained, instructed and alternately soothed and maddened. He spoke his mind, and his words were both heeded and winced at. If I can apply a lofty term to so grounded a character, he was of the oral tradition.

His life spanned most of the 20th Century (b. circa 1906, d. 2000). His birthdate and paternal lineage are uncertain, which casts into question my grandpaternal lineage. He was the third of six children, following two sisters who emigrated with him to the U.S., my aunts Dorothy and Frieda, the latter not to be confused with my mother, another Frieda. Like my father, the older sisters made it into their 90s, Dorothy to 95, Frieda to 98. The U.S.-born siblings died younger — Abe 87, Rose 86, Hymie 74 — but they all were cigarette smokers and contracted emphysema, whereas Dorothy and Frieda avoided tobacco while my father stuck to his cigars, which he didn't smoke so much as chew. His La Palinas came in a box bearing the illustration of a veiled Spanish-looking woman and the word *excellente*. When I was a tyke, after Dad removed a cigar from the box, I liked to slip the paper cigar band onto my ring finger to see how long I could keep it from breaking.

In his early years my father spoke, dreamed and cussed in Yiddish — what the Nobel Prize-winning Yiddish novelist Isaac Bashevis Singer called "the language of exile." As a youth, Pop was both idler and go-getter, at first more the former than the latter, later the reverse. In time, financial rewards came his way. Many early Jewish immigrants were scavengers, peddling rags, scrap metal, bolts of cloth and pots and pans from pushcarts and horse-drawn carriages. Dad, scavenging at a later date, had his trucks for transporting the used produce bags that were his stock-in-trade.

For him the path from buying low to selling high was often circular. Farmers, after taking their apples, potatoes, onions, cucumbers, tomatoes and soybeans to market, were left with empty bags, which were dirty and often torn. Dad bought and reconditioned the bags, then sold them, often to the same parties from whom he purchased them. He also did business with food processing plants, flour mills, flood-control agencies and tree nurseries. From boisterous Benton Harbor in the southwestern corner of Michigan next to its smaller, better-behaved Twin City of St. Joseph, he traversed Michigan's Lower Peninsula, Illinois, Indiana and occasionally as far away as western Ohio and eastern Iowa.

When business was good, he employed other drivers, but he always drove one truck himself. On the road, he faced temptation. I read that if an early peddler didn't own a horse and carriage, those could be rented for a dollar a day plus 50 cents for feed for the horse. This factoid jumped out at me because I remembered Dad telling of a hotel in Huntington, Indiana, where the services rendered were scaled the same: the hotel charged a dollar a night for the room and would send a woman up for 50 cents more.

WHEN MY FATHER asked what a headache felt like, he should have been more specific. There are literal headaches, but there also are figurative headaches. The figurative headaches are what the Jewish people call *tsuris*. We have a saying about *tsuris*, as we do about everything in life. "Don't worry about tomorrow," we say. "Who knows what will befall us today?"

Tsuris was something Mook knew well.

My mother was a high achiever but brittle. She cried a lot

and had screaming jags that came on unpredictably and in time all too predictably. Dad tried to jolly her out of her pinwheeling moods, calling her "dearie" or "sweetie." When it worked, they hugged, and he said, "Stay as sweet as you are right now, dearie." Other times his efforts at amelioration failed. I hated Mom's hysterics. If her screaming was directed at me, I screamed back. With Mother, Dad did some jollying. To me he counseled, "I worry about your temper, Jerry. Always be slow to anger." My father issued many life lessons. Be slow to anger was one of them.

I'm one of three children — Roberta, or Bobbie, the oldest; me six years her junior; Joel six years younger still, a spacing of ages more orderly than anything else that can be said about our family. Bobbie had a congenital heart condition. She also was retarded (the word then in currency) and at 13 was diagnosed with Juvenile, or Type 1, diabetes. The burden of dealing with this extraordinary constellation of ills fell largely on Mom. She administered Bobbie's daily insulin shots; weighed her food in grams on the metal scale on the kitchen counter next to the Mixmaster and the electric can opener; tracked her sugar levels by dipping a specially-coated strip in her urine and watching the strip change colors, blue meaning no worries for the moment, green signaling uh-oh; handled arrangements for the historic heart surgery Bobbie underwent at Johns Hopkins Hospital in Baltimore; and found the special-needs schools that her daughter attended. My mother discharged these tasks tirelessly but not uncomplainingly. My father's roles were to pay the steep bills for my sister's care and deal with his wife's outbursts, which he did with an unflappability that defied understanding.

Dinnertime scene: Mother is in the kitchen preparing a meal with all the fixings — everything from soup to nuttiness.

The potatoes are on the stove, the brisket is in the oven, Frieda is on the warpath. Serving the meal, she slams the dishes on the table with such force I'm afraid they'll shatter. She won't be joining us for dinner tonight. With sobs, gasps and shrieks, she rushes to the bedroom, slamming the door behind her.

My father places a napkin on his lap and positions his knife and fork. "One thing about her, she always puts a meal on the table," he says.

"How can you stand this?" I ask.

"When you take those vows...."

His voice trails off and he starts to eat.

———

As children, my brother and I heard picaresque stories about our father — born in a distant and hostile land, kicked out of home as a boy in his new country, waylaid by mobsters as a taxi driver in Chicago, double-teamed in a dirty-tricks business rivalry with his two brothers, and more. Joel and I thought our father's life was an open book, but we were wrong. Only as adults did we learn of a burglary he committed that was too tragic in an immediate consequence — another man's wife shot to death in his arms — to be fully mitigated by how young he was when it happened.

Chapter 2

Wyatt Earpszki

A MONUMENT on Ellis Island bears the name of a man who may or may not be my paternal grandfather. This man and the 800,000 other people memorialized on the American Immigrant Wall of Honor — a circular assemblage of stainless-steel panels in a grove next to the Ellis Island National Museum of Immigration — are recognized not for any wondrous deeds they may have performed, nor did all of them necessarily come through Ellis Island. Indeed, my could-be grandfather was a man of modest achievement who first stepped ashore in the United States in Philadelphia. For an immigrant to be immortalized on the Wall of Honor, there is but one strictly pecuniary requirement: that a contribution ($100 when the wall was created in 1990, now $225) be made to the museum in one's honor. My possibly-not grandfather's name is seen — on Panel 223 — thanks to Dad's brother Abe, who paid the requisite fee and provided the information found on the Ellis Island website.

In memory of
MENDEL KIRSHENBAUM
Donated by
ABE KIRSHENBAUM
Country of origin
SOVIET UNION

The words on Abe Kirshenbaum's tombstone in Benton Harbor's B'nai Sholom cemetery read BELOVED FATHER. HUSBAND. SCHOLAR. but since I never heard Uncle Abe referred to as a scholar while he was alive, I regard one-third of this inscription as posthumous résumé inflation. Like my father and other members of their scrappy generation, Abie, as he was diminutively called, was endowed with street smarts that my cousins, when planning their father's headstone, may have mistaken for erudition. Whatever they imagined Abe's field of scholarship to be, I trust it wasn't 19th Century European history, because the information he imparted to Ellis Island is in error. Mendel Kirshenbaum's country of origin wasn't the Soviet Union, which at the time of his birth in 1873 didn't yet exist. Mendel originated, as it were, in Poland, which was then part of the Russian Empire, a different kettle of carp than the nation of Lenin and Stalin that thundered to life in 1922. Abie was off by nearly half a century.

The Kirshenbaum ancestral home — and my father's birthplace — is the Polish hamlet of Radziłów, which lies 100 miles northeast of Warsaw, near the city of Bialystok hard by the border of Belarus. At the time of Dad's birth, Radziłów had some 2,000 residents, nearly half of them Jews. This part of Poland, along with Belarus, Moldova, Ukraine, the Baltic states and western Russia, was within the Pale of Settlement, a swath of territory to which Jews were confined by czarist fiat and restricted to menial trades. Jews could be butchers, harness makers, shopkeepers and laborers, but professions like medicine, banking and the law were closed to them.

Mendel Kirshenbaum was a blacksmith, although one wouldn't have guessed it to look at him. Unlike the village smithy extolled by Longfellow as a mighty man with arms like iron bands, Mendel was thin and lacked brawn. Furthermore, being a man of piety, he was as likely to be found bent in study over the Talmud as in toil over the anvil.

On March 17, 1899, in "the synagogue of Radziłów," Mendel married Gitla Bursztyn, also known as Gittel, and who, in the U.S., would sometimes go by Gertrude. About her, there is no doubt: She is my grandmother. Gitla's mother, Rochla, was deceased, but her father, Chaim, was in attendance, as were Mendel's parents, Aron and Dwejra. The wedding ceremony was performed by Rabbi Jankel Wegdenbaum, an eminence in his 80th year. In a world in which couples customarily married young to get a jump on fulfilling the Biblical commandment to go forth and multiply, Mendel and Gitla, both in their late 20s, must have seemed almost as ancient as Rabbi Wegdenbaum.

In Radziłów as elsewhere in the Russian Empire, Jews were subjected to murderous pogroms, and the men faced conscription in the Czar's army, where they suffered abuse and humiliation. Never have the cruelties visited on *shtetl* Jews been more succinctly recounted than by the Austrian Jewish author Joseph Roth: "Their Christian neighbors threaten them. The local squires beat them. The official has them locked up. The army officer fires his gun at them with impunity. The dog barks at them because their garb seems to provoke animal and primitive people alike."

The years between 1880 and 1910 saw some two million Eastern European Jews emigrate to the United States, most of them downtrodden and desperate for a better life. The first family member to join this wave of strivers and disaffected was Mendel's younger brother, Samuel Kirschenbaum, representing the "c" branch of the family. In 1895, 19-year-old Sam left Radziłów and found his way to Chicago, where he would operate bakeries on the West Side, first at 14th and Halsted, then in the 3400 block of Roosevelt Road. At each location, the family lived above the shop, making it convenient for Sam's wife, Kadie, and their five children — one of them the original Milton/Mook — to help prepare muffins, cakes and other baked goods downstairs.[1]

Nine years after his brother's departure, it was Mendel's turn to undertake the journey. He traveled alone to Liverpool and sailed on a Philadelphia-bound American steamship, *SS Merion*, which would be stranded off the Grand Banks of Newfoundland because of fog. The ship arrived, two days behind schedule, on December 28, 1904, depositing Mendel and 700 other passengers on Philadelphia's Pier 53. Mendel followed Sam to Chicago and found employment with a bedspring manufacturer, an enterprise involving metalwork for which a blacksmith proficient at forging and casting may have been suited.

Left behind in Radziłów were Mendel's two or three children. The hedge is necessitated by uncertainty about whether my father was Mendel's son. While Dwoire and Freide —

---

[1]. A knack for the creation of confections ran in the family. Kadie's sister Edie married another Polish Jewish immigrant, Harry Baskin, and raised a family with him in Streator, Ill. Edie and Harry's son Burt Baskin partnered with his brother-in-law Irv Robbins to create Baskin-Robbins, which grew into a global colossus of 5,000 ice cream shops.

Aunts Dorothy and Frieda — had assuredly been born by the time Mendel left Poland, my father's date of birth has resisted efforts to pin down. When Mendel departed Radziłów, Dad may have been months, weeks or days old, or Gitla could have been pregnant with him. Another possibility cannot be ruled out: that he was born later, sired by another man. All we can be certain of is that a great many bedsprings needed to be assembled before Mendel had the means to send for Gitla; further, that she now had in her care Schmul in addition to his two older sisters.

When Mendel left Poland, he and Gitla had been married five years. They spent the next three years an ocean apart. Finally, Grandma and her children, ages five, four and anybody's guess, traveled to Bremen, Germany, like Liverpool a major European port of embarkation for Atlantic crossings, and boarded a U.S.-bound German liner, *Kronprinzessin Cecille*. They would live out their days in the United States, as would the ship that carried them. Seized by the U.S. Navy from Germany in World War I, *Kronprinzessin Cecille* was known as the *SS Mount Vernon* until it was scrapped in 1940.

Unlike Mendel, Grandma and children came through Ellis Island, arriving on that hallowed speck of land in Upper New York Harbor on December 4, 1907. Aboard *Kronprinzessin Cecille*, to be buried in California, was the body of the celebrated American dancer known as Papinta, who had died at age 30 of "apoplexy" — the word at the time for a stroke — during a performance on stage in Düsseldorf. Among passengers still drawing breath was Baron von Itterson of the Netherlands, who lost $1,600 in a marathon on-board poker game to Burt Goldy, real name Boro Goldblatt. On arrival in New York, Goldy would be arrested at the Waldorf Astoria Hotel on the baron's complaint that he'd been swindled. Grandma Kirshenbaum, traveling with her three children, one of them himself a future poker player, doubtlessly was unaware of the alleged fleecing going on in surroundings far superior — high deck, plush furnishings, fresh ocean breezes — to the steerage quarters to which she and her brood were consigned.

The ship delivering my father to America docked on a blustery New York City morning, temperature in the 30s. Gitla and children were processed in Ellis Island's massive Registry Hall beneath a large overhead U.S. flag newly stitched with a 47th star marking the admission to statehood of Oklahoma 19 days earlier. Three years almost to the day after Mendel's arrival in Philadelphia, Schmul's age was entered in an Ellis Island logbook as "1y 6m." If this was accurate, Mendel couldn't have been Mook's father or my grandfather.

Could the entry have been wrong? If so, the mistake wouldn't have been Ellis Island's alone. That Schmul was 1y 6m first appeared, denoted in the same bureaucratic shorthand, on *Kronprinzessin Cecille's* manifest, then was repeated at Ellis Island, where officials routinely relied on ship records for immigrants' ages, name spellings and other basic information. It can be theorized that Dad was older than 18 months, his age fudged to secure whatever break was afforded the youngest children on Atlantic crossings. Arguing against this thesis, however, is the likelihood that agents of North German Lloyd, *Kronprinzessin Cecille's* shipping line, would have been on guard against attempted fare beating.

In any case, Ellis Island officials had more important worries than this or that child's age. They were too busy rooting out Bolsheviks, anarchists, prostitutes, polygamists and others for whom the Statue of Liberty lowered her torch. Additionally, doctors at Ellis Island watched for arrivals with disqualifying diseases like cholera and tuberculosis. For their part, immigrants presented fake documents, suppressed telltale coughs and pulled other fast ones to avoid detection. Processing as many as 6,000 newcomers a day amid shouting, pleading and weeping, harried immigration officials relying on translators in a dozen languages made snap decisions about who should or shouldn't be waved through — a scene suggesting a running of the bulls at the Tower of Babel.

Grandma and her children made it through the heaven-hell of Ellis Island and joined Mendel in Chicago. In his book *On the Trail of the Immigrant*, Edward A. Steiner, a Hungarian Jewish author who himself had emigrated to the U.S. (and converted to Christianity), imagines such a moment as one of untrammeled joy. "Jacob meets his Leah," Steiner writes, "for whom he has toiled and suffered these five years, for whose sake he ate hard rye bread and onions that he might save money to bring her to him — when Jacob meets his Leah, there are warm embraces and kisses through the tears. Here, men embrace and kiss each other, and children are held up to the father's gaze — fathers who left them as infants and now see them grown."

Like the fictional Jacob, Mendel likely scrimped and saved to bring Gitla and the children to him. When little Schmul was held up to his gaze, did Mendel beam with joy at the sight of a child he had no reason to question was his? Or was his visage darkened by the realization that to save face and preserve a life with Gitla, he from this day forward would pass off as his eldest son a boy he knew or suspected was fathered by another man?

Opportunity would arise far in the future for Grandma Kirshenbaum, there being no better source to seek out on the matter, to address the question of my father's paternity. Three years after Mendel's death, my father, in his 50s, got around to seeking U.S. citizenship papers. In 1911, while living in Chicago, Mendel had been naturalized as a citizen, which by law conferred citizenship on his foreign-born children, but it had to be shown that Mook was his child. To that end, Dad's younger sister, Rose, took my elderly grandmother to the Berrien County courthouse in St. Joseph to provide a sworn statement. According to Aunt Rose, an impertinent functionary asked Grandma point-blank if she had experienced intimate relations with anyone other than her husband, to which she replied, "Von man, dot's enough." Rose told it that way, exaggerated accent and all. Grandma's interrogator buckled, and it was accepted that Dad was Mendel Kirshenbaum's son. However, somebody was too quick with the rubber stamp and too careless with the math, because the citizenship papers my father received as a result of that acceptance bear a birthdate of February 12, 1906, which was 14 months after Mendel took leave of Gitla in Radziłów. In other words, the document certifying that my father was Mendel Kirshenbaum's son provides evidence indicating that he was no such thing.

Meaning no disrespect to my grandmother, I note that saying "one man is enough" isn't the same as simply saying no. I raise the possibility that a young woman living for three years without knowing if she would see her husband again could have been driven by loneliness and despair into another man's arms. Alternatively, such a woman could have been taken advantage of. Was my biological grandfather a Polish peasant? A marauding Cossack? A Jewish bounder who seized that which wasn't his?

I picture Radziłów as a Polish Deadwood. Women in bonnets and long dresses and black-garbed men emerge from houses and shops, attracted by the ruckus in the street. There are whispers that the commotion has to do with the terrible thing that happened to the poor woman with the two little ones and a third on the way. The crowd watches as suspects are taken on horse-drawn carriages that clip-clop to the hoosegow, where the chief lawman, Wyatt Earpszki, stages a lineup, hoping to bring to justice the no-goodnik who did the woman wrong. Alas, no positive identification can be made.

For Christmas one year, my wife, Susan, and I received Ancestry DNA kits as gifts. Ordinarily I'm less desirous of finding new relatives than I am of offloading some I already have, but I thought that through DNA testing, I might solve the mystery of Mook's paternal pedigree. Following instructions, I spat into the provided vial and mailed off the sample. By the miracles of expectoration and DNA analysis, my family tree sprouted new branches and twigs populated by individuals said to be my third, fourth, even fifth cousins. Many of these heretofore unknown kin were on my mother's side, and to the extent that I was able to make sense of the centimorgans and segments employed for establishing genetic connections, none on the Kirshenbaum side linked me to Mendel independently of Grandma, with whom it was certain I had a biological bond.

There are reasons besides a ship manifest and Ellis Island logbook to question whether my father was of legitimate birth. Of the three Kirshenbaum brothers, only Mook was kicked out of the house at a tender age by Mendel, who never stopped favoring the other two, Hymie and Abe, over him. Also to be considered are physical characteristics. Where Hymie and Abe shared Mendel's lean build and swarthiness, Mook was of softer construction and fairer-skinned. Shown side-by-side photos of my father and Mendel, people shake their heads and say, "I just don't see it."

My father's official birthdate of February 12, 1906, puts his conception five months after Mendel departed Poland. The date was conferred on him when he was a child, perhaps to give him the same birthday as another individual of humble beginnings, Abraham Lincoln. But it also could be that the date was chosen to be as accurate as possible, regardless of the uncomfortable implications.

A verifiable birthdate for my father became my holy grail. I combed the genealogical records at the Center for Jewish History in New York City and checked and rechecked the JRI-Poland online database thinking I might have missed something or that the database had been updated with new information. I reached out to the Polish Institute for Jewish History in Warsaw, where a researcher, Anna Przybyszewska Drozd, located Mendel and Gitla's wedding certificate, the details of which I've shared in this chapter, but couldn't find a birth record for Schmul. I asked Ms. Drozd if a birth certificate could have been destroyed in a pogrom or the Holocaust, but she thought that in a backwater like Radziłów, one probably never existed.

And there matters stand. February 12, 1906, was the birthdate on my father's citizenship papers, driver's license, passport and every other document that called for a DOB, and it's a date my brother and I had no choice but to put on his tombstone in B'nai Sholom Cemetery.

MILTON KIRSHENBAUM
BELOVED HUSBAND & FATHER
FEB. 12, 1906-APR. 3, 2000

Considering the setting, one might think this the final say on the matter, but just as the word *scholar* on Uncle Abe's nearby grave marker doesn't mean he matriculated at Oxford, neither can it be written in stone that Dad's birthdate is February 12, 1906 — even if it *is* written in stone.

Mook and Mendel never got along. "We have no use for

each other," my father said many times and in many ways. For that reason, he might have been happy to learn that somebody else — anybody else — was his birth father. But I think he would have laughed at me for going to such lengths trying to find his birthdate. I can imagine him saying, in his insouciant way, "What does it matter when I was born? I'm here, aren't I?"

Mook grew up being told that Mendel was his father and unquestioningly addressed him as "Pa." Similarly, to me Mendel was Grandpa. That's how I referred to him when talking with any of my 14 Kirshenbaum cousins, and it's what I won't hesitate to call him when it's convenient for me to do so in the pages that follow. Still, I can't help wondering if those 14 are only my half-cousins.

Chapter 3

"It Was All Funny"

MENDEL — that is to say, Grandpa — suffered from asthma and thought the open spaces of rural Michigan would be beneficial to his health, but his decision to become a farmer was audacious. Jews in the Pale of Settlement generally had been forbidden to own land, with the result, observed Joseph Roth, that "the majority don't understand the soil that feeds them."

This was a shortcoming that the Jewish Agricultural Society set out to correct. Created in 1900 by a fund underwritten by Baron Moritz von Hirsch, a German Jewish financier and philanthropist, the Society assisted Jewish immigrants to America who wished to escape the teeming big-city tenements and become farmers. It provided low-interest loans, discounts on fertilizer, seed and tractors, and instruction on farming techniques. In 1900, by one estimate, there were 200 Jewish farmers in the U.S. By 1923, that number had swollen to nearly 75,000. The Jewish Agricultural Society was in no small part responsible for the explosive increase.

The countryside across Lake Michigan from Chicago was fertile ground for Baron von Hirsch's efforts. Truck farming for vegetables flourished in Southwestern Michigan, but fruit was king. The area was long known as "The Fruit Belt." With rich sandy-loam soil and breezes off Lake Michigan that kept growing seasons long and productive, orchards and fields on the lake's eastern shore yielded a bounty of pears, peaches, apples, melons, berries and cherries. The beating heart of this fruit-growing Eden was Benton Harbor. What made it so, besides the abundance of fruit farms thereabouts, was the Benton Harbor Fruit Market, said to be the largest non-citrus fruit exchange in the world. Located a few blocks from Benton Harbor's downtown retail nexus, the 15-acre "cash to growers" market was jammed on summer days with farmers clamorously bringing their produce for sale. Laden with bushel baskets, cartons and bags packed with freshly picked fruit, trucks were massed at the market seven wide and a dozen deep. No sooner did one truckload of fruit arrive than out went another, to be transported by road, ship and rail to points throughout the Midwest and beyond.

With the Jewish Agricultural Society standing by to help, the *Forverts* (*The Forward*), *Daily Jewish Courier* and other Yiddish-language newspapers in Chicago — there were racks of them on the city's newsstands in the first years of the 20th Century — carried ads offering farmland in Benton Harbor and nearby communities such as Cassopolis, Bangor, Eau Claire and Dowagiac. Everything was in place for Grandpa and Grandma Kirshenbaum, so recently transplanted from Poland, to experience another uprooting. In 1912, for $8,500 in borrowed money, they bought a 75-acre spread on the southeastern edge of Benton Harbor.[1]

---

1. They purchased the farm from Jacob Miller and his wife, Lena. Seven months earlier, the property had been the scene of a tragic accident. Jacob and

By the time the Kirshenbaums arrived, there were some 50 other Jewish farm families in the Benton Harbor area, with more to come. Like Mendel and Gitla, most of the settlers were religiously orthodox. They shopped for their rabbinically approved meat at Barney Alberts's kosher butcher shop on Wall Street and worshiped at Ohava Sholem synagogue on Highland Avenue, where the women sat upstairs while the men, freed from weaker-sex distraction, *davened* in the sanctuary below, their bodies bobbing in movements choreographed, it was easy to believe, by God Himself.

Benton Harbor's Jewish farmers formed the nucleus of what would become an unusually large and vibrant Jewish community for an average Midwestern town. Few second-generation family members would work the land as their elders did, but many remained in Benton Harbor and made their mark in other walks of life. Our family dentist, Sid Berliner, hailed from a farm family, as did lawyer Seymour Zaban, clothiers Dave Pollyea and Oscar Hennes and other Benton Harbor professional people and merchants. The offspring of the pioneers established conservative and reform synagogues to go with the orthodox *shul*, and Jewish clubs and philanthropies were created, which helped attract later-arriving coreligionists. The more who came, the more who followed, and by 1940, Benton Harbor had some 250 Jewish families, accounting for more than 1,000 Jews in Benton Harbor's population of 16,600.

Early on Jews distinguished themselves in every aspect of Benton Harbor life, including sports. There were outstanding

---

Lena were away when Eulla Eberhardt, a 24-year-old woman caring for the Miller children, died when she lit a fire in the kitchen stove and, trying to make it burn better, threw gasoline on the blaze, causing a burst of flames that enveloped her.

Jewish athletes in the city in the 1910s and '20s, none more accomplished than Leonard "Ladybug" Goldstein, who owed his nickname to his quicksilver moves on the basketball court and gridiron. Another of his moves was to legally change his name between his junior and senior years at Benton Harbor High School so that when he quarterbacked the school's football team to the 1929 Michigan state championship with a 26-0 thrashing of Detroit Northwestern High, he did so as Leonard "Ladybug" Bishop.

Benton Harbor also had a Jewish demimonde. Its denizens included Alex Goldbaum, owner of the Regent pool hall on East Main Street, who sold whiskey of his making during Prohibition. In 1923, after creating a witch's brew of wood alcohol that resulted in the agonizing deaths of a clerk at the Benton Hotel and a salesman from Battle Creek, Goldbaum was charged with murder. His attorney, John J. Sterling, mindful of recent cross burnings in the area, questioned prospective jurors on whether any were members of the Ku Klux Klan. All answered no, but Sterling, who one day would be Benton Harbor's mayor, took those assurances for what they were worth and negotiated a deal that sent his unsavory client to prison only for violating state liquor laws.

A Benton Harbor Jewish businessman with the same surname as the pool hall moonshiner but of higher repute was Mose Goldbaum, whose Goodman and Goldbaum men's store kept the town's gentleman class outfitted in Florsheim shoes, Stetson hats and Arrow shirts. Goldbaum was president of both the Benton Harbor Merchants Association and the Benton Harbor Chamber of Commerce, and on his death in 1942, the city's downtown stores closed for an hour in his memory. Mose's university-educated son Dave Goldbaum took over the business and added a photography department featuring Bell & Howell movie projectors and Argus cameras with built-in light-exposure meters. Things didn't get any fancier than at Goodman and Goldbaum, where in spring the mayor would be pictured in the newspaper getting his new straw hat to see him through the warm months.

My putative grandfather, Mendel Kirshenbaum, was active in a different civic realm than Mose Goldbaum. Mendel co-founded and for several years was president of the Berrien County Jewish Farmers Association, which imported Yiddish-language vaudeville shows from Chicago and hosted Chanukah parties for the children. Mendel was better at farm politics than at farming. He grew pears, cherries, grapes and berries — straw, black, blue, rasp and elder — but struggled to make a living. To help out, Sam Kirschenbaum sent day-old bread by bus from his Chicago bakery to his brother in Benton Harbor.

Some of my father's recollections about his youth are captured on tape by Susan's and my son, David. In his pre-teen years, David was a pipsqueak version of the title character in the Beckett play *Krapp's Last Tape,* chronicling life around him by conducting interviews on an ever-present cassette tape recorder.

"Grandpa, tell me stories and stuff."

"What do you mean?"

"Some funny things in your life."

"It was all funny."

The recordings capture Mook's easy cadences and rhetorical tics. He says, "You hear?" "How about that?" and "Isn't that something?" and if he's sharing a joke that he fears a listener might not get, he throws in, "You follow?" or "Catch on?" Telling of hard times on the farm, he says, "We had no telephone, no electric lights — we used a lantern, you hear? We didn't have a toilet. You had to go outside for the toilet. Can you imagine having to do that in winter?"

Dad told people he went barefoot in the summer months to save shoe leather for the winter. He also claimed that he bathed only when the Paw Paw River thawed in the spring. If this was true, he may not have gotten himself completely clean because he never learned to swim and, after having been rescued from drowning in Lake Michigan by a lifeguard, he always was cautious around water. He may have ventured only far enough into the river to scrub to his knees and stopped right there.

My father and his brothers had the three Rs drilled into them at the Fair Plain Pioneer elementary school, a wooden, three-room structure that harked to the days of inkwells and dunce caps. The schoolhouse would be torn down and replaced at the same location, the corner of Colfax and Napier Avenues, by the larger Fair Plain School that I later attended, a standard-issue brick building with less charm but better heating. When I made the mile-long walk home from school, I was barked at by dogs who wanted only to say hello. When Dad and his brothers walked the same distance but in the opposite direction to the farm, they fought hooligans spewing antisemitic slurs, one of which had extra mustard on it because it was the middle brother's name. The most valuable lesson that Mook, Hymie and Abie learned during their schooldays was that six fists were better than two.

Grandpa Kirshenbaum was a taskmaster. Having suffered under three Russian monarchs — two Alexanders and a Nicholas — he wouldn't have appreciated my calling him the family czar, but his despotic tendencies are well sourced. He demanded his meals at exact hours, and his sleep was not to be disturbed. During middle-of-the night electrical storms,

Grandma, out of ancient superstition, roused the children and made them get fully dressed until the foul weather passed. Grandpa was allowed to sleep lest he unleash thunderclaps of his own. He was said to be undemanding in one way only. When it came to the presentation as distinct from the timing of his meals, he didn't care if the eggs, herring, pickles and beets were served all mixed up because, he reasoned, everything wound up in the same place anyway.

Dad and his brothers were peas in a pod. Within the family, they were "the boys." It was: "Go tell the boys it's time for dinner." Or: "Ma, the boys are picking on me again." Or: "The boys are driving me *meshuga!*" When Mook came home one day and found his meager belongings on the lawn, the pod lost one of its peas. His schooling short-circuited — he'd made it to the eighth grade — he found refuge in Chicago working at his uncle Sam's bakery. On tape with David, he says, "I was learning to be a baker, but I ran out of dough, catch on?" He says that Mendel threw him out of the house because "he didn't like the way I worked on the farm." Giving David a grandfatherly dig, he adds: "You see, I was like you. I didn't obey."

While it's true that Mook ducked out of his chores — picking fruit, sweeping the barn, collecting eggs from the henhouse — it's known that Hymie and Abe also shirked farmwork, yet they weren't sent packing as their older brother was, which prompts the question: Did Mendel find insubordination harder to take from a boy he knew wasn't his?

In any event, my father's banishment was enforced loosely enough that he was able to return from Chicago for brief visits, less a sinner absolved than a youth lured by the siren call of his hometown. Chicago in the 1910s and '20s was rocked by race riots, fixed World Series games and spectacular bank robberies, and although Benton Harbor came up short in those areas, it was no Podunk. Besides thriving as an agricultural center, Benton Harbor was an emergent manufacturing hub, with foundries, assembly lines and well-paid lunchpail-toting workers who kept cash registers in downtown stores ca-chinging There were major companies like Auto Specialties, Clark Equipment, Benton Harbor Malleable, Modern Plastics and, above all, Whirlpool, which grew from a small St. Joseph producer of washing machines called The Nineteenth Century Corporation to become the world's largest appliance maker and today still maintains its global headquarters in Benton Harbor.

There also was tourism. Before the growth of air travel allowed Midwest holiday-goers to jet off to Florida, Las Vegas and Europe, fun-seekers descended on the Twin Cities by road and rail and on excursion steamships that crossed Lake Michigan from Chicago, depositing as many as 1,000 vacationers a day on Benton Harbor's Central Docks. In summer the attractions included golf courses, boat rentals and pristine Lake Michigan beaches. Year-round there were mineral springs from which visitors took the baths at hotels, the Whitcomb in St. Joseph and the Dwan, Earle, Premier and Saltzman in Benton Harbor — all offering, as an ad for the Whitcomb promised, relief from "rheumatism, colds, neuritis, arthritis, nervousness, blood and skin disease, lack of vitality etc."

The Twin Cities also had two amusement parks, so unalike that they belonged on different planets instead of just four miles apart. The parks also seemed to have switched places. Well-mannered St. Joseph was home to raucous Silver Beach, with a roller coaster, Ferris wheel, fun house ("Hilarity Hall") and rides like the Whip, Airplane Swing and The Scooter. On Silver Beach's boardwalk, guys tossed baseballs to win kewpie dolls for their gals and tough-looking barkers filled the air with their aggressive come-ons.

Also incongruously, rowdier Benton Harbor boasted the tranquil House of David, where a miniature train chugged through wooded grounds in a scene from a children's picture book. Among the House of David's homespun pleasures were a vegetarian restaurant, zoo, pony rides, picture-framing shop and ice cream served in sugar cones so good that some customers threw away the ice cream and just ate the cones, which was foolish of them because the ice cream was excellent too. At night there was a beer garden where visitors danced under the stars to the syncopated strains of Manny Woodworth's lushly bearded and braided orchestra.

The House of David was a fundamentalist Christian sect whose male acolytes kept their hair unshorn in emulation of Jesus. Along with its spiritual side, the colony was a many-tentacled business enterprise with the amusement park, valuable real estate, the Grande Vista resort south of St. Joseph and a huge cold storage plant next to the Fruit Market where the Welch company stored the grapes it used to make its juices. The House of David was famed nationally for its barnstorming baseball team comprised of bearded and long-haired colony members and an occasional ringer with ringlets. The team traveled the land spreading The Word, earning money for the colony and delighting spectators with players running the bases backwards, hiding the ball in their whiskers and performing other horseplay while also playing high-level baseball.

The House of David was founded by an itinerant, illiterate and charismatic preacher named Benjamin Purnell, who proclaimed himself God's seventh angelic messenger. King Ben greeted tourists on the park's grounds resplendent in white suit and white hat and astride a snow-white steed. Foremost among the commandments Ben imposed on his flock was celibacy, but he himself came to be criminally accused of seducing female followers, including underage girls, in "purification rites." He eluded capture for two years until, on November 16, 1926, a police raid found him, sick and emaciated, in secret quarters in a building on the colony's grounds. He was brought to trial on sex and fraud charges but died before legal judgment could be made.

In an injustice to the House of David faithful, who on the whole were humble and hard-working, Purnell's story is sensationalized in a book, *King of the Harem Heaven*, luridly subtitled *The Amazing True Story of a Daring Charlatan Who Ran a Virgin Love Cult in America*. The House of David is depicted, also with license but more gently, by the humorist Ring Lardner, a native of the nearby Berrien County town of Niles, who tells in his comic dialect of arriving by excursion boat from Chicago and visiting the colony: "It sounds like a road house, but it was even better'n that. You couldn't get nothin' to drink, but they was plenty to see and hear — band concerts, male and female; movin' pitchers; a zoo; a bowlin' alley; and more funny-lookin' people than I ever seen at an amusement park...it ain't a regular amusement park but fifty-fifty between that and a kind of religious sex."

King Ben's debaucheries were only part of Benton Harbor's indecorous early history. The town was also, in the words of one scribe, "the glamour venue for bloodletting." This was owing to an enterprising homegrown boxing promoter, Floyd Fitzsimmons, who in 1920 staged two headline-grabbing fights in his 11,000-seat outdoor arena at Fair and Britain Avenues. On July 5, world lightweight champion Benny Leonard knocked out Charley White, and on Labor Day, newly crowned heavyweight champ Jack Dempsey, a close friend of Fitzsimmons, put his title on the line for the first time, against Billy Miske. In the days before the Dempsey-Miske fight, as gamblers, grifters, swells and roguish characters like One-Eyed Connelly, the famous gate crasher, descended, Benton Harbor was also the glamour venue of price-gouging. A wire service story reported that "rooms in private houses are $8.00 per day if you please" and "restaurants have not reduced their prices — nay, nay, in fact they have been increased."

Mook wasn't about to remain in Chicago when such a spectacle was unfolding at home. Decades later, some old-timers told of climbing the Fitzsimmons Arena fence as youths to watch Dempsey disassemble Miske in a third-round knockout, but my father did no such thing. Nay, nay, he and his 14-year-old pal Sammy Price teamed to sell jugs of water, if you please, to thirsty spectators.

Soon Sammy Price himself joined the pugilist ranks. This was the era of outstanding Jewish fighters, including world champions Leonard, Barney Ross, Jackie Fields and Slapsie Maxie Rosenbloom,[2] and Sammy aspired to a go at world lightweight champion Sammy Mandell, who Mike Tyson, a student of the Sweet Science, called the greatest Jewish fighter ever. Mike should have studied harder. Gentile boxers in those days sometimes changed their names to appeal to Jewish fight fans. Sammy Mandell, born Salvatore Mandala, is enshrined in the National Italian American Sports Hall of Fame.

---

2. After hanging up his gloves, Rosenbloom became a stage and nightclub performer. For the *Minneapolis Tribune*, I covered him when he appeared at a suburban St. Paul night spot, Diamond Jim's. I wrote that as a prizefighter, Slapsie Maxie had a style resembling a windmill and that on stage, "his mumbling diction suggests he swallowed the windmill." The line was picked up by syndicated columnist Hy Gardner, who wrote: "Jerry might like to know that Maxie is not only a look-alike and sound-alike for Noel Coward, but claims he gave Noel diction lessons."

Sammy Price was fast on his feet and featured a jaw-snapping left jab. Sportswriters wrote that he had "a slam-bang style" and was "a dancing master." One told of his having "mixed a sleeping potion" for a vanquished foe. Sammy lit up the ring in Indianapolis, Fort Wayne, Louisville, Terre Haute, Cincinnati and elsewhere, and when he fought in Benton Harbor, which he did many times and usually victoriously, he was hailed as a hometown hero. But he suffered broken fingers and after a couple of tough losses and with other opportunities knocking, he quit the fight game. One day my father and he would partner — Mook the money, Sammy the muscle — in a bail bond firm, Twin City Bonders, which for Pop was one more sideline to his bag business.

In 1922 a visit home by Dad was noted on the Benton Harbor *News-Palladium's* society page. Next to items about a travel talk on Italy at the Methodist church and a bridge party at the A.B. Carter residence in St. Joseph, it was reported that "Miss Dorothy [Dad's eldest sister] and Milton Kirshenbaum, of Chicago, have been the guests of their parents, Mr. and Mrs. M.H. Kirshenbaum for the past week." Readers had no reason to doubt that Milton was on best of terms with his family, and, in fact, M.H. [Mendel] Kirshenbaum was in a forgiving frame of mind. Failing in agriculture, he was trying his hand at something agriculture-related, the burlap bag business, and he wanted "the boys" to help. That meant all of them, my father's presence not merely tolerated but now insisted upon.

To get his fledgling operation off the ground, Mendel marketed bags through the newspaper classifieds.

Early: *"Potato Bags — 2,000, all sizes. M. Kirshenbaum."*

Later: *"Potato Bags — 10,000. All sizes and kinds. M. Kirshenbaum."*

From quantity to quality: *"Grain bags — guaranteed free of holes. M. Kirshenbaum."*

Grandpa dreamed that from this acorn would grow an oak to be called "Mendel Kirshenbaum & Sons." As Dad told it, Mendel worked into the wee hours night after night drawing up instructions for the boys to follow in the mornings, so exhausting himself in the process that he slept the days away. Left unsupervised, the brothers too often ignored the tasks assigned them and instead checked out the Chicago girls visiting the amusement parks or the local lasses sunning themselves on the Lake Michigan beaches. At this stage of their lives, Mook, Hymie and Abie were more interested in sowing wild oats than in trafficking in the bags meant to hold them. Mendel's scheme went nowhere, leaving him, my father said, "a general without an army."

Returning to Chicago, Mook no longer worked at Sam Kirschenbaum's bakery but now was driving a taxi, enjoying greater independence and earning better pay. But the work was not without risk and discomfort. Chicago in the 1920s was in the throes of a violent taxi turf war in which Checker and Yellow cabs were firebombed and drivers murdered. Driving a Yellow, Mook dodged those dangers, but there were unpleasantries he couldn't, starting with the Chicago weather. In winter, with monster winds blasting off Lake Michigan, taxicab passengers sat in enclosed spaces, leaving drivers exposed to the bitter cold. "We only had blankets on our laps, you hear?" Dad said. "Some days we froze our asses off."

Worse was the time that gangsters with guns drawn pulled Mook out of his cab and accused him of messing with their boss's girlfriend. "I tried telling them they had the wrong guy, but I thought for sure they were going to kill me," Dad said. He didn't know how it happened, but they finally accepted his claim of mistaken identity and let him go.

Before long, however, there would occur another incident involving my father and firearms that didn't end as happily. And this time he indeed may have been messing with somebody else's woman.

Chapter 4

Milton Kramer

The revelation was a bombshell, the detonation a question: "Did you know your father was in prison?"

My brother and I were on opposite coasts, Joel a lawyer in San Francisco, I a writer for *Time* in New York, when Cousin Deana shared her discovery with us. Why hadn't we known about this earlier? Working on an oral history of the Kirshenbaum clan for her graduate studies in family therapy at Georgetown, Deana learned that her uncle Mook had gotten into serious trouble in South Haven, a resort town on the Lake Michigan littoral 25 miles north of Benton Harbor that came to be known as "the Catskills of the Midwest." Deana told us that our father freely reminisced about other things, but when she asked about what happened in South Haven, he clammed up. Joel and I assumed that Dad wouldn't want to discuss the matter with us either, and we didn't have to try. From public records and reams of newspaper coverage, it's possible to piece together an account of tragic events in South Haven during the first week of August 1925.

When people speak of the Catskills, often they're referring

not to that New York mountain range in its craggy and forested totality but to a portion of it jocularly called the Jewish Alps. Through the first half of the 20th Century, Jews were denied access to many of the nation's leading hotels and resorts, which posted signs reading "Jewish patronage not desired" or "no Hebrews or pulmonary patients entertained." In response, an alternative hospitality industry came into existence in the Catskills that allowed Jews to vacation among their own in hotels and resorts often more lavish than those that excluded them. At Grossinger's, the Concord, the Nevele and other famed resorts, there were championship-level golf courses, indoor and outdoor swimming pools and amenities and extravagances of every kind. Grossinger's had its own post office and airfield. The Concord, with 1,500 guest rooms and a 3,000-seat dining room, was noted for its architectural excesses. Its founder, Arthur Winarick, was asked by the writer Mordecai Richler how he thought his hotel compared to the grand hotels and spas of Europe. Winarick witheringly dismissed the European establishments as "Garages with drapes. Warehouses."

Catskills resorts fed guests gargantuan quantities of brisket, kreplach and chopped liver — "Too much is not enough" was the byword — and generous servings of world-class entertainment. The resorts were famous for their Borscht Belt comedians, many of whom became stars of radio, stage and screen. Milton Berle, Danny Kaye and Jerry Lewis (born Mendel Berliner, Daniel Kaminsky and Joseph Levich) got their starts in the Catskills, as did, to one degree or another, Mel Brooks (Melvin Kaminsky), George Burns (Nathan Birnbaum), Sid Caesar (Isaac Sidney Caesar), Rodney Dangerfield (Jacob Cohen), Buddy Hackett (Leonard Hacker), Alan King (Irwin Alan Kniberg), Jackie Mason (Yaakov Moshe Maza) and Joan

Rivers (Joan Molinsky) — the list stretches on to also include Myron Cohen, Shecky Greene and Henny Youngman, comics whose styles hewed more closely to their Catskills roots and who tinkered only slightly (Myron Cohen not at all) with their birth names. Shunned by Gentile hotels, Jewish vacationers had not just the last laugh but lots of laughs.

Similar pleasures abounded in the Catskills of the Midwest. Like Benton Harbor, South Haven was a Fruit Belt community populated by Jewish farmers. In both South Haven and Benton Harbor, farmers took in boarders, which sometimes proved more profitable than farming. This was especially the case in South Haven, where many farms were converted to inns and resorts, and a thriving tourist industry took hold. With a year-round population of 4,000, South Haven became home to some 60 hotels and resorts and scores of beachfront tourist cottages. South Haven vacationers hailed from Detroit, Indianapolis and, most of all, Chicago. As in Benton Harbor, daily excursion boats from Chicago brought a summertime crush of visitors to South Haven, the majority of whom were Jewish.

South Haven establishments such as Steuben's Summer Hotel and Mendelson's Atlantic Resort attracted regulars who faithfully returned year after year. Another prominent resort, Fidelman's, advertised "80 acres of instant happiness," as opposed to the 80 acres of drudgery that the owners, Morris and Belle Fidelman, had experienced as farmers.

Where the Jewish Alps treated residents of New York and other Eastern cities to fresh mountain air, South Haven offered Midwesterners beaches, boating and fishing. For the younger set, there was a dance hall, The Casino, a vaulted-ceiling structure resembling an athletic fieldhouse that boasted "the highest paid and best dance bands in America." Despite the name, the only gambling done at the Casino were chances taken on romance, which could pay off for a night or a lifetime or come up snake eyes.

South Haven's best-known landmark is its lighthouse, which, since 1872, has guided Lake Michigan ships through darkness, fog and storms. Milton Kirshenbaum could have benefited from a beacon of his own to keep himself on course. Instead, in South Haven, he participated in wrongdoing that led to the violent death of a 20-year-old married Chicago woman named Ethel Shapiro Esrig.

Ethel, one of four children of a tailor, Louis Shapiro, and his wife, Lena, was vacationing in South Haven with her mother while her father and her husband, Harry Esrig, remained in Chicago. There would be press reports that Ethel and Harry were having marital problems, which Harry, described as either a real estate man or laundry service worker, denied. But in South Haven, Ethel wasn't using her married name and was spending time with my father. They were friends and possibly more.

An incident suggesting their closeness occurred on Monday, August 3, 1925. The South Haven *Daily Tribune* would later report that my father had been horseback riding that day and was arrested for having "over-driven" his horse against a car, for which he was fined $25. Ethel either was riding with him or was close by because, the newspaper said, she was believed to have helped Dad pay the fine.

In South Haven my father was also palling around with two other Chicagoans, Sam "Scotty" Brown and Solomon "Solly" Crystal, both 18. (Dad reportedly also was 18, though his true age was, as always, uncertain.) Brown, like Mook, was a Chicago cab driver. On Wednesday, August 5, two days after the horseback riding mishap, at approximately four in the afternoon, my father, Brown and Crystal broke into a cottage belonging to Louis Meyers, the owner of a Chicago auto supply store. Many South Haven cottages were used on weekends only, and Louis, his wife, Lillian, and their young son, Melvin, were away. In the cottage, the burglars broke open a locked trunk and, police said, removed $15.40 in cash, a Waterman fountain pen, pocketknife, cap, necktie, child's watch and pearl-handled .38 caliber revolver. They might have gotten away with the burglary if it hadn't been for Brown's recklessness. After events took a tragic turn, the Chicago *Tribune* referred to him in a headline as REVOLVER JOKER.

At 11:30 that night, my father met up outside a South Haven drugstore with Ethel, who was wearing dark slacks, slipover sweater, oxfords and hat, and at 5'7" was three inches shorter than Dad. According to the Kalamazoo *Gazette*, Ethel and Mook attended a dance together, after which they were joined by Solly Crystal and other young people, including Ethel's friend Molly Boiko, the daughter of the owner of the resort hotel where Ethel and her mother were staying. The group headed toward Lake Michigan. Passing the Casino, they were joined by Sam Brown. A procession formed — Molly, Solly and others up ahead, with my father, Ethel and Sam Brown following. Sam had the revolver from the burglary with him and began twirling and pointing it as if he were Tom Mix, the Western movie star of the day, taking aim at desperadoes. There were pleas for Sam to put the gun away, but he said it wasn't loaded. To prove it, he pulled the trigger. Nothing happened. At the coroner's inquest, Van Buren County Sheriff Glen Weaver would testify that the revolver's six chambers contained five cartridges. Evidently Sam chanced on the one empty chamber.

Sam now pointed the weapon teasingly at Ethel. One wonders if he was interested in her and was jealous seeing her with my father. Screaming at Brown to stop, Ethel flung her arms around my father as Sam again pulled the trigger. This time the gun discharged. The bullet, fired at close range, struck Ethel on the left side of her head, singeing her hat as she leaned against my father's shoulder. The South Haven *Daily Tribune* reported that my father "was stunned by the impact and momentarily blinded by the powder flash and at first believed he too had been struck [and] upon realizing the situation, he whirled and caught Miss Shapiro."

According to eyewitnesses, Sam dropped the gun and ran, calling for my father and Solly to follow, but they remained with the stricken woman. Sam was last seen heading toward the Black River, which creases South Haven and flows into Lake Michigan at the location of the lighthouse. My father and Solly took the wounded Ethel in a passing car to the hospital, where, at 2:11 a.m., Thursday, August 6, she was pronounced dead. Even then Dad didn't leave her. The South Haven newspaper said he accompanied the body to Calvin's undertaking rooms on Phoenix Street.

A burglary for which my father was responsible had led to a homicide for which he wasn't. Questioned by police, Dad and Solly confessed to the break-in at the Meyers cottage and disclosed that it was the source of the revolver that killed Ethel. I take heart that my father didn't flee the scene as Sam did, but instead of being completely aboveboard, he identified himself to police as Milton Kramer. It's unclear whether this was a name he made up on the spot or an alias he'd been using in South Haven all along.

With Crystal and "Kramer" in custody, Sam Brown was missing. United Press reported that a police cordon had been set up around the Brown family home at 1121 South Mozart Street in Chicago. There were rumors that Sam had committed suicide. The shooting death of Ethel was sensational news in Chicago, Benton Harbor and elsewhere. Sheriff Weaver issued a public alert that the fugitive had "a Roman nose that spreads over his face" and a tattoo of "a sailor boy" on his arm. The headline dominating the front page of the *News-Palladium* screamed MYSTERY IN GIRL'S DEATH, the mystery being Brown's whereabouts. Readers didn't yet know that the Milton Kramer mentioned in the story was Milton Kirshenbaum from a local farm family.

The next day, with Brown still on the lam, the *News-Palladium's* lead headline was NET OUT FOR GIRL KILLER. By now my father had given authorities his real name, and his identity became known to Benton Harbor friends and neighbors. On Saturday, August 8, Ethel's body was taken to Chicago for burial. That morning my father testified at the coroner's inquest. The South Haven paper reported his account of the shooting. "Sam had the revolver, Kirshenbaum said. Ethel said, 'Throw it away. I don't want to see it.'" The newspaper quoted Dad as saying, "Ethel must have had her head on my left shoulder and Brown must have been standing close, as the shock of the shot made me deaf in the left ear."

Crystal also testified. He said that he and Brown had inspected the revolver. He said he believed that the weapon had "six cartridges, six or five, he wasn't sure." Although this indicates that Brown knew the gun was loaded, Crystal and other witnesses testified that Sam appeared to be shocked when it fired. They said he cried, "My God, I've shot her" or "What have I done?" The jury ruled the shooting accidental. Sam Brown was charged in absentia with manslaughter for "the reckless and negligent killing of Ethel Shapiro Esrig." He also was charged with breaking and entering, as were Crystal and my father, both of whom were remanded to the Van Buren

County jail to await trial. Mook faced an additional reckoning. According to Van Buren Circuit Court records, his $1,000 bond was posted by Mendel Kirshenbaum, no doubt through a bail bondsman. There surely was cause for new strain between Mook and Mendel.

After two weeks, Brown surrendered. He said that after the shooting, he had hidden for two days in South Haven in a haystack, then hitched a ride to Chicago. Appearing before Circuit Court Judge Glenn E. Warner, the three men entered guilty pleas. Warner sentenced Brown to three to 15 years in prison on the manslaughter charge, and all three defendants to one to five years for burglary. The judge recommended that Crystal serve 18 months and my father 16 months, the difference being that Solly had committed a previous crime in the area, the theft of an overcoat at a dance, while Mook's prior slate was clean. (Like Crystal, Brown had a previous rap, a forgery allegedly committed while he worked as a messenger at a post office in Chicago.)

On September 3, 1925, brought low by bad company and his own bad intentions, my father entered the Michigan Reformatory at Ionia, where he remained until December 1, 1926, when he was freed with scores of other inmates in time for Christmas. He served 15 months, one month less than Judge Warner recommended. To go by his recognized birthdate, he was, on release, 21 years old.

AS A CHILD I was unwavering in my regard for my father. If you'd told me he committed thievery, I would have said of course he did. I knew from reading Dickens, Twain and other truthtellers that when a child was poor, he might be driven to filch an apple off a grocer's cart to ease his hunger or steal a loaf of bread to help feed his family. But if you'd said, don't be ridiculous, little Jerry, your father broke into a home and stole a loaded revolver that killed a married woman with whom he may have been romantically involved and who was fatally wounded in his arms, and that he went to prison for his crime, I would have been thrown into a state of tearful confusion.

Even today I have trouble squaring the miscreant under examination here with the man I knew as my father. My father was as non-violent as Gandhi. He never took a hand to me, and I can't remember him raising his voice more than a decibel or two no matter the provocation. He wanted no part of firearms. I can't say how much this might have been as a result of his South Haven experience, but when I begged for a Red Ryder BB gun like those that other boys had for shooting at tin cans and squirrels, he refused, forcing me to settle for toy cap pistols that emitted sorry wisps of smoke and sounds no more credible than the snap, crackle and pop of my morning Rice Krispies.

While researching my father's South Haven lawbreaking, I came across a clipping in the Benton Harbor newspaper telling of a lesser slip-up of his that occurred two years after he left prison. It was reported in a brief item inside the paper that Mook and his brother Hymie were jailed along with a third man for starting "a near riot" in a Benton Harbor dance hall called — so help me — Jap-O-Land.[1] News of disposition of

---

1. Jap-O-Land was festooned with Oriental parasols and lanterns. The day after Pearl Harbor, the owner, Percy Bulley, renamed the establishment "Bulley's Night Club," saying with patriotic fervor, "I don't want anything that smacks of the Japanese." After V-J Day, Bulley changed the name back to Jap-O-Land. When the Big Band Era ended, dance halls in Southwestern Michigan including Shadowland in St. Joseph, Crystal Palace in Coloma and Ramona in Sister Lakes disappeared, as did Jap-O-Land in Benton Harbor.

the case — the brothers pleaded guilty to disorderly conduct and paid $5 fines plus court costs — was buried even deeper in the paper, overshadowed by front-page coverage of far greater criminality. On February 14, 1929, the day Mook and Hymie were released from the Benton Harbor jail, seven members of Bugsy Moran's gang were gunned down by Al Capone's hitmen in a Chicago garage in what would come to be known as the Saint Valentine Day's Massacre.

There were moments when my father may have had stronger than usual reminders of his troubles in the Catskills of the Midwest. When I was little, our family went for dinner in a much diminished South Haven, where the few resorts still in operation were scraping the bottom of the entertainment barrel, presenting acts such as Sally Dermer, the Jewish Kate Smith, or Jerry Stern, the One-Man Band, or cha-cha demonstrations by the dance master up from Florida, Sy Braun. We ate at Mendelson's Atlantic Resort, where my parents said the gefilte fish, knishes and other dishes were as good as ever, though little of it was to my taste, which ran more toward hot dogs and hamburgers. I wonder what thoughts may have been awakened in Dad's mind by his being in such close proximity to the sites of the burglary of Louis Meyers's cottage and the fatal shooting of Ethel Shapiro Esrig.

There was another time when memories of his wrongdoing may have been strongly jogged. After graduating from the University of California (Berkeley) Law School, my brother was working in San Francisco on the legal team defending the Soledad Brothers, three Black inmates — George Jackson, John Clutchette and Fleeta Drumgo — charged and ultimately acquitted of murdering a white prison guard, John Vincent Mills, in California's Soledad State Prison. Visiting Joel, Dad attended sessions of the nationally publicized trial. Did hearing testimony about events at Soledad trigger thoughts of his own time spent within prison walls?

One ever-present reminder: For the rest of his life, my father had slight hearing loss in his left ear, likely the result of the gunshot discharging so near his head that, as he testified, it temporarily deafened him. He made light of his hearing impairment, saying winkingly, "Sometimes, with my wife, I wish I didn't hear as well as I do."

IN THE 1920S the Benton Harbor *News-Palladium* carried wire-service photos of national and world events but few pictures of local happenings, and the South Haven *Daily Tribune* ran no photos at all. It was different in Chicago, where newspapering was fiercely competitive and infused with an anything-goes ethos that placed a premium on the garish and pictorial. This was the era of Ben Hecht and Charles MacArthur, Chicago newsmen who wrote *The Front Page*, the play of a thousand stage and film incarnations depicting that city's newspapering at its most rip-roaring. At the Chicago *Daily News*, Hecht, who would become one of the most prolific screenwriters in Hollywood history, was a "picture chaser," the term for a breed of reporters who sneaked into homes and brazenly snatched photos of the principals in sensational crimes and sordid sex scandals off end tables and bedroom dressers.

Whether obtained by stealth or by other means, a photo of Ethel Shapiro Esrig appeared in the Chicago *Tribune*, referenced to a story about the case on another page in which my father is identified as Milton Kramer. Captioned CHICAGO WOMAN KILLED AT MICHIGAN BEACH RESORT, the photo shows Ethel in profile, dark-haired, strong-jawed and pensive, as if she's about to share a confidence. She stares into the distance, toward a future she will be denied. I do a double-take. She bears a strong resemblance to another Chicago woman — my mother — whom my father would marry six years later.

Chapter 5

Roosevelt Road

MOTHER WAS "AMERICAN, CHICAGO BORN," a locution I borrow from the first line of Saul Bellow's novel *The Adventures of Augie March* for a dual purpose: to establish Frieda Goldberg Kirshenbaum's USA bona fides while noting as an aside that Bellow's older brother Maurice (né Moshe) was in her 1926 graduating class at Chicago's John Marshall High School.

Marshall High was huge, 4,000 students, and overwhelmingly Jewish. Like many of her schoolmates, my mother was a child of immigrants, while others were themselves immigrants, including Maurice Bellow, who was born in Russia. Maurice's brother Saul, who came into the world during a family pit stop in Montreal, attended a different predominantly Jewish school on Chicago's West Side, Tuley High (now Roberto Clemente Community Academy). Not to be outdone by Tuley's Nobel Prize winner, Marshall claims a distinguished Old Grad of its own from the same era, Admiral Hyman Rickover, the visionary responsible for the U.S. nuclear Navy. By the time my mother entered Marshall as a freshman, Hyman had dropped anchor in Annapolis, but she overlapped in the school's crowded hallways with his sister, Augusta "Ricky" Rickover, Class of '24.

My mother's schoolfriends called her Fritz. At Lawson Elementary, the sentiments her eighth-grade classmates wrote in her autograph book were the kind found embroidered on throw pillows. "Leaves may wither, flowers may die, friends may forget you, but never will I," vowed Esther Kaplan. A boy named Ben may have mistaken eighth-grade graduation for Valentine's Day. "Dear Fritz," he wrote, "our eyes have met, our lips not yet, but O, you kid, I'll get there yet." By contrast, the valedictions penned in my mother's copy of the Marshall High yearbook, *Review*, were largely confined to signoffs like "Best Wishes" and "Yours Truly." The future was at hand, and the time for silliness had passed.

Fritz coasted through Marshall in three and a half years. At graduation, she sat on stage with other top students. In a red leather diary she maintained that year, she writes, "Only officers and honor students had that privilege...thrilling."

Her senior class bio in *Review* breathlessly sums up her achievements:

If activities make a girl then "Fritz" is A No. 1. Here they go: Sec. C.I.C. '25, Sec. Photography Club '26, member of Les Joyeux Francais, Spanish, Science, Girl Reserves, French, Art, Literary and Honor Clubs. Students' Council, News Reporter '26. Led the Volleyball team in '25 and was on the Championship Captainball Team '26 and made the Honor Roll.

Her diary chronicles a flurry of non-school activities — bridge games, golf outings, shopping and moviegoing. Tribulations are few. "Mom and Dad are on the outs — it makes me so miserable," she writes in early May. Come Mother's Day: "Dad bought Mother a beautiful diamond studded wristwatch."

My parents both came from orthodox stock, raised in homes where the kitchens were kosher and the Jewish holidays strictly observed. The differences in their upbringings were in educational opportunities and creature comforts, of which Mook had few, Fritz many. Yet they may have crossed paths early in Chicago because Mom and her family lived at 3420 Roosevelt Road across the street from Sam Kirschenbaum's bakery at 3421, where Dad was employed after his banishment from Benton Harbor.

Mom's father, Jacob Goldberg, was a saloonkeeper sidelined by the enactment of Prohibition in 1920, but he kept the wolf at bay with real estate holdings and a bit of bootlegging. He and his wife, Rose, got to know the Kirschenbaums, and young Frieda Goldberg became best friends with two of the Kirschenbaum daughters, Florence and Bernice. Fritz and Mook must have been at least aware of each other. She was the girl tee-heeing with Dad's cousins; he was the farm boy from Michigan covered in flour dust.

Roosevelt Road, originally 12th Street, was a world unto itself, as much Odessa or Vilnius as Chicago. On its bustling east-west expanse, one could buy vegetables, galoshes, pickled tongue, chickens live or cooked, a drink of seltzer, and yarn for the knitting, jars for the canning and coal for the furnace. One needn't go far to get his shoes cobbled or her hem shortened. Shoppers went from store to store by foot or, if one's lumbago was acting up, on trolley cars that ran the length of the thoroughfare. Roosevelt Road even had its own department store, the seven-story 12th Street Store at the corner of Halsted Street. There was nothing fancy about any of this. If you needed lawn furniture to lounge in next to your backyard swimming pool or cruisewear for yachting with the Vanderbilts, you could find these things at Marshall Field's in the Loop, the nation's first department store with a tearoom and personal shopping service. The everyday needs of folks like the Kirschenbaums and Goldbergs could be satisfied right there on Roosevelt Road.

Before Prohibition, Sam Kirschenbaum may have enjoyed a schnapps at the Goldberg saloon. Chances are, Rose Goldberg bought challahs at the Kirschenbaum bakery. On Saturday mornings, the two families may have walked the few blocks side by side to sabbath services at the Anshe Shalom synagogue at Independence Boulevard and West Polk. One way or another, the couples learned they were from the same Lomza region of Poland — Grandpa Goldberg a native of Zambrow, 35 miles from Radziłów, Grandma Goldberg hailing from the city of Lomza, closer still. Bonding over their common roots, they shared reminiscences of the Old Country and news received from those left behind.

Both of Mom's parents had been previously married. Grandma Rose, born Rifka Rochel Kokozhka, was wed in Poland at 17 and had two children, a son, Mashe, and a daughter, Ancholy. When her husband was killed in the Russo-Japanese war, Rose came to Chicago and worked in a sweatshop to earn money to send for the children. Sadly, both died in Europe, and she never saw them again. Grandpa was born Jakob Gebel and in the U.S. changed his name to Goldberg because he thought it sounded more American. Jakob and his first wife, Schactel, were childless, and it was said that he wanted children. After securing a divorce from Schactel by paying her a court-ordered sum of $265, he married Rose, with whom his wish for children was granted five-fold: Mom born first, followed by a son, Irving, and three more girls, Gere, Mirian and Edna.

The connection between my parents' families flourished to the point that Sam and Kadie Kirschenbaum took Jake and Rose Goldberg on visits to Sam's brother's farm in Benton Harbor. Swaddled in *Yiddishkeit* bonhomie, the couples could not have foreseen that they would one day be linked by marriage as well as by friendship. As a girl, Mom visited the Kirshenbaums in Benton Harbor, never imagining that her future lay in that town. She writes in her diary of going to Benton Harbor with Dad's cousin Florence Kirschenbaum. A photo shows them at Mendel and Gittel's farm posing in bibbed overalls as if they were taking a breather from the rigors of plowing and planting. A closer look gives the game away. Florence is wearing sandals secured by three straps, footwear less suited for farmwork than for showing off a pedicure.

My mother's diary tells us that July 1926 was a busy month for her. Over the Fourth of July weekend, she took an excursion steamer to Benton Harbor with Florence and two other friends and stopped at the Kirschenbaum farm only long enough to drop off their suitcases and say hello, goodbye. "Got in at 8 and rushed into dif. clothes, then out to Silver Beach... had a nice time," she writes. The next day they returned to Silver Beach, where she attracted admirers, allowing, "I did look stunning with my white dress and hair slicked back."

The month's biggest event was the wedding in Chicago of Dad's namesake cousin, Milton Kirschenbaum, to Ann Patis. Fritz gushes in her diary about excitement in the household above the bakery. The women were treated to mud baths, and there were two "butlers" and, "ah the confusion... the Baskins from Streator [Illinois], the Kirschenbaums [sic] from Benton Harbor..."

My father, behind bars, didn't attend the wedding. His absence goes unmentioned in my mother's diary.

After his release from prison, Dad returned to Chicago and resumed driving a taxi. He paid visits to his uncle Sam's bakery and reconnected with the owner of a pool hall two doors away at 3417 Roosevelt Road, an older man named Benny Adler. When Mook worked at the bakery, Adler had taken a liking to him, and now a deeper friendship developed. Not far from Adler's were Davey Miller's boxing gym, the scene of illicit gambling as well as fisticuffs, and the bookmaking and bootlegging emporium of Benjamin "Zookie the Bookie" Zuckerman, whose life was cut short in 1927 by a gunman's bullet. Benny Adler held his own among these dodgy characters. Poker and craps games flourished in Adler's back room, and in 1932 Benny and a bakers' union organizer were charged with hiring two men to bomb a bakery, not the Kirschenbaum bakery but one at 1602 South St. Louis Avenue that may not have been playing ball with the union. The two men were caught planting sticks of dynamite on the bakery's roof and went to prison, but Benny avoided the slammer, ably represented by an attorney who was a brother of the judge presiding over the case.

Dad considered Adler a fine man. He said, "You've heard the expression, 'There's no honor among thieves?' Well, I'd take Benny Adler over a priest or rabbi any day." This makes Adler sound as one with a Chicago mobster named Pete Penovich. In his book *A Corner of Chicago*, the journalist and radio soap opera writer Robert Hardy Andrews writes that Penovich attended mass but never took confession, explaining, "I ain't honest but I'm honorable."

Somewhere — I advise against putting your money on any

place other than Roosevelt Road — my parents' eyes met. Mook was showing interest in the better-bred high school graduate (who'd spent a semester taking business courses at Northwestern University's Chicago campus), while Fritz was drawn to a lightly schooled taxi driver consorting with ruffians in a pool hall. Trying to account for how my mother fell for my father, the best I can do is to note that she was a risk-taker. In photos of her as a teenager cavorting with friends on the Lake Michigan beach in Fremont, Indiana, she's the one atop the human pyramid and anchoring the tug-of-war rope. And she had a mind of her own. In her diary, she writes of a suitor who was too forward with her. "I allowed him to kiss me," she says. Of that lapse she vows, "He will never take such liberties again."

But was she adventurous enough to take up with a man with Dad's history? The question of why Joel and I hadn't known earlier of our father's burglary, the woman shot to death in his arms and his imprisonment is wrapped in the greater mystery of whether our mother found out about that part of his life at all. During her many bursts of anger at Dad, she threw in his face every negative thing about him, real or imagined, yet never did Joel or I hear her speak of his trouble in South Haven. To think that she knew and kept her lips sealed would credit her with restraint and discretion she never otherwise displayed. Remaining silent wasn't in her makeup. Although the killing of Ethel Shapiro Esrig had been headline news in Benton Harbor, where Mother lived most of her life, it seems possible, hard though it is to believe, that she never learned of Dad's wrongdoing in the Catskills of the Midwest.

THE START OF MY PARENTS' courtship coincided with the onset of the Great Depression. Before the Wall Street crash of 1929, Mom was working a $25-a-week job as a bookkeeper for a manufacturer on Chicago's South Side of upholstered davenports, tufted wing chairs and brass beds, and helping her father, Grandpa Jake, with the books for a mortgaged garage he owned in the Chicago suburb of Oak Park. As the Depression deepened, Fritz was let go at the furniture company, and Grandpa lost the garage.

Amid the economic gloom, my father returned to Benton Harbor and set out to prove that he could be the breadwinner for the woman he had his eye on. Mendel's efforts to draw Mook and his brothers into the bag business a decade earlier had been unavailing, but now Dad saw that there might be money to be made in that line of work. He bought a truck and launched a business while at the same time wooing Mom. His pursuit of her included letters that made up in ardor for what they lacked in artfulness. The letters, which Mother saved, reveal that he didn't immediately close the deal. On August 12, 1929, six months after the Jap-O-Land fracas and three months before the stock market crash, he wrote her, "Maybe someday you could learn to love me. I've always enjoyed your company Fritzie, and believe me kid there's no one I'd rather go out with." He said he was coming to Chicago the next weekend and promised to take her to a movie.

Soon there was a rendezvous in Benton Harbor after which Mook accompanied Fritz home to Chicago, then took a train back because he had a business trip to make in the morning. "I got in B.H. about 4 a.m. so you see I didn't get any sleep last night," he wrote. "I had to wait about 2 hours for the train and the time sure did drag. I certainly hated to see you leave so soon honey, but I guess it just couldn't be helped. If I hadn't gone back to Chicago with you, I wouldn't be so tired now. But honey I'll never regret that trip back, will you? I could have kept on riding to the end of the world with just you, baby."

Those impassioned words appear under the letterhead of the Lakeview Hotel in Lakeville, Michigan. Other letters reached Mom from the Ross House in Plymouth, Indiana, ("Dining room in connection"), the Whiting Hotel in Traverse City, Michigan, (Telephone 61), and, also in Michigan, the Hotel Northern in Manistee (F.M. McMann, Prop.) and the Wesley in Saginaw (Glen E. Whaley, Mgr.).

After a pause in his epistolary romancing, he apologized, explaining, "Last night I stayed in a small town that didn't even have stationary. Sounds like a poor excuse doesn't it baby? But it's the truth so you see I'm writing the first possible chance." He was offering these amends from the Hotel Barnett in Logansport, Indiana, on writing paper containing a wealth of information: "Strictly Modern European; 50 rooms, 18 with bath; rates $1.25 to $2.50; one-half block from Interurban station."

Driving a truck in wintry Michigan was tough going. Writing from Saginaw: "Terrible driving, slippery and plenty of snow, might not be able to get back. I'm all in, driving more than 200 miles without a windshield wiper is no fun." Another time: "It's pouring outside and I can't think of anything better to do than write a few words to my baby." He was having trouble with his car. "I don't know what I'm going to do with it yet, it needs an overhauling, and the rear end went bad." Even so: "Business has been pretty good."

There was talk of their fixing up Sammy Price with a friend of Mom's named Kiki, but Dad wrote, "[I] was planning on coming in with Sam Price this Sat, but Sammy has got another fight for the 28th, so you see he's in training and cant [sic] step out. I know Sammy would like Kiki very much. Why shouldn't he. Well maybe we can arrange it for some other time."

Sammy and Kiki never happened. In the bout Dad referred to, Sammy, despite suffering a dislocated shoulder in the second round, won a unanimous 10-round decision over Cleveland's Al Kline. The next year, fighting out of Indianapolis, he wed Betty Brown of that city. That marriage ended, and Sammy would enter into a lasting one with Josephine Pantaleo from an Italian family in the Benton Harbor area.

Letters that Mom wrote to Dad during this period don't survive, but they evidently were lengthy. "Well honey I suppose I'll have a nice long letter waiting for me when I get back," he wrote at one point. "That's something to hurry back for." She was keeping him on his toes. From Muskegon, he wrote, "I think I'll take your advice about joining a gym. Honey, you know you pass out some pretty good lectures at that." Another time he wrote: "I didn't take your books with me. I left them in BH but I'll read them when I get back. Looks like I'll have to be studious if I want to get along with you." Seems Mom viewed him as a project as well as a prospect.

On March 15, 1931, my parents married. The wedding reception was held at Alex and Bella Zweig's kosher banquet hall upstairs of the Stream Dine cafeteria at 3146 Roosevelt Road, corner of Kedzie Avenue. The briefest of honeymoons followed, two nights at the Book Cadillac Hotel in Detroit, at 33 stories the tallest hotel in the U.S. That was all my father could afford in time or money. On the drive to and from Detroit, he could point out to his bride some of the places — the Kalamazoos and Battle Creeks, the Albions and Parmas — where he had begun earning a living and now would be doing it for both of them.

On the Roman calendar, March 15 is the Ides of March, a

date signifying doom for Julius Caesar. Two millennia later, there were early portents of trouble for my parents' marriage. When my mother was visiting her family in Chicago a month after the wedding, my father wrote her from Benton Harbor about a bracelet she had misplaced. "It seems as though your [sic] always losing something, aren't you honey?" In another letter: "I don't know what Gerry [her sister Gere] could have told you to make you so excited.... You better learn to control yourself a little more." Once, he sent a telegram that said sharply: COME HOME ON NEXT TRAIN. MILTON. But there was fondness as well as friction between the newlyweds. In a letter to her husband from Chicago, Mom calls him "honey boy" and "daddy" and signs off with, "Your most loving and adoring wife and sweetheart, Frieda."

As my quick-tempered mother was beginning married life in Benton Harbor, other Chicagoans of an even more volatile nature also were drawn to the area. W. Somerset Maugham famously called the French Riviera "a sunny place for shady people," too good a line, in my estimation, to be wasted on small-time operators like the Côte d'Azur's jewel thieves and gigolos. A better summer setting for Somerset — spring, fall, winter too — would have been the Twin Cities and surroundings, which attracted the real deal: gangsters who came from Chicago to play and sometimes to stay.

Al Capone's bodyguard Phil D'Andrea built a large house in St. Joseph near the St. Joseph River, a waterway that divides Benton Harbor and St. Joseph. D'Andrea's house was rumored to have a tunnel leading to the river should an escape by water become necessary. Fifteen miles upriver in Berrien Springs, another Capone henchman, Louis "Little New York" Campagna, raised cattle and alfalfa on an 80-acre farm later acquired by Muhammad Ali, who spent some of his final years there. And in Stevensville, a burg bordering St. Joseph to the south, a man calling himself Fred Dane who told neighbors he owned gas stations in Indiana lived in a two-story shingled house with a woman named Viola and a snarling German shepherd. On Saturday, December 14, 1929, a Hudson coupe driven by a drunken "Fred Dane" collided with another car in downtown St. Joseph, which was abustle with Christmas shoppers. When a policeman walking his beat, Charles Skelly, arrived to investigate, Dane shot him dead and fled.

It was quickly established that Dane was Fred "Killer" Burke, a cold-blooded Capone gunslinger who had committed bank robberies and murders and was a key figure in the St. Valentine's Day Massacre 10 months earlier. Searching Dane/Burke's house, Berrien County sheriff's deputies found in a locked closet submachine guns that ballistics tests proved had been used in the Chicago mass killings. Burke was tracked down in Missouri and brought back to St. Joseph for trial. He was convicted of murdering Skelly and was sent to Marquette State Prison in Michigan's Upper Peninsula, where he died at the age of 47.

Capone himself was a frequent visitor to the Twin Cities, sometimes staying at the Vincent Hotel, at eight stories Benton Harbor's tallest building. Capone and his retinue occupied the top floor, with armed guards stationed at the elevators and stairways. My father told of seeing convoys of Packards, a luxury car of that era, transporting Scarface and his pals to the Twin City Golf and Aviation course east of town. It was rumored that some of the golf bags in the cars contained Tommy guns instead of niblicks and mashies.

Capone made his final visit to Benton Harbor in July 1931, four months after my parents' wedding. Recently convicted of tax evasion, which would send him to a Georgia penitentiary and then to Alcatraz, Capone hosted 75 guests in the Vincent Hotel's Rose Room in what amounted to a going-away party. The room had been reserved by a women's group, which was booted to a smaller space, causing a kerfuffle that hotel manager Dannie O'Connor was forced to address. "When Capone comes here, he's a guest and nothing more," O'Connor told the press. "You hear all kinds of stories, I suppose."

Some of the stories had to do with Capone's munificence. In the Spielberg movie *Jaws*, sharks in a resort town's waters were bad for business. In Benton Harbor, the presence of human sharks was a boon. Mark Bass, my brother Joel's closest high school friend, was the son and grandson of barbers, Floyd and Frank Bass, light-skinned African Americans whose clientele was mostly white. Mark's older brother, Floyd Jr., known as Hige (pronounced *high*-ghee), was Muhammad Ali's Berrien Springs property manager and chauffeur. Mark told me that Hige's and his grandfather Frank was summoned to the Vincent Hotel to give Capone a haircut and shave, and Capone tipped him $100. At the time, a haircut at the Bass Barber Shop on Empire Avenue was 25 cents, a shave 15 cents.

It was to Benton Harbor, a town hospitable to a fault, that my father brought my mother to live. Marital storm clouds were gathering, but life proceeded apace, Mook growing his bag business and playing his poker, Fritz proving herself a dynamo reminiscent of her days at Marshall High:

> *If activities make a woman, then Frieda Kirshenbaum is A No. 1. Here they go: President Benton Harbor B'nai*

B'rith Auxiliary. President Benton Harbor Chapter of Hadassah. President Temple Beth El Sisterhood. Delegate B'nai B'rith District convention Mackinac Island. Donor chairman Hadassah. Reservations chairman Israel Bond dinner.

Chapter 6

Relathieves

My father was friendly with both of his brothers but was closer in age to Hymie and closer to him period. I was surprised to learn of the fight at Jap-O-Land, but not that Hymie was with Dad when the fists started flying. Hymie was the toughest Kirshenbaum. If he'd lived in Poland, he might have taken beatings from the Cossacks as so many other Jews did, but not, I think, without throwing a few of them down a well.

In common with Dad, Hymie drove a cab in Chicago and hung out at Benny Adler's pool hall. The story is told of Hymie taking his leisure at Adler's with a pack of other malingerers when he fell asleep in a chair and was given a hotfoot. There was expectant chuckling as the burning match inched closer to the sole of his shoe. Waking in pain and at a loss to establish which dirtbag in a room full of dirtbags was responsible, he grabbed a pool ball and had to be restrained from using it to clear out the whole crummy lot of them. Hymie was Benny Adler's kind of guy and Benny's daughter's kind as well. He married Jeanette Adler, brought her to Benton Harbor and had four children with her.

When my father was starting out in the bag business, Hymie worked for him. Dad's first trucks were clunkers barely able to transport heavy loads of bags. Hymie sometimes joined Dad on the road for help in case the truck broke down. Mook told of a time he and Hymie were traveling in Michigan in a loaded truck that was having trouble negotiating a hill. The truck edged part-way up the hill, then slipped back. With the gas pedal pressed to the floor and with the brothers' expletive-filled encouragement, the vehicle lurched forward and back a couple more times, finally heaving up and over. Mook and Hymie rejoiced as if they had conquered Mount Kanchenjunga in Nepal.[1]

Minutes later a factory's noon whistle sounded, Hymie's stomach churned. Like Grandpa Mendel, he was programmed to eat at an exact time — lunch at 12, dinner at six. Alerted that it was time to chow down, he thought of a roadside restaurant they'd passed a couple of miles back.

"Mook, turn around. That place looked good."

"We'll find something up ahead."

"What if there isn't anything? Go back. I'm hungry."

"We were lucky to make it up that hill, Hymie. I'm sure as hell not going to risk it again."

Not one to trifle with at mealtime, Hymie told his brother to pull over. He exited the truck and began walking toward the

---

1. Jewish folklore: A coachman and his decrepit horse Toby are taking a rabbi to Minsk. Coming to a hill, the coachman says, "Toby can't make it up the hill with both of us," and he orders the rabbi to get out and walk. At a second hill, the coachman volunteers to be the one who walks. A third hill is so daunting that it's necessary for both men to walk. At journey's end, the rabbi says to the coachman, "I came to Minsk to serve my congregation. You came to Minsk because I was paying you. But please tell me, why did we bring Toby?"

restaurant below the hill. "He must have hitchhiked home," Dad said. "Neither of us ever said another word about it."

There were moments of togetherness that included the youngest brother, Abe. Escaping a spell of frigid Michigan winter, the three brothers took a road trip to Florida, Abe driving. Dad told of an escapade in Miami that made the sojourn particularly memorable for him. He was in Abe's car riding shotgun, he said, when a beautiful blonde in a red convertible pulled alongside and motioned to him. With hurried goodbyes to Abe and Hymie, he joined the woman in her car.

It isn't essential for us to know whether the woman really was driving a red convertible or if she might have been a hooker. For all I know, she was a maiden on her way from choir practice to the pet store to buy food for her goldfish when she was turned to mush by the sight of the Adonis she took my father to be. The story's one indispensable element is that she was a beautiful blonde. To Mook, that was one word. Jean Harlow and Lana Turner weren't just blondes, they were *beautifulblondes*. Dark-haired sirens like Dorothy Lamour and Claudette Colbert were also easy on the eyes, but they were disadvantaged by not being *beautifulblondes*. Nor was it only blonde movie stars who caught my father's fancy. For him, being blonde went a long way toward making any woman beautiful.

Of the *beautifulblonde* in Miami, my father said, "I was with her three days, you hear? She showed me a helluva good time."

"When was this, Dad?"

He replied right away. "1932."

"But you married Mom in 1931."

"So?"

Whether Dad's dalliances were few or many, Mom never mentioned them in my hearing, or in Joel's either. She must have had her suspicions, but she had married a traveling man, and traveling men, we know, can swerve off course. It may even be that part of his appeal to her was that he was a man's man, with all that implied, both good and bad.

Insofar as business was concerned, things were getting to be quite good. Harbor Bag Company, which previously existed only as a post office box number, now had a brick-and-mortar presence at Eighth and Lake Streets in the Flats, a low-lying former wetland that was home to much of Benton Harbor's African American population and light industry — tool-and-die shops, auto repair garages and junkyards. Mook's building was a short walk from the Fruit Market and on the same block as two African American establishments with soul-stirring music, the Second Baptist Church, which had served Benton Harbor's Black community since shortly after the end of the Civil War, and the intriguingly named night spot, The Research Pleasure Club.

My father soon outgrew the first building and built a larger one a block away at Eighth and Bond, a structure that accommodated greater quantities of baled bags as well as heavy machinery. This is the first of Dad's buildings I remember. For cleaning bags, metal chutes hanging from the ceiling functioned like upside-down vacuum cleaners. Workers held bags under the chutes, and powerful suction turned them inside out with a whoosh, removing what needed to be removed. Nearby was a row of sewing machines for mending torn bags. If a farm or mill wanted its name on bags, a gigantic floor-to-ceiling printing press existed for that purpose. Dad's business card: WE PRINT BAGS TO ORDER. PRESENTED BY M. KIRSHENBAUM.

Harbor Bag Co. began as a shared enterprise between Mook and his bride. In January 1932, my mother, seven months pregnant with Roberta, was visiting her family in Chicago when a breezy letter arrived from Dad. "Hello Honey! How are you? I just called you a little while ago but I decided to write you a few lines anyway. I don't know for sure if I'll be in Chicago this week end or not, but I thought the best thing to do is send the checks in and let you deposit them. What have you been doing lately, taking good care of yourself? You better baby or your daddy won't love you any more." Continuing: "Listen honey deposit the checks as soon as you get them. And I'll straighten things out when I come in. I haven't any more to say and listen I'm sending a bye-bye dearie. With lots of love, Milton. P.S. there are six checks — total 277.75."

Mom noted the checks on the back of the envelope.

J.L. Hillyard, Fremont, Michigan $6.00
Warsaw Milling, Warsaw, Indiana $67.50
Farmers Mill & Elevator, Columbia City, Indiana $62.50
Gratz & Lemmlie, Waterloo, Indiana $9.00
W.W. Sopher & Son, Angola, Indiana $42.75
Thomas Milling Co., Lansing, Michigan $90

Many businesspeople lost everything in the Depression, but Mook, having started with nothing, had nowhere to go but up. As his business grew, he advertised for a parttime bookkeeper and operators of "bag-patching" machines. Willie, who would mend bags for him for 30 years, was hired, followed by another woman, Charlene. He bought newer trucks and lined up drivers. For loading trucks in those hard times, unemployed men were easy to find on street corners in the Flats. Word got around that this Mook fellow with the cigar was good for a dollar or two.

That my father was on the upward curve didn't go unnoticed by Grandpa Kirshenbaum. Having introduced Dad, unsuccessfully at the time, to the rudiments of the bag business a decade earlier, Grandpa demanded what he considered his due and asked him to take on Hymie and Abe as partners. But Mook had no wish to let Mendel in the door as dealmaker, much less as Hymie and Abe's probable silent partner. When he said no, the blowback was immediate. His brothers went into competition with him, and Grandpa told him, "We're going to ruin you." Such a harsh thing to say to one's son — if, one wonders anew, Mook was in fact Mendel's son.

What followed was a bare-knuckle fight between my father and his brothers that was an unsettling backdrop to my childhood. I understood that I had uncles in Benton Harbor, but the only reason I even knew their names was from hearing Mom rail against them. She made Hymie and Abe sound like ogres, and I tried to imagine what tortures awaited me if I ran into them and was caught unawares. Adding to my dread was knowing that there were aunts and cousins in town I wouldn't recognize if I saw them and who I was sure were also bad news. But when Mom called Hymie and Abe good-for-nothings, Dad told her to cut it out. He wasn't disagreeing with her, only taking the long view. He said — life lesson — "If somebody's no good, you don't have to tell other people. The time will come when other people tell you."

The uncles called their business United Bag Company. They operated at first out of Mendel's barn but soon moved into a building in the Flats a block from Harbor Bag Company. My father crossed paths with them when picking up cold cuts at Abe Frank's grocery store on Bond Street or when servicing a truck at Hy Firehammer's General Tire shop at Lake and Tenth. Hymie and Abe could peer down the street and see when Mook was getting a truck ready, and he could see when they were doing the same. If the bags on the Harbor Bag loading dock had printing on them, his brothers might have been able to make out the identity of Mook's customers.

Hymie and Abe got off to a bumpy start. They couldn't keep up payments on their building, and it went into receivership. To stay afloat, they engaged in dubious side hustles, selling hog feed and dealing in animal skins discarded by butchers. And as Dad foresaw, people had reason to speak ill of them. On September 6, 1941, a front page story in the *News-Palladium* reported the arrest of Hymie and Abe on charges of assault and battery against a former employee, Nate Cohen. Cohen, the story said, claimed that "the Kirshenbaum brothers beat him severely during an argument over a dispute of longstanding."

My father was a footloose teenager when he committed a burglary in South Haven, while Hymie and Abe were in their mid-30s with wives and children when they allegedly dragged Cohen from his truck and beat him bloody. Whatever the cause of their original quarrel with Cohen, the brothers may have been further upset that he now was driving a truck parttime for my father. What's more, Mook was throwing business Cohen's way and allowing him to work out of the Harbor Bag Company building, which Nate was doing under the name Benton Bag Company. Essentially, Hymie and Abe's exemployee was competing against them in league with their enemy brother.

Dad told me he received a call from a distraught Mendel urging him to persuade Cohen to drop the charges. He said he told Mendel that the matter was something his brothers and

Cohen had to work out themselves. On the eve of the scheduled trial, Nate withdrew his complaint. I suspect that Mook may have had a hand in that decision after all but wasn't about to show weakness by admitting it to Mendel.

Hymie and Abe were dogged by rumors of devious dealings. In 1947 the insurance company covering their International two-ton truck canceled the policy, determining that the United Bag Company brothers had shady Chicago connections and were suspected of dealing in stolen goods. As if to further damn them, the company's report telling of the cancellation made it a point to identify the brothers as "Hebrew."

By appearance, Hymie and Abe called to mind the principals in Steinbeck's *Of Mice and Men*, the crafty migrant worker George and his lumbering sidekick Lennie. Abie was small and canny like George, while Hymie was stronger and more deliberate in manner, not unlike Lennie, but after that, the comparisons fall flat. Hymie was no lummox, and he was Abe's willing partner in the war against Mook, which included a bonkers but dead-serious battle waged in the Benton Harbor-St. Joseph Yellow Pages. To steal business from Mook's Harbor Bag Company and, conveniently, at the same time from Nate Cohen's Benton Bag Company, the United Bag partners took a second listing under the directory's BAGS-BURLAP heading as "Benton Harbor Bag Co." resulting in:

Benton Bag Co, 308 Eighth St 51371
Harbor Bag Co, 308 Eighth St 51371
United Bag Co, 402 Eighth St 54822
Benton Harbor Bag Co, 402 Eighth St 54822

Counterattacking against the United Bag Company brothers, Mook the next year listed Harbor Bag Company secondarily in the Yellow Pages as "United Bag Supply Co." whereupon:

Benton Bag Co, 308 Eighth St 51371
Benton Harbor Bag Co, 402 Eighth St 54822
Harbor Bag Co, 308 Eighth St 51371
United Bag Co, 402 Eighth St 54822
United Bag Supply Co, 308 Eighth St 51371

Michigan is known for its single-industry cities — Detroit automobiles, Grand Rapids furniture, Battle Creek breakfast cereal, and there's even Mackinac Island for fudge. With only the telephone directory to go by, one might have thought that Benton Harbor was the Michigan town synonymous with burlap bags.

In the end, the Battle of the Yellow Pages was probably a standoff, each side stealing business from the other. My father told of a time when he bested his brothers as a result of Yellow Pages confusion. "I got a phone call, and this fellow said the bags were ready," Pop said. "I could tell the call was meant for my brothers. I said, 'Let's go over the order again.' It sounded like a good deal, you follow? The guy confirmed the time to pick up the bags, and I made sure to arrive early. I loaded up and was out of there." Dad said that on his way back to Benton Harbor, he recognized Abe and Hymie coming up the road toward him in their truck. "I honked because I wanted to make sure they saw me. If they didn't guess that I had the bags meant for them, they were about to find out."

Pop referred to Hymie and Abe as his "relathieves." They could have called him the same and probably did.

My father wasn't ruined by Mendel, not even close. He

succeeded in business because he was well-liked and hardworking and because being a road warrior suited him. Alone in a truck, crisscrossing Midwestern highways and byways, he was at peace. Having Hymie with him in a truck was history. He no longer needed companionship, not even over the airwaves. He rarely turned on a truck's radio, and he disdained CB radio — none of that "good buddy" foolishness for him. All he needed to transact business on the road were the maps available for free in those days at gas stations, and once he knew the territory, he didn't need those.

Then too, he was lucky. He was a hoarder of burlap bags, amassing far more of them than he ordinarily could have hoped to sell. If bags were available at the right price, he bought them, truckload after truckload, and even truckloads weren't enough. His acquisitiveness led him to Campbell Soup Company's Chicago plant, which had huge quantities of bags to dispose of that had held tomatoes, carrots, beans and other vegetables. Dad befriended a well-placed Campbell Soup operative with whose connivance bags were loaded onto barges and shipped across Lake Michigan to Benton Harbor. Mook bought the bags for next to nothing, and the barges kept coming. Once he gave the Campbell Soup insider keys to a new car as, shall we say, a token of their friendship.

With every inch of his shop filled with bags, Mook was in constant need of additional space. He built a warehouse on Britain Avenue and bought and rented storage facilities elsewhere in Berrien County and in neighboring Van Buren County. His heedless buildup of inventory was an MBA-worthy case study of what not to do in business, but during World War II, he found himself with the mother lode. Bags were still needed for farm products but now also were in demand for use as sandbags in foxholes and as armor on tanks.

At the same time, global war cut off importation to the U.S. of burlap from Asia. Other dealers ran out of stock, but my father's storehouses bulged. Up to and through the war and for several years thereafter, his business was the best it had been or would be ever again.

Hymie and Abe never fared as well in the bag business as my father did, but in the end they made out all right with United Bag Company, earning livings for their families, and with no further blemishes on their names as far as I know. Just as there was room for both Kellogg and Post cereal in Battle Creek, so, it turned out, could Benton Harbor accommodate coexisting bag companies — even those operated by brothers who didn't trust each other for a single minute.

Chapter 7

Peeling Onions

IN THE FIRST decade of their marriage, my parents lived in a succession of small, rented houses in Benton Harbor that my mother called "bungalows." She kept finding fault with them — ceiling too low, closet space insufficient, neighborhood sketchy — and my father could be choosy too. After inspecting a house while Mom was visiting her family in Chicago, he wrote her, "I didn't care for it so much. It's got too many doors."

Eventually they put small and rented behind them and moved into a palatial Tudor house that made my father's improved circumstances plain for the world to see. The house was large, with a gabled roof, tri-colored chimneys, and carved and chiseled wood and stone inside and out. There was a stately front lawn shaded by maples and elms. In the back, a screened porch opened onto a smaller lawn on a bluff overlooking the St. Joseph River, which flows from its origins in northern Indiana and easternmost Michigan before reaching its mouth at Lake Michigan three miles from the house. At the house's location the river was bordered on both banks by dense thickets of woods.

The house was in Fair Plain, an unincorporated residential area of Benton Harbor and, more narrowly, in a real estate development called the Indian Hills Country Club District. The name was a nod to the onetime prevalence in the area of Potawatomi and Miami tribes and traded on the cachet of the nearby Berrien Hills Country Club, which excluded Blacks and Jews from membership. The Indian Hills Country Club District was created in the 1920s with a floridly worded prospectus that spoke of "winding walks, tree-arched drives and flower-edged roadways," surroundings that "down through the ages of time we find human fancies still seeking." The prospectus promised that "inviolable restrictions on building and ownership" would "at all times protect the dwellers of Indian Hills" — here, too, plain and simple, no Blacks or Jews.

My father was too live-and-let-live to butt up against discriminatory barriers simply for the satisfaction of seeing them fall. I offer a more prosaic explanation for how we came to be the first Jewish family on Miami Road, the development's "newly created main drive." The Depression was in its late stages, but money remained tight, and for a house that on, say, Chicago's North Shore or in Connecticut's Fairfield County would one day command many millions, Dad made a $20,000 all-cash offer that was too good to refuse, even coming from a Jewish buyer. Paying cash was Mook's way. He didn't believe in mortgages and never learned that debt could be an investor's friend. "You shouldn't buy anything until you can afford it," was his stated belief.

Mom, Dad, Roberta and I took up occupancy in the house at 1530 Miami Road on December 1, 1941, six days before

Pearl Harbor. There, our family of four, to be five with Joel's arrival in 1944, lived in comfort if not always in harmony.[1]

From the start, Miami Road was one of Benton Harbor's most prestigious streets. Nearly a mile long, it was lined with several other houses as splendid or nearly so as ours, and none less than fine. Feeding into Miami Road like tributaries of the mighty Mississippi were streets with Native American names: Seneca, Onondaga, Cayuga, North Ottawa, South Ottawa, Chippewa and Montezuma. These street names survive but the term Indian Hills Country Club District, having served its purpose as a marketing tool, fell into disuse.

One side of our house was defined by a row of firs, beyond which lived the Van Antwerps, who moved in different circles than my parents. Robert Van Antwerp was commodore of the St. Joseph Yacht Club and a pillar of the Benton Harbor Congregational Church. He and his wife, Vera, had four children, one of whom, Robert Jr., went to West Point and ascended to captain of cadets, the highest position in the academy's student chain of command. Afterward, climbing the military ranks, Lt. General Robert L. Van Antwerp Jr. became head of the Army Corps of Engineers. He was 12 years younger than I. Had we been closer in age, perhaps some of his spit and polish would have rubbed off on me. More likely, next to such a paragon, I would have suffered feelings of utter worthlessness.

On our property's other, unobstructed, side were the Gideons. John Gideon was in the sundries business with his

---

[1]. Saul Colef, a dentist, his wife, Sara, and their daughters, Helyn and Evelon, became the second Jewish family on Miami Road. When Helyn married Herman Presser in the Colef living room, I was the ring bearer, carrying the rings down the aisle dressed head to toe in white, looking like a vanilla milkshake. (Saul's brother Irving was the Benton Harbor physician who five years earlier delivered all 8 lb. 11 oz. of me at Mercy Hospital.)

brother Leon, for six years Benton Harbor's mayor. The brothers distributed candy, including some of their making, such as their popular "nut balls" and "pride clusters." John's wife, Monica, was crippled after crashing her Volkswagen Phaeton into a tree when she swerved to avoid hitting a dog. A gregarious housekeeper, Hilda Dean, minded the Gideon children, Jack, Jimmy and Anne. Jack had polio. On summer days he and his mother could be seen outside taking the sun together in their wheelchairs. Jimmy Gideon was a sour-faced child. In a home movie of a party on our back lawn for my ninth birthday, games are being played, but Jimmy looks like he can't wait for Hilda to come rescue him.

Where Bob Van Antwerp strutted, Jimmy Gideon stumbled. He graduated from Notre Dame, dropped out of University of Detroit Law School, had business setbacks and went to prison twice — for making false statements to obtain a federal loan, then for conspiring, unsuccessfully, to kill his ex-wife and his brother-in-law, Anne's husband.

The lot opposite us was heavily wooded, and I enjoyed exploring its secrets until Edwin J. Bartz, owner of the Dodge-Plymouth dealership, and his wife, Ruth, ruined my fun by building a house there. Where a thick entanglement of trees had been, a tidy lawn and gardens appeared, cared for by a House of David hired hand with full beard and flowing locks who gave me half waves while keeping the Bartz foliage more neatly tended than his own.

I was a just turned one-year-old when World War II broke out and six when it ended. My father, too old to serve in the armed forces, helped on the home front as a civilian air-raid warden, participating in drills to protect the Twin Cities in case Luftwaffe bombers reached the heartland. On a shelf in our front closet was his white warden's helmet, which I liked to wear. It was heavy and covered my eyes and ears.

"Take that off — it's not a toy," Mother commanded in a faraway voice.

Father, always more lenient, said, words muffled, "Careful you don't run into something," but added, "That hat looks good on you, boy."

Dad also was on the Berrien County war bond committee, and Mom belonged to a women's group that collected waste fats and oils for the military to make medicine and gunpowder. Because of the awful things happening to the Jews in Europe — first in Germany, then in one Hitler-conquered country after another — they felt they had an extra stake in the war's outcome. In the U.S., there was gas rationing, with signs asking motorists IS THIS TRIP NECESSARY? After the war, Dad employed this phrase for other purposes. An authority on the shortcomings of ladies' beauty salons ("some of those dames look better when they arrive than when they leave"), he ensured that when my mother made an appointment to get her hair done, she had considered the matter carefully. "Is this trip necessary?" he inquired of her.

My father had Herculean stamina. He often played poker into the wee hours, came home, grabbed three or four hours of sleep, then went out on the road. To facilitate faster getaways, he sometimes brought a loaded truck to the house the night before. Our neighbors didn't know the truck had been there because he was gone before morning light, leaving me to contend with Mother alone.

Dad's long hours and hard work, I came to understand, accounted for the material advantages we enjoyed. We always had two cars, one and sometimes both of them Cadillacs. A towering antenna affixed to the back of the house allowed us to get all three Chicago television stations on our enormous 16-inch Motorola. Benton Harbor was closer to Chicago than to Detroit — 90 vs. 185 road miles, and even closer, 60 miles, across Lake Michigan. Although I cheered for the home-state Tigers, I could follow them only on the radio because Detroit television stations were out of range, whereas the fuzzy black-and-white transmissions of Cubs and White Sox home games were viewable on Chicago's WGN-TV, Channel 9, the teams sharing the same announcer, the neighborly Jack Brickhouse. [2]

Business success gave Dad stature. I was in boyhood heaven when he took me downtown with him. While he went to "get my ears lowered" at the barbershop in the Fidelity Building, I perused the newsstand at the cigar store on Territorial Road. I leafed through *Boys' Life, Collier's, Time* and *The Saturday Evening Post* and peeked at *Latest Hit Songs, Hit Parade* or *Song Hits,* on whose tissue-thin pages were printed the words of pop songs along with ads for acne treatments and magic sets for wowing your friends. These publications kept me lyrics literate during the period when Tin Pan Alley was transitioning from wartime rousers like "Who's Gonna Fear Der Fuehrer (When Der Fuehrer Fears Himself)" to peacetime ditties such as "Rag Mop" and "I've Got a Lovely Bunch of Coconuts." Here I learned that when the Merry Macs sang "Mairzy doats and dozy doats and liddle lamzy divey," what they were saying — why, of course! — was "Mares eat oats and does eat oats and little lambs eat ivy." But the only publication

---

2. I also watched wrestling televised from Chicago's Rainbow Arena and Marigold Gardens. To get the dope on grapplers like Lou Thesz, Farmer Don Marlin and Hombre Montana, I subscribed to a Chicago magazine called *Wrestling As You Like It*. I assume that the clunky title was inspired by the wrestling match won by Orlando in *As You Like It*. Somebody at the grunt-and-groan publication must have known his Shakespeare.

I bought with my allowance money was "The Bible of Baseball," *The Sporting News*, which published the box scores even of minor league games. That alone made it worth the 20 cents I shelled out for it.[3]

Later I met Dad at the bank, where he knew everybody — officers, tellers, other customers. The Farmers and Merchants Bank was the most imposing building on Main Street, with two columns rising to a pediment housing a clock that told the time in Roman numerals, merging, as I saw it, the glory of Rome with the grandeur of Benton Harbor. I went with Dad into the vault area, where two keys, his and a clerk's, opened "our" safe-deposit box. He placed papers in the box and took papers out and did the same, in and out, with cash. The roll of greenbacks he put in his pocket as we exited was secured by a rubber band. Whenever he removed a bill from the roll to buy something, it looked like he was peeling an onion. If expenses made him peel too many onions, he said, "All I've got left is the rubber band."

Other times I went with him to the Benton Harbor Fruit Market, which was alive with the cacophony of trucks rumbling, horns blowing and growers and brokers shouting. Dad was greeted by farmers he knew who gave him, gratis, sacks of peaches, apples and strawberries that I took to be tribute paid to a man of high station. If we had time, we stopped at the Market Restaurant. Seated at the counter, the

---

3. *The Sporting News* also printed the box scores of American Legion state and territorial championship games. When I was 14, I went through that year's 49 American Legion box scores and ascertained that 37 of the winning teams made fewer errors than the losers, eight made more errors, and four committed an equal number. I wrote *The Sporting News* citing those figures as evidence of "how many games are lost because of poor fielding." Simplistic though my analysis was, *The Sporting News* published the letter from JERRY KIRSHENBAUM, Benton Harbor, Mich.

bags of fruit at our feet, Mook had his slice of apple pie ("and a glass of water, dearie, no ice") and I my chocolate ice cream or cherry Coke.

Best of all was when I was six or seven and my father took me with him by truck on a daylong trip to Indiana. It was to north central Indiana — Logansport, Wabash, Bluffton, those parts. We dropped off a load of bags at a farm and made stops at other farms where he had done business. These side visits were happen-to-be-in-the-neighborhood showings of the colors. I especially remember two things about the trip. One was the sweet smell wafting from the distilleries that converted harvested mint plants into oil. Until then, I hadn't known that it was from God's green earth that Mr. Wrigley got the spearmint for his chewing gum or where Santa acquired the peppermint flavor for his sugar canes. Dad told me that Indiana was a major mint producer. He said Michigan was too. He knew a lot of things, Pop did.

My other memory was of how warmly he was welcomed at each farm. I can't say what was discussed with the slow-talking men in the overalls and mud-covered boots — possibly commodity prices or road conditions, almost certainly the weather — only that they were in no hurry to get back to their tractors. I could tell that they liked my father, and I knew that the reason they were nice to me was that I was his son.

Mom was glad when Dad began to do well in business but complained about his "hoodlum friends." For him, it was a matter of loyalty. These were the fellows he knew on the escalator up and to whom he might need to turn if he found himself on the freight elevator down. "Don't forget where you came from," was how he put it. Mom got on his case for loaning money to cronies not paid back. Another of Dad's life lessons was that if you float somebody a loan, you should think of it as a gift so as to soften the blow if you don't see your money again. This lesson was lost on Mom, who badgered him about errant loans. He might be forced to reply, "Frieda, you can say Kaddish for that money. Don't let it aggravate you." For my father, aggravation was to be avoided. He considered peace of mind more important than riches. "What good is owning silk sheets if you're too worried to fall asleep on them?" he asked.

One evening a black car with Illinois license plates pulled up our long driveway. Mother seemed concerned. I followed her to the window and made out two figures in the front of the car and two in the back. A small man in the back got out. He hurried to the side door by our garage. My father listened to him and went upstairs, returning with an envelope. My parents had alerted me to a hatbox on a high shelf in a bedroom closet containing cash in case of an emergency. Apparently, the man had an emergency. Dad gave him the envelope. "Thanks, Mook, I'll pay you back," he said. He returned to the black car. Headlights back on, it sped away.

Our visitor, I learned, was Joey Kamin, a truck driver who split his time between Benton Harbor and Chicago. A gambler and convicted car thief, Joey once was busted for fencing stolen television sets. I would see him in Dad's shop. He had a five o'clock shadow no matter the hour and was in the curious practice of keeping one pant leg rolled up to the knee but not the other.

He appears in a photo of celebrants at a New Year's Eve party, an image as evocative for me as *Our Town* has been for generations of theatergoers. A smiling Alice Becker, who will die at age 40 of a heart attack, is hugging Lake Price, who playfully sticks her tongue out and makes a face at the camera. Charlotte Alberts is sharing a laugh with her sister-in-law Pearl

Grau, who will make it to 105, outliving all others in the photo. Bertha Mindel has one arm draped around her husband, Irv, who will hang himself in his junkyard office in the Flats by means described in the *News-Palladium* in enough irresponsible detail to be a procedural on committing suicide, the other on the shoulder of Harold Friedman, owner with his wife Helen of Helaine's, the women's clothing store that one day will be run by Hillard Friedman, Harold's son from a previous marriage. Mom, wearing a long sleeveless dress that flatters her well-toned shoulders, is in the arms of Charlotte Alberts's husband, Harold, an insurance broker and, like the others mentioned, a family friend. Dad isn't in the photo. He may be in another room, with somebody in *his* arms.

Alone in the back row, Joey Kamin is blowing up a balloon.

I WAS at work in the Nation section of *Time* when the daily stack of newspapers and wire-service clippings thudded onto my desk. A front-page story in *The Miami News* caught my eye.

> TRUCKER'S MURDER HERE HAS GANGLAND TOUCH
> *A husky gunman invaded a North Dade trucking firm last night and fatally shot its owner — who had a long police record — a crime carried out with gangland efficiency. The victim was Joey Kamin..."it looked like a contract job," said a Miami Police source....*

I phoned Dad. He was sorry to hear the news but sounded unsurprised. The Miami papers said Joey was connected to Frankie Dio, an underworld figure recently convicted in an international dope-smuggling operation. The killing was never solved. Mook said nothing of the night Joey Kamin came to our house or the envelope that changed hands.

Chapter 8

Goo-Goo Eyes

I HAVE A MEMORY, one buried so deep in my consciousness that it actually may be only a remembered dream. My four-year-old self is playing on the front lawn of 1530 Miami Road. My sister is standing on the grass next to the house, and I call for her to join me. Roberta is 10 but isn't as given to playing as I am. She mulls my invitation and picks at her lips, a nervous habit of hers, while I take care not to trip over any of the water sprinklers on the lawn. Underground sprinkling systems are new to residential properties and are glitch-prone. They're meant to recede flush to the ground, but sometimes one remains upright, a hazard for the unwary.

Bobbie takes steps in my direction, then squats to catch her breath. She needs to rest like this when she exerts herself even slightly. When I am older, I will learn the reason. She was born a blue baby, so called because of cyanosis, a condition in which the faces of afflicted children take on a bluish hue. To me, Bobbie's color leans more toward purple. Did I not mention that my memory is in Technicolor? I can also say that I was wearing green shorts and a yellow striped shirt, but I'd be making that part up. The Technicolor here is as wonky as our sprinkling system.

Blue babies have a congenital heart malformation called tetralogy of Fallot, which limits the oxygenated blood circulating from the lungs to the heart. The exhaustion and fainting spells Bobbie experienced because of the defect were impairment enough. That she also was mentally handicapped was discovered when she was an infant. Her retardation was blamed on a stoppage of her heart that caused brain damage. Shaken by their daughter's disabilities, my parents questioned whether to have more children but were assured by doctors that there was little risk that any additional offspring of theirs would suffer similar problems. It's to the dispensers of these assurances, no doubt issued with fingers crossed, that my brother and I owe our existence.

In my sister's time, special-needs education programs were almost non-existent, and she was thrown into the public school population with predictably poor results. Starting in kindergarten and through first and part of second grade, she attended Fair Plain School. She had trouble keeping up and was too incapacitated to join other children at recess or for play dates. When she was diagnosed with diabetes, one more cruel trick fate played on her, she could no longer even go through the motions in public school. But she had stuck it out long enough to learn to read and write. For the rest of her life, the books by her bedside were of the see-Spot-run variety, and her penmanship was childlike, but she was able to write simple thank-you notes and letters to the family when she was away from home, which turned out to be much of the time.

In 1943, when Roberta was 11, my parents found a school

for her in Florida. The Tanglewood Boarding School for Handicapped Children occupied a white stucco building in Fort Lauderdale two miles from the Atlantic Ocean, close enough for the school to promote itself as being "by the sea." To be near their daughter, my parents rented a small house in the Little River section of Northwest Miami. The house was a half-hour drive from the school. Joel spent some of the first months of his life in Miami, and I attended kindergarten there.

I recall little of Florida in those World War II years other than my membership in Clayton's Gang, a pack of small fry whose primary activity was to run around, fall on the ground and get up. Clayton, who may have been as old as seven, wore his mantle of leadership with aplomb. He must have liked me because he kept doing favors for me. A creek said to be infested with alligators separated our house from a wooded area, and Clayton built a bridge for me so I could check out the other side. The minute I stepped on the bridge, a piece of crumbling plasterboard, I plunged into the water, drenched to the waist. In fear of my flesh being torn to pieces by jagged teeth and canyon-sized jaws, I clambered onto dry land in a panic.

Another time Clayton relieved me of my treasured U.S. Army water canteen, a gift from my Uncle Irving, Mom's brother, who was in the Army helping win the war. I traded Clayton the canteen for a sword consisting of two pieces of nailed-together driftwood that he said was magical. Dad told me I'd been bamboozled but said I probably could get by in the years remaining in my life without the canteen. My getting snookered may have been an early indication to him that I wasn't cut out to follow in his footsteps as a businessman. For me there was a different takeaway: the world was full of Claytons, and my father could protect me from them only to a point.

My parents eased into the pleasures of Florida living. A home movie shows my mother dolled up and my father in sunglasses and with a raffish George Raft look. They sampled South Florida nightlife. In Miami Beach, they went with friends to the Five O'Clock Club, a dinner-and-dance nightclub where drinks were on the house at 5 p.m., an alcohol-infused analogue of the early-bird special. Another night they treated Bobbie to a big-girl night out at the Clover Club, a supper club on Biscayne Boulevard that presented Latin-flavored floor shows and billed itself as "the showplace of the tropics." In a photo taken at the Clover Club, Mom has a gardenia in her hair, Dad wears a double-breasted sport coat with shirt buttoned to the neck, and Bobbie is in a striped dress and clutches a fan. In photos taken at other times, she sometimes has a faraway look. Here she is alert and smiling.

My parents were desperate to find help for my sister. In 1942, before our time in Florida, Mother contacted Dr. Richard Overholt, a thoracic surgeon at Boston's Deaconess Hospital and one of the first medical professionals to warn of the hazards of cigarette smoking. He agreed to see Roberta, and Mom took her by Pullman train to Boston, which was under wartime blackout, signs everywhere warning of German air attacks: DON'T GIVE 'EM A TARGET. Dr. Overholt examined Bobbie and corresponded with Mom for a year, finally writing, "I am sorry that we found a situation that could not be corrected surgically."

As it happened, down the Eastern Seaboard in Baltimore, efforts were underway at this time at Johns Hopkins Medical School and Hospital to address that very "situation." The driving force at Johns Hopkins behind what would be an historic medical breakthrough was Dr. Helen Taussig, a woman regarded as the founder of pediatric cardiology. Taussig overcame daunting obstacles to carve her name in the annals of medical history. She worked in a profession dominated by men, she had dyslexia, and she was partially deaf. To overcome the last of these impediments, she used her fingers to feel the heartbeats of her young patients.

Encountering children with tetralogy of Fallot, Taussig theorized that the defect could be repaired by rerouting the flow of oxygenated blood to the lungs by means of a shunt. She sold Johns Hopkins' surgeon-in-chief Alfred Blalock on the idea, but it took a third team member, an unassuming man named Vivien Thomas, to turn the concept into reality by working out the surgical details. Together, Taussig, Blalock and Thomas developed the so-called blue baby operation, which is credited for ushering in a new era of cardiac surgery that led ultimately to coronary bypasses and heart transplants.

An African American, Thomas wasn't a doctor and had only a high school education, yet he was a skilled technician. Blalock previously worked at Vanderbilt University, where he hired the Louisiana-born Thomas as a lab assistant and came to rely on him so completely that when he was offered the Hopkins position, he insisted on taking Thomas with him.

Walking the halls of Johns Hopkins Hospital, a Black man in a Southern city at an institution where members of his race were rare in any position, Thomas was mistaken for a janitor and paid like one. He was a second-class citizen even to Blalock, who, much as he valued Thomas working alongside him, treated him differently after hours. At parties Blalock hosted at home for his white friends and fellow surgeons, Thomas was the Negro hired to tend bar.

Thomas overcame his challenges as impressively as Taussig did hers. After developing the methodology used in the blue baby surgery — performing more than 200 operations on laboratory animals to demonstrate that the procedure could be safe and effective on humans — he became a trusted member of the Johns Hopkins faculty, teaching techniques for lung as well as heart operations to young surgeons, some of them the guests he served drinks to at Blalock's parties.

The blue baby collaborators earned wide acclaim. Taussig received the Presidential Medal of Freedom from Lyndon Johnson, Blalock's name adorns Johns Hopkins' 15-story Alfred Blalock Clinical Sciences Building, and one of Johns Hopkins Medical School's four advisory colleges is named after Taussig, another after Thomas. Thomas became the hospital's director of surgical research, and in 1976 Johns Hopkins awarded him an honorary doctorate. He is the central figure in two movies — a PBS documentary *Partners of the Heart* narrated by Denzel Washington and an HBO feature film *Something the Lord Made* in which Mos Def, Alan Rickman and Mary Stuart Masterson play Thomas, Blalock and Taussig, respectively.

On November 29, 1944, with Taussig close by and Thomas even closer, advising Blalock about suture placement and the exact instruments to use, a critically ill nine-month-old girl, Eileen Saxon, became the first child to undergo surgery to correct tetralogy of Fallot. Eileen died seven months later but was believed to have lived longer than she would have had the operation not been performed. For that reason, the surgery was considered a success. On February 3, 1945, a 12-year-old girl became the second patient to be operated on by Blalock. She fared better than Eileen, and others fared better still. By November 1, 1945, 55 children had undergone the surgery.

The achievement at Johns Hopkins was hailed in medical journals, newspapers and magazines around the world, and the hospital was deluged with inquiries from parents hoping their blue baby children could be helped by the miracle procedure. In late 1945, with our family back in Michigan, my mother had Roberta's medical records sent to Johns Hopkins. Dr. Taussig decided she was a candidate for the surgery, but acceptance came with a warning. The death rate from blue baby operations was running about 20%, and Bobbie's recently discovered diabetes, Taussig cautioned, made the mortality risk for her even greater. Their daughter's quality of life was so poor that my parents decided to go forward with the surgery, and on March 7, 1946, my 13-year-old sister was admitted to Johns Hopkins Hospital, with Mom and Dad at her side.

Examining her new patient, Taussig wrote in her notes that she thought Roberta "could be benefited by the operation but it will not be easy." Of the chances for success, she wrote, "I do not feel a bit too sure."

Dad left Mom in Baltimore and returned to Benton Harbor for business and to watch over me, seven, and Joel, almost two. On Friday, March 15, my parents' 15th wedding anniversary, Roberta became the 102nd patient to receive the Blalock-Taussig shunt, later renamed the Blalock-Taussig-Thomas shunt, correcting a slight to the Black man without whom the breakthrough wouldn't have happened. Bobbie's surgery lasted three hours and 15 minutes. "The patient had a very deep chest," Blalock wrote in his surgical notes. "Exposure was somewhat more difficult than usual. I have not seen a patient in whom there was so great a distance between the subclavian artery and the pulmonary artery." Blalock noted that Bobbie had been "quite cyanotic" at the start of the operation, but her color improved greatly after [it] was over." He guardedly foresaw "an excellent result."

The day after the operation, settling in for the evening at Lord Baltimore Hotel, Mom wrote my father on hotel stationary. "My darling, Saturday nite is the loneliest night in the week — for both of us. Roberta — well, I knocked on her door and she said, 'come in' and there she was sitting in a chair, moving around. Her speech is clearer than before the operation & her eyes clearer. She's going into a wheelchair tomorrow. Oh darling, it's the miracle we always hoped would happen. God has certainly been wonderful to us." She wrote that Dad's brother Hymie and his wife, Jeanette, sent flowers. The brothers were bitter business rivals, which made the gesture all the kinder.

Bobbie's recovery was long and difficult. Poked and prodded by waves of medics, she didn't fully understand what was happening. "She is not very cooperative," a post-op report said. "She appears quite suspicious ... For about 2 weeks her mental status was very poor, and she was terribly belligerent and paranoid. However, after that time, when she was allowed up and realized how much improved she was, she seemed more friendly and well adjusted."

Bobbie spent her 14th birthday — March 29, 1946 — at Johns Hopkins. She was kept a week longer than expected to allow doctors to get her diabetes under control. On April 10, she came home. She had been in the hospital 34 days.

The blue baby operation was new and imperfect, and my sister would be hospitalized for heart issues and other problems many times in her too-short life, but her bluish-purplish coloring was gone, and she could walk greater distances without tiring. No longer did Dad have to carry her from room to room in the house, or from the house to the car, or from the car to her doctors' appointments. She was stronger and her spirits high enough that a search began for a school that would be right for her.

The year in Fort Lauderdale had been basically a holding

action. Other than taking students to the beach, Tanglewood Boarding School for Handicapped Children offered few social activities and little in the way of academic instruction. Stays at other institutions followed. They were brief and for one reason or another unsatisfactory — the Hazelwood School in Union City, Michigan, the Woods School in Langhorne, Pennsylvania, and the Mary E. Pogue School and Sanitarium in Wheaton, Illinois, a Catholic institution where there were other Jewish youngsters, one of them a rabbi's child.

Finally, Roberta landed at Brown School in Austin, Texas, which she would attend on and off for more than a decade. Brown School served mentally disabled children and young adults, most of them from the South and Southwest, and provided dances, school outings and academic tutoring.

My sister's letters home from Brown School, obviously written with help, were cheery. "My Dearest Mother," one began, "you may stay happy because I am happy. I am taking History, Homemaking, Ceramics and Physical Ed." She thanked Mom for newspaper clippings she'd received about family friends, and ended by noting, "Jane Miller isn't here anymore she went to a school in Okla [sic] near her home town."

Writing me: "My Dearest Jerry. How are you? I am feeling fine. I miss you very much. I hope you had a nice Christmas. The history Class took a field trip to San Antonio and we took our lunch. We saw the Missions. New Year's Eve we celebrated late." She closed with a request. "Please tell mother to send me some assorted cards. Your loving sister, Roberta."

My parents visited Bobbie in Texas half a dozen times. When she developed a mastoid infection requiring surgery — more misfortune for the poor girl — they flew to be with her, otherwise Dad drove down. Many roadside accommodations in those days were guest cabins with lumpy beds and rusty bathroom fixtures, and my parents kept stayovers enroute to a minimum. The sooner they got to Texas, the better.

I came along on three of the trips, the first when I was eight. I was fascinated by the names of towns along the way like Cape Girardeau, Poplar Bluff, Bald Knob and Arkadelphia, but we zipped by them so fast I couldn't tell if they were as fabulous as they sounded. However, I made sure that Dad slowed down during the homage-paying seconds it took to pass through Swifton, Arkansas, population 500, hometown of the Tigers' Hall of Fame-bound third baseman George Kell. I also had him ease up on the gas when we came upon Burma-Shave signs, those treasures of roadside Americana spaced one after another along the highways, parceling out doggerel, line by hilarious line.

HARDLY A DRIVER... IS NOW ALIVE...WHO PASSED... ON HILLS... AT 75.

A MAN A MISS... A CAR A CURVE... HE KISSED THE MISS... AND MISSED... THE CURVE.

Only rarely did the verse pertain to Burma-Shave's product, brushless shaving cream: THE WOLF... IS SHAVED... SO NEAT AND TRIM... RED RIDING HOOD... IS CHASING HIM.

I read aloud these lines, and Mom and Dad laughed with me. I thought the poetry department at Burma-Shave headquarters must be a jolly place to work.

My father called himself a "wheel beater," meaning he was an indefatigable driver who could press on for many miles with few rest stops. One of our infrequent pullovers was in Texarkana, where we had lunch in Arkansas, then strolled across State Line Avenue for ice cream in Texas. I thought that was swell, but I was otherwise unimpressed by Texarkana, considering it neither here nor there.

Only when we reached Texas did we do any true sightseeing. From Austin we traveled to the border city of Brownsville and had a glimpse of the Rio Grande and Mexico on the other side. We visited Houston and stayed at the ultra-posh Shamrock Hotel, which Dad had read about. The Shamrock was built by the oil wildcatter Glenn McCarthy, the inspiration for Jett Rink, the character in Edna Ferber's novel *Giant* portrayed in the film adaptation by James Dean. The Shamrock was stupendous, with a swimming pool so oceanic that motorboat races were said to be held on it.

In Austin we stayed at a different hotel each visit. The most fun was the lushly landscaped Terrace Motor Hotel. Half motel and half resort, it was the last word in post-war roadside lodging, featuring a cocktail lounge, steakhouse, room service, bellhops who traveled the grounds in Jeeps and, potentially best of all, a barbershop with a singing barber. I say "potentially" because when I went for a look-see and listen-to, the barbershop was closed. The singing barber was on vacation, resting his chops.

The Terrace Motor Hotel's swimming pool was smaller than the Shamrock's, but it had a three-meter diving board from which my mother snapped off several smartly executed dives. "She must be a professional diver," my father overheard a man at poolside say. Pop wasn't always proud of Mother in public, but on this occasion, he was.

While we were visiting Brown School, a girl student two or three years older than I followed me around smiling and giggling. Dad teased me, "She's making goo-goo eyes at you." I pleaded, "*Dad...!*" When Joel was five and joined us for the first time, he bragged that he was going to ride the fastest horse in

Texas. At a stable outside Austin, Joel was asked if he wanted a fast horse or slow one. He whispered, "a slow one." Dad overheard and ribbed Joel as he did me about Miss Goo-Goo-Eyes.

Bobbie returned from Brown School to Benton Harbor for two or three months at a time, making our family complete and our lives richer. Sitting on the couch with my father, I liked it when he rubbed his stubbly cheek against mine. I said, "Whisker me again, Daddy," and he sandpapered me harder. Bobbie didn't like being whiskered, but she could handle gentle hugs and a bit of tickling. Joel and I played War and Go Fish with her, and our father sometimes joined in. Away from the poker table, playing children's card games, he fared no better than we did.

My sister loved movies, especially musicals, anything with singing, dancing, a love story and a happy ending. Before I was old enough to drive her myself, Dad dropped Bobbie and me off on Saturdays at the Liberty Theater on Main Street. At Popcorn John's two doors from the theater, I bought five-cent bags of popcorn for each of us. John Moutstason's popcorn was the best the world has ever known. In four decades on the same block, he sold enough popcorn, spice drops, taffy, jawbreakers and lollipops, first from a wheeled cart, later out of his cramped shop, to retire comfortably to his native Greece. When word of his death reached Benton Harbor, popcorn lovers grieved.

After the movies, we went to Holly's, the restaurant across from the theater, where I had a cherry Coke and Bobbie unsweetened iced tea. The waitress working the counter on weekends was a super-friendly and to me beautiful Benton Harbor High School student, Marilyn Kullenberg. Marilyn's friendliness and beauty weren't the whole of it. She also was famous because I kept seeing her name on the *News-Palladium* sports page for her victories in junior girls' tennis tournaments. And I knew her in person! Marilyn addressed Bobbie and me by name, questioned us about the movie we'd just seen as if our opinions mattered and teased me in a way easier to take than when my father did it. On the ride home, we told Dad how friendly Marilyn had been, and he said, "Good to hear." I didn't tell him I had made goo-goo eyes at her.

Roberta loved children. If they tried to wriggle away from her when she reached down to kiss them, they were in for a battle. One of her pastimes was to make potholders by weaving loops of multi-colored fabric around hooks on a children's loom. She gave the potholders as birthday, Christmas and Chanukah presents, even, oddly, as baby gifts. She checked the newspaper for hospital admissions and wrote get-well cards when she recognized the name of a family friend or of somebody from a store or a doctor's office she'd been taken to. Dad sometimes drove her to the post office so she could drop the cards in the mail slot herself.

Bad heart but good-hearted — that was my sister Roberta. At *Sports Illustrated*, writing in the Scorecard section about the Special Olympics, I said that the mentally disabled youngsters who participated in those competitions exhibited joy too often lacking in big-time sport. I wrote that in the Special Olympics, cheating is virtually unknown "and if somebody falls during a race, competitors can usually be counted on to stop and lend a hand."

I received a letter from a reader taking me to task. The letter writer accused me of making the mentally challenged seem even more apart than they already were. Handicapped children, the complainant said, were capable of selfishness and poor sportsmanship like everyone else. My immediate reaction was, hey, you don't know my gentle and kind sister, but I realized that my correspondent was right. Thinking of my sister and others with similar disabilities as unfailingly selfless and joyful was wrongheaded. Writing about the Special Olympics, I had Roberta's loving nature in mind but overlooked the times when she was angry and rebellious, which would become more frequent as she got older.

Chapter 9

Sleeping With Cats

After their honeymoon, my parents never again motored together to the Motor City. Chicago, closer than Detroit, was where Benton Harbor residents more often shopped for hard-to-get goods and went for medical care beyond the capabilities of local doctors. Chicago attracted my parents for those and more particular reasons — Mom because it was where her family lived and where she had "my jeweler" and "my furrier," Dad because he knew every inch of the city from his taxi-driving days and enjoyed revisiting old haunts.

They also sampled Chicago nightlife. I have the record jacket that the chanteuse Sophie Tucker autographed "with love to Milton Kirshenbaum" when my parents saw her perform at the supper club Chez Paree. The jacket is intact, but the 78 rpm record it housed — "My Yiddishe Momme" on Side A, "Some of These Days" on the reverse — shattered, leaving two shards in the inconvenient 39 rpm format.

When I was little, I enjoyed visiting Mom's Chicago relatives, but I had one quibble. Welcoming us, Grandma Goldberg and Aunts Gere and Mirian kissed us on the lips. It was nice that they were glad to see us, but as far as I was concerned, they didn't need to get all yucky about it.

As we prepared for Chicago, we were often in a state of heightened anticipation amid sighs and foot-shuffling while Mom kept thinking of another dress, blouse or pair of shoes to add to the too many of each she had already packed.

"If we want to get there in time for dinner — " said Dad.

"Stop rushing me," said Mom.

Loading the car, Mook complained, "All I do is schlep," but from how ingeniously he squeezed our luggage into the car's trunk, you could tell he had the art of schlepping down cold.

If Roberta was home, she joined us on our Chicago visits. Otherwise, it was just the folks, Joel and me. Our trips were arranged around school holidays — shorter over Christmas vacation, longer in the summer. Sometimes we also went in for Passover seders or Thanksgiving, which can be thought of as the national seder.

The route from Benton Harbor to Chicago formed a U around the bottom of Lake Michigan: south from the Twin Cities skirting Michigan beach communities like Sawyer, Harbert and Union Pier that one day would be prime second-home territory for wealthy Chicagoans; west past the Indiana Dunes and a Dairy Queen where Joel's and my pestering sometimes got Dad to stop; and north into Chicago. Near the end, we experienced a stretch of northern Indiana — Gary, East Chicago, Hammond — where steel mill smokestacks belched sulfur so strong that you smelled it even with the car windows closed. This was a blue-collar area that the locals referred to as Da Region, spoken with the same swagger that moved Chicagoans to call their pro football team Da Bears.

The drive to Chicago was ordinarily two hours, but we had

to allow extra time because a Cadillac with out-of-state license plates was catnip for Chicago police. The minute we crossed the Calumet Skyway onto Chicago's South Side, Dad was on the alert for Nabby, his name for ticket-writing officers of the law. Chicago cops were the nabbiest, inclined to pull over out-of-state motorists driving expensive cars for speeding even when they were practically going backwards.

Wrongly stopped by Nabby, my father knew better than to waste time informing the uniformed figure on the other side of the rolled-down window that he'd been observing the speed limit. He let matters get quickly to where he knew they had to go, the recitation of a sob story by the officer that could break the hardest heart. It was amazing how many of Chicago's men in blue had wives who were sickly and children who lacked proper school clothes. In Mook they found a sympathetic ear and outstretched hand. Usually a ten-dollar bill changed ownership, and he was on his way.

But Dad spoke of one time in Chicago when the script changed. There was the usual siren-and-flashing-lights greeting, followed by the do-you-realize-how-fast-you-were-going song and dance, but this Nabby had no heartbreaking story to share, forcing my father to improvise. As he recounted: "I said, 'Officer, can we settle this right here?' He said, 'Don't try that funny stuff with me.' He told me I had to follow him to the police station."

Dad said that at the station he was taken before a desk sergeant who was a chatty sort. What he was chatty about was his ailing wife and his little ones with clothes in tatters.

"If I can help — "

The sergeant wordlessly opened a desk drawer, and Mook dropped a tenner on top of other offerings already there. "It was still a shakedown," he said of the rigamarole, "only this time by the desk sergeant."

For me, there was unpleasantness in Chicago besides crooked cops. I wanted no part of stickball or kick the can, Chicago games contested on pavement less forgiving than the dirt and grassy terrain on which I played softball and touch football in Benton Harbor. I also spurned phosphates, syrup-and-seltzer concoctions (called egg creams in New York) that were too medicinal tasting for my liking. But in a moment of weakness, I allowed myself to become a fan of those perennial also-rans, the Chicago Cubs. The bargain I struck with myself was that the Cubs were my National League team while I continued to root for the Tigers in the American League. When those two clubs chanced to meet in the 1945 World Series, I was a conflicted seven-year-old. Of course Detroit won, another disappointment in a century of them for a team never fearsome enough to be called Da Cubs.

My mother's family lived on the West Side, in a neighborhood that had, I swear, a synagogue on every block and a kosher butcher shop on every other. The Goldbergs, enough of them to make a *minyan* (if you cheated and counted the women and children), occupied adjacent buildings at Independence Boulevard and Arthington Avenue, a setup as cozy as the Kennedy compound in Hyannis Port about which much soon would be heard.

Grandpa and Grandma Goldberg lived on Arthington in an apartment whose dominant theme was doilies and slipcovers. The building next door, which was owned by Grandpa, faced Independence Boulevard. Here resided Aunt Mirian with her family and Aunt Gere with hers in apartments one above the other, identical in footprint, distinguishable by the furnishings. Upstairs were Gere, Uncle Jack and their four children.

On the floor below were Mirian and Uncle Sam with their two. The apartments were reachable by two sets of stairs, wooden in back for deliveries, stonework in front for guests. The layouts would have been ideal for playing tag or hide-and-seek, but we children were under orders to not be "wild."

Independence Boulevard was a parkway with a tree-lined median where kids played catch and couples strolled. One day when Bobbie was with us, our family gathered with the Chicago relatives on the boulevard to film a home movie that looked as if it had been taken in the countryside instead of in a concrete cityscape. Before air conditioning, residents of Independence Boulevard and nearby blocks encamped on sweltering nights on the grassy expanse in giant neighborhood slumber parties.

We always slept at Mirian and Sam's, which was ideal for me because their son, my cousin Ron, had a first-rate comic book collection. On a wall in Mirian and Sam's apartment was a *pushka*, a small metal box into which Aunt Mirian placed coins that a man in beard and side curls regularly came by to collect. One night when we were staying there, a burglar climbed onto a landing, reached through an open window and made off with the *pushka*. That this happened while I was asleep nearby was both frightening and exciting. The next time the man came, Mirian found a few coins in her purse so he wouldn't leave empty-handed.

At Mirian and Sam's, people were always stopping by — Grandma and Grandpa from around the corner, members of Aunt Gere's family from upstairs, and an endless parade of friends, neighbors and delivery men. Uncle Irving also appeared. An insurance agent who didn't marry until his mid-40s and then unhappily and briefly, Irving came by when he wanted a home-cooked meal, or to say hello to his sister Frieda's family visiting from Michigan, or to get any of his many grievances off his chest. Things were always hopping at Mirian and Sam's.

Activities included my mother's fashion show. Now was revealed the reason for her overpacking. Out of her luggage came garments, one after another — a "darling" dress for Mirian, a skirt "just right" for Gere or a "stunning" blouse to be shipped to Edna, the youngest sister, who was always off somewhere teaching school. Mom also brought forth outfits acquired for herself, which she modeled for Gere and Mirian's approval. The clothes bore tags from Twin Cities stores like Helaine's, Terri's and Enders. These were the latest stylings for milady direct from the salons of Benton Harbor and St. Joseph, and one could only hope that Chicago one day would have access to such fine raiment. During the fashion show, Dad kept his distance. "She's always putting on the dog," he muttered.

During the day, Mother's brothers-in-law were at work, Sam Bailis at his health food store, where Aunt Mirian sometimes pitched in, and Jack Netboy at his shoe store. Mom's relatives borrowed money from Dad. In my parents' papers are an IOU from Grandpa Goldberg for $3,000 and a note from Jack on La Belle Shoe Store stationery promising to pay a balance of $1,500 on a $3,000 loan "as soon as I can." I assume the loans were paid off. I never heard otherwise.

There were times when life with the in-laws became too humdrum for my father. Over breakfast one day, he called attention to a bowl on Mirian and Sam's kitchen table containing vitamins, some loose, others in small plastic containers. "What are those?" he inquired. He knew perfectly well what they were, and they knew he knew, but instead of crediting Mirian and Sam with having enough faith in the wares they sold at their health food shop to bring home samples for their own use, he volunteered that he didn't take vitamins and didn't believe in them. That got their goat, but they had long since accepted that Frieda had married a goat-getter.

The member of Mom's family whose company Dad most enjoyed was Grandma Goldberg. He liked talking Yiddish with his mother-in-law, as he did with his own mother. "I like their *bubbe-mayses,*" he said. Because *bubbe-mayses* translates literally as "grandmother stories," it's tempting to think of them as old wives' tales, but *bubbe-mayses* most often were true, recounting experiences in the Old Country. I understood little of the conversation, but I liked sitting with my father and grandmother as he listened happily to her stories in Yiddish of a world from which he had been removed at too young an age to remember.

Jewish kids like me didn't learn Yiddish. We wanted to assimilate, a goal at odds with speaking Yiddish. Besides, we weren't *supposed* to learn it. Yiddish was what our parents spoke to discuss private matters, and cracking the code would have been a violation, like entering their bedroom at the wrong time. But the language was in our bloodstream. We intuited when to call somebody a *shlemiel* instead of a *shmegegge,* a *shlimazl* rather than a *shmendrick,* a *shlub* but not a *schlump,* a *nebbish* in lieu of a *nudnik.* We winced when non-Jews said *shmuck* or *putz* without realizing that those words referred to a male's maleness, and we laughed when our Gentile girlfriends and wives pronounced *Pesach,* the word for Passover, to rhyme with "gray sock." We coached them to say it the correct way, with a guttural flourish, drawing out the "ach" to make it sound like air coming out of a tire. The fun we made of Yiddish was done lovingly. Billy Crystal, who grew up around

Yiddish-speaking uncles, calls Yiddish a cross between German and phlegm. "This is a language of coughing and spitting," he says. "Until I was 11, I wore a raincoat."

Hearing my father say something in Yiddish that made others laugh, I asked him to translate, but he cautioned, "It doesn't come out the same in English." He spoke of people "drinking black coffee by the mailbox," which he said was a Yiddish expression. Pressed to explain, he said: "If a rich man wants people to think he's poor, he'll drink black coffee near the street so people passing by will think he can't afford cream." In Yiddish, "drinking black coffee by the mailbox" is six words." It took 27 words for Dad to say the same thing in English.

Mook was, in essence, the anti-Mendel, giving his children pleasures he never experienced when he was young. His idea of childrearing was to spoil his kids, and in Chicago, away from work, he had time to do a lot of spoiling. Not a baseball fan, he contentedly sat in the stands with Joel and me at Wrigley Field or Comiskey Park and waited patiently after games while we stationed ourselves outside the clubhouses and cadged autographs, a Phil Cavaretta or Rex Barney at Wrigley, a Nellie Fox or Snuffy Stirnweiss at Comiskey. Back at Mirian and Sam's, Dad told the relatives that the fans seated around us had been amazed hearing little Joel rattle off batting averages and other baseball minutiae.

He also took us to the Balaban and Katz movie houses, those gilded and chandeliered entertainment palaces with ushers in white gloves and epaulets and offering live stage shows along with first-run films. The glitziest establishments were the Chicago and Oriental Theaters in the Loop, but Balaban and Katz also had many neighborhood theaters, a few of which also offered live shows. In the 3,600-seat Chicago

Theater, we saw the Ink Spots, Martin and Lewis, and the Will Mastin Trio featuring a "skyrocketing headliner," Mastin's nephew, Sammy Davis Jr. Sammy was born in 1925, the same year as Mel Tormé, the pride of Chicago's Hyde Park area, who we caught at Balaban and Katz's Marbro Theater on the West Side. It's hard to say which of them, Davis or Tormé, was more precocious. Sammy sang, tap-danced, played the drums and did impressions. Mel sang, drummed, played the piano and wrote wonderful songs, including "The Christmas Song," the chestnuts-roasting-on-an-open-fire classic associated with Nat King Cole, who, by the way, we saw at the Oriental. Of course he was then billed Nat-lessly as King Cole. From our Chicago peregrinations with our father, Joel and I knew cool stuff like that.

Sometimes our cousins joined us on our outings. This was usually the case when Dad ferried us to the Museum of Science and Industry, the Field Museum of Natural History or Riverview, the Chicago amusement park with The Bobs, said to be the most terrifying roller coaster anywhere. I wanted no part of The Bobs, but to avoid appearing wimpy in front of my more adventurous cousins, I forced myself to go on Pair-O-Chutes, a 200-foot-high tower assembly on which two people were strapped side by side into seats like those on playground swings and were carried high into the firmament as the great city stretched out beneath and beyond. My heart hammering and with a hollow feeling in my nether regions, I watched Dad become a speck on a bench far below as I ascended heavenward until a jolt sent me freefalling under an open parachute that swayed so much that I feared it had become untethered. Landing, I was surprised to discover I was intact.

Dad endeared himself to his Chicago nieces and nephews. "Did you bring your gum, Uncle Milton?" they asked, and he didn't disappoint. He made sure to have enough Black Jack chewing gum to parcel out to each of them. He liked Black Jack because it was easy on his dentures, my cousins because it turned their tongues black. Sometimes he said things that made them almost swallow their gum.

"I know a woman who sleeps with cats."

They sensed something hilarious was coming.

Again, he didn't disappoint.

"Mrs. Katz."

OCCASIONALLY MOM and Dad visited Chicago by themselves. In October 1947, while Bobbie was in Texas, they spent a weekend in Chicago, leaving Joel and me in Benton Harbor with their friends Bill and Alice Becker. On Saturday, October 25, Mrs. Becker had the kitchen radio on while she made breakfast. I was listening with hometown pride because the radio was tuned to WHFB (Heart of the Fruit Belt), which had come into existence only a month before, giving Benton Harbor its very own radio station. Suddenly I froze. Over WHFB, 1060 on the dial, a voice delivering the news shockingly said that a Benton Harbor couple, Mr. and Mrs. Milton Kirshenbaum, had been held up at gunpoint the night before in Chicago.

This was different than Dad's encounters with Nabby and as heart-pounding as the time mobsters accosted him in his taxi-driving days. As he told it, he and Mom had gone to a movie with Uncle Irving and stopped at a cocktail lounge for nightcaps. They were driving Irving home when a car cut them off. "We're being robbed," Mook said. Mother slipped off her diamond rings and put them in an ashtray. Two masked men approached the car. One pointed a gun at my father and demanded his wristwatch, which he handed over. The second addressed my mother: "And your rings."

"I don't have any."

"Frieda — " Dad's voice was urgent.

"I don't — "

"Frieda — "

Reluctantly, Mom surrendered her rings.

"She could have gotten us killed," Mook said. "Those guys must have been in the bar. They knew she had rings because they saw them on her."

He said that after the thieves sped away, Irving, mute to this point, shouted from the back seat, "Let's go after them!"

"When the holdup was happening, Irving was shitting bricks," Pop said. "Now he was talking tough. I said, 'Irving, they've got guns, and we don't. We're not going after them.'"

IN THE 1950S, blockbusting and white flight inflamed Chicago. Overnight the West Side was transformed from a Jewish ghetto into an African American ghetto. The synagogues became Black churches, with faded Stars of David and Hebrew letters visible on buildings now filled with Baptist and African Methodist Evangelical worshipers. Jews dispersed from the West Side, many settling in Skokie, Glencoe, Highland Park and other northern and western Chicago suburbs. These second-generation émigrés looked back nostalgically on what they called, gently mocking the Yiddish accents of their immigrant parents, the "Great Vest Side." They formed the Great Vest Side Club, which holds annual dinners at which guest speakers are greeted with hosannas for doing no more than mentioning a fondly remembered West Side landmark or institution like the Douglas Park lagoon, or Flukey's, the hot dog stand run by Abe "Flukey" Dressler, or the 1,780-seat Central Park Theater, the world's first movie house with air conditioning. The theater would become a Black church, the default fate of repurposed West Side structures.

The Goldbergs joined the exodus. Aunt Mirian and Uncle Sam moved to Skokie. Grandma Rose, alone since Grandpa's death in 1953, went to Los Angeles to be near her brother Enoch and Aunt Edna. (Grandma would later emigrate to Israel and be buried there.) Aunt Gere and Uncle Jack relocated first to Wisconsin — "Other Jews have relatives in medicine, we have them in Madison," Dad said — and then to Florida, heeding what the comedian Freddie Roman called a Biblical injunction: "When Jews turn 60, they have to move to Florida, It's in the Torah."[1]

Only Uncle Irving remained in the city. Once athletic and leading-man handsome, Irving was beaten down by health and financial setbacks. He wrote my parents desperate letters. In one, he said he'd lost 30 pounds and, "the walls have closed on me, and I get horrible thoughts." Another: "I have no more tears. I'm drowning in a sea of loneliness and have reached my limit...I have been terribly ill for over a year, and it won't take much to push me over a clift [sic]."

Sometimes Irving arrived in Benton Harbor unannounced, argued with my mother and overstayed his welcome. After one

---

1. Roman's real name was Fred Kirschenbaum, no relation to the Benton Harbor Kirshenbaums. The New York-born Roman performed in the Borscht Belt, Las Vegas and Atlantic City and created and starred in *Catskills on Broadway*, an extravaganza of one-liners that enjoyed a year-long run in New York's Lunt-Fontanne Theater. For many years he was abbot of the New York City Friars Club, famed for its off-color celebrity roasts. Freddie joked that his family name was Roman, but his relatives were so ashamed of his comedy career that they changed it to Kirschenbaum.

visit, he apologized, "Your home was my haven, but I realize that my being there causes complications. I was terribly depressed when I came out and had intended to stay a day. Instead, I imposed."

My mother had troubles of her own and was easily distracted. On the back of a letter in which Irving wrote, "I have no one else to turn to," Mom scribbled the ingredients for pie crust. It wasn't that she was unsympathetic. She just needed something to write on in a pinch.

My father reached Uncle Irving as others couldn't. My brother remembers Irving on a rampage in Mirian and Sam's apartment. "He was yelling and wouldn't stop," Joel says. "Dad put a hand on his shoulder and said, 'Irving, let's go outside.' They walked around the block. When they came back, Irving was calm."

Joel recalls Irving at another time telling him, "Your father is a man of infinite patience."

In a letter to Dad, Irving asked, "I wish you could give me a ring at the office or at my home when you are in town and maybe you can help me get over the rough spots thru your experiences." In another letter: "Milt, I know that it is hard for a person like you to understand what is happening to me. You are so strong mentally." When Irving was no longer capable of making the trip by himself, my father drove him from Chicago to Benton Harbor and back. Irving wrote Mother, "Milt drove me all the way home although he had south side appointments and I appreciate it. Please thank him for his kindness to me."

But one time in Benton Harbor, Irving and Mom had a fight so heated that Dad told his brother-in-law that maybe he shouldn't visit for a while.

Irving inherited Grandpa's building on Independence Boulevard and came to regret it. The neighborhood had become a quagmire of poverty and crime, and the building was beset by arson, broken windows and burst steam pipes. Irving had difficulty collecting rent from the tenants and was issued health code violations but couldn't find repairmen willing to go into the neighborhood. "I would take any price for the building" he wrote my parents, "but no one wants it even as a gift."

Irving died of a heart attack in 1971. He was 61. Mom's family now was entirely gone from the West Side, but Dad still had reason to visit the old neighborhood. The Goldberg buildings were a few short blocks from Sears, Roebuck and Company's world headquarters, where Mook sometimes picked up unused appliance cartons to resell, just as he acquired bags on a far greater scale from Campbell Soup. Driving through the Great Vest Side, he saw dramatic changes. "Nowadays if you tried to sleep outside on Independence Boulevard, you wouldn't survive the night," he said.

Chapter 10

Educated Fools

My father's parenting portfolio notably included infrastructure. Thanks to him, there arose in our backyard a set of swings, not the store-bought, assembly-required kind meant to be stored away in the fall, but an all-season public playground-worthy behemoth with steel girders anchored in concrete. While Joel and I and sometimes Roberta played on the swings and on a seesaw that was also part of the setup, Mom checked on us from the kitchen window or Dad from the screened porch with the in-the-wall barbecue pit and the wrought-iron patio furniture.

When my interest turned to photography, Pop had a darkroom built that transformed part of our basement into a phantasmagoria. I was a crazed scientist hunched over trays of elixirs — developer, fixer and stop bath — in a red-lit enclosure outside of which loomed Mom's mangle for ironing sheets, a steel monstrosity as forbidding as an iron lung, and on a wall, shelves of bottled preserves resembling the dream-haunting jars of animal specimens at the Field Museum in Chicago. I told myself that by processing photos at home, I was saving the expense of having it done at the drugstore, but who was I kidding? The cost of building the darkroom was never recouped, savings realized only when my interest in photography waned, and the darkroom was dismantled.

The most enduring installation was the basketball hoop Dad put up in the turnaround area of our driveway. There I imagined myself John Stevens or Norm Reidel starring for the Benton Harbor Junior College team that in 1951 did our town proud by finishing fifth in the national Jaycee tournament in Hutchinson, Kansas. Neighborhood kids came to shoot baskets with me, and once in a while an arriving delivery man or family friend called for the ball. Mook also may have let one fly, but if so, I've put it safely out of mind. Playing basketball wasn't in his portfolio.

I can mention other activities that weren't either. Other boys but not I bonded with their fathers on camping trips, pitching tents in the wild and sharing fellowship and hot dogs over blazing fires. As adults my friends but not I grew misty-eyed watching *Field of Dreams* and recalling the times they played catch with the old man. The teams my contemporaries cheered for and the country clubs they belonged to were their fathers' teams and country clubs. Mook had no favorite teams and, never having played golf or tennis, he probably wouldn't have joined a country club in Benton Harbor even if there'd been one that accepted Jews.

But I'm not complaining. Let other men hold dear their memories of catching thrown balls and poison ivy with their fathers. Mine are of Mook at ticket windows peeling onions to gain us admission to events in the Twin Cities as he did in Chicago. If there were a Spectator Hall of Fame, my father would be a first-ballot inductee. Until Joel was old enough to join us, I had Dad to myself, and I took full advantage. When I learned, for example, that Gorgeous George was coming to town, I exulted, "Gorgeous George! This is the first time he's been to Benton Harbor!"

"Gorgeous George?" Dad scoffed. "What I'd like to know is, what's so gorgeous about him?"

"If we go, you'll find out," I said, clinching the deal.

And there we were, indulgent father and rapt son, seated ringside in the ramshackle old House of David ballpark as Gorgeous George's valet, Jeffries, set up a candelabrum in the ring and laid a carpet of rose petals at the feet of his villainous master, who entered to lusty boos. While Jeffries bowed and scraped, Gorgeous George sprayed the air with the perfume he called Chanel N°10 ("why be half safe?" he reasoned), a scent that inflicted more pain on those of us within sniffing distance than anything the vainglorious wrestler and his opponent did to each other during the match. I understood that much of the wrestling was scripted, and my father enlightened me further, advising in too loud a whisper, "You know, he isn't really a fairy."

Among the Twin Cities' other delights were two outstanding semipro baseball teams, the Benton Harbor Buds and St. Joseph Auscos. The Buds and Auscos waged a rivalry that divided Twin Cities fandom. I of course rooted for the Buds, but I had to admit that the Auscos were the classier outfit. Sponsored by Auto Specialties Corporation, they played home games in Edgewater Park, a gem of a ballpark that the company's owner, Waldo Tiscornia, for 13 years the mayor of St. Joseph, tricked out with gadgetry. When the home plate umpire stepped on a pedal, up sprang a container filled with a dozen new baseballs. Another pedal produced a gust of air that dusted off the plate, no umpire's whiskbroom needed. After the Auscos disbanded, the gizmos were acquired by the

Chicago White Sox showman owner Bill Veeck, who installed them for a time in Comiskey Park.

Mook and I were in Edgewater Park the night the Auscos hosted a Negro League team, the Indianapolis Clowns, who were touring with a 17-year-old shortstop who had just signed with the Boston Braves and was touted as a can't-miss prospect. In a 10-5 Clowns loss, young Henry Aaron had a double and a single, faltering only as an evaluator of his own gifts. After the game, the future Milwaukee/Atlanta Braves outfielder who would break Babe Ruth's career home run record told a reporter, "I'm not a long-ball hitter, but I manage to turn a lot of ordinary singles into doubles."

Besides catching sight of Hank Aaron before his big-league playing days began, Mook and I saw another Hall of Famer, Harry Heilmann, after his were over. Heilmann was the Tigers' radio announcer following a major league career during which he was one of 23 players in history to hit .400 in a season. On the air Heilmann had a catchphrase relating to one of the broadcast's sponsors, Bug-a-Boo insect repellant. Calling a fly ball out, he exclaimed, "Bug-a-Boo, another dead fly!" At an appearance before the St. Joseph Lions Club by this man who knocked the rock and later talked the talk, I think even Dad could tell we were in the presence of an immortal.

My father was there for me when I needed him but made himself scarce when I didn't. Driving me to St. Joseph Office Supply, he didn't ask why I was buying green and brown desk blotters, and he didn't intrude when I shut myself in my bedroom and scissored and pasted, using the brown for the infield dirt and the green for the outfield grass, with leftover scraps of blotter placed upright to represent the outfield fence. My self-crafted ballpark allowed me to picture Hoot Evers in center, Johnny Lipon at short and the other Tigers manning their positions in Briggs Stadium, which I had never seen, not even on television. At such times, Dad's and my lives were siloed off. He was concerned with making payroll, fending off business attacks by his brothers, caring for Roberta and keeping the lid on with Mom. I worried about whether I should have made right field shallower.

I didn't always require Mook's help to experience Twin Cities pleasures. For five cents, kids under 12 could ride a bus almost anywhere in Benton Harbor and St. Joseph (the fare for adults was a dime, or three rides for a quarter), and when my best friend, Buddy Alberts, and I felt like visiting record stores or buying comic books, we caught a bus at the corner of his street, Elvern Drive, and traveled to the downtown retail district along Colfax Avenue, passing the Flats and the Fruit Market on the left and the House of David yonder to the right. Or we saved our nickels and hitchhiked and were picked up by townspeople without our ever having to worry if they were axe murderers.

I also got around on my Schwinn, the "truly modern post-war bicycle" with the cantilevered frame, tubular front fork and built-in headlight, which I rode to have ice cream at Olds Dairy on May Street or to watch through the studio window at WHFB as Ray Mittan read the news to the radio audience or Don Buehler delivered the sports scores. When I was nine, I bicycled to WHFB to participate in a weekly kids' sports quiz show hosted by Jumping Joe Savoldi. The program pitted boys 12 and under (girls presumably could have taken part, but none did) against a panel of high school lads laughably called "experts." When Jumping Joe asked who Herman Hickman was, the know-nothing high schoolers scratched their heads and studied their white bucks while I raised my hand in the peanut gallery and squeaked correctly that Mr. Hickman was the football coach at Yale. I won a softball from the show's sponsor, the sporting goods store Gardner's.

"And you got it for free?" Dad asked.

"Yep."

"Hmmm," he said, which I could tell meant he was proud of me. He also hmmm-ed when I came home with a lantern, metal folding chair and other prizes. My pal Steve Findley was also good at answering Jumping Joe's questions. Between us, Steve and I must have created some empty shelves at Gardner's.

Savoldi played fullback at Notre Dame for Knute Rockne, then knocked heads on the pro wrestling circuit. He supposedly owed his nickname to once having flung himself over opposing linemen to score a critical touchdown for the Irish, a daring maneuver in the days of thin moleskin football helmets. After one broadcast, Steve and I stuck around to ask Jumping Joe what it was like being Jumping Joe. To prove he still had the goods, Joe removed his shoes and from a near-standing start, jumped stocking-footed onto his desk, which shuddered under the force of what must have been 250 pounds of out-of-shape ex-jock. It was an impressive feat and a miracle he didn't break his neck.

Improbably for a Jewish father and son, Dad and I bonded over Savoldi's alma mater. The connection was forged when a Notre Dame football booster Pop did business with gave him tickets to a Fighting Irish game. South Bend, Indiana, is 30 miles south of Benton Harbor in an interstate area bearing a portmanteau name, Michiana, and on a balmy October afternoon, my father and I watched Frank Leahy's juggernaut starring Johnny Lujack, big Leon Hart and Emil "Six Yard" Sitko defeat Iowa 21-0 enroute to a second straight national championship and the conferring of the Heisman Trophy on Lujack.

It was the first football game I ever saw — nothing like starting at the top.

For *Sports Illustrated*, I would write a "bonus piece," the name given the long, in-depth stories that ran toward the end of each of the magazine's issues, entitled, "The Greening of the Fighting Irish." The story detailed Notre Dame's success under its president, the Rev. Theodore Hesburgh, at turning a conservative Catholic school seen as little more than a football factory into a world-class institution open to fresh ideas and bold influences. In his office in the administration building crowned by Notre Dame's famed Golden Dome, Father Hesburgh told me, "I rather like the proportion football is in now. I think we've proved it's possible to play competent, effective football and have a good university, too."

Historically male only, Notre Dame had begun admitting women at the graduate level and relaxing the monastic demands it imposed on its students. Ray Kennedy, a Notre Dame alum I worked with at *Time* and *Sports Illustrated*, told me that when he was in college, a master switch turned off lights in dorms at 11 p.m., and maids rummaged through wastebaskets looking for beer cans. "After Notre Dame, my two years in the Army were a breeze," Ray said.

A Notre Dame priest I made it a point to interview was the Rev. Charles McCarragher, the school's former prefect of discipline. Legend had it that Black Mac, as he was known, patrolled the dorms wearing one street shoe and one sneaker so that when he ran through the halls pursuing wrongdoers, his footfalls sounded as if he was walking. As we talked, I took careful note of Father McCarragher's shoes visible beneath his ankle-length cassock. They were black and they matched.

While I worked on the bonus piece, Dad drove down from Benton Harbor a couple of times to be with me. After my

Sports Illustrated story appeared, Hesburgh's publicity chief, Dick Conklin, invited me to write two freelance stories for the Notre Dame alumni magazine. One was about my experience as a journalist writing about Notre Dame, the other a profile of the school's colorful basketball coach, the undertaker's son, Digger Phelps. The two stories meant more trips for me to South Bend and more visits with my father. At the campus hotel, Morris Inn, we had lunch in the company of priests, professors and alumni. In the South Dining Hall, we ate amid the din of textbook-toting students grabbing bites between classes. I'd gotten to know Notre Dame well enough to point out to Mook landmarks such as the Grotto (a replica of the shrine at Lourdes), the library (later named the Theodore Hesburgh Library) and "Fair Catch Corby," the statue of Father William Corby, an early Notre Dame president, raising his hand to the sky as if fielding a punt.

"What a beautiful campus," Pop exclaimed, as if he knew a thing or two about college campuses. Striding Notre Dame's manicured grounds ringed by its stolid Gothic buildings, he could have been Professor Schmul Kirzhenbaum, the eminent Old Testament scholar hired in another of Hesburgh's moves to broaden the university's horizons.

In reality, Dad was never at ease with academia. At the start of every elementary school year, he was reduced to asking me, "What grade are you in now?" When I reached high school and told him I was taking physics, he asked, "What's that for?" and darned if I could tell him. But he didn't stand in the way of his sons' schooling. He didn't expect Joel or me to join him in the bag business, telling us, "There are easier ways for you to earn livings. I had no choice because I wasn't educated." At the same time, he couldn't understand why academic achievement didn't always translate into riches. He considered it a grave injustice that two of my best friends, Elden Butzbaugh and Bruce Conybeare, whose grades were no better than mine, became powerhouse lawyers and made much more money than I did.

Dad believed that some people with sheepskins on their walls were "educated fools." He was good with numbers, as were some of the farmers he did business with. Negotiating with a farmer over the sale of, say, 6,500 bags he'd bought for 4 ½ cents each, Dad knew that if he priced them at 22 ½ cents, he would realize a profit north of $1,000. He didn't have to figure it "down to a gnat's ass," as he put it. On the other side, the farmer understood that the bags would set him back roughly $1,400. The guesstimate each man made would be good enough for a handshake deal to be struck.

When the farmer died, his innumerate college graduate son took over and relied on a calculator. My father complained, "If you asked the kid to add two and two, he'd pull out the damn calculator. You should see him." There followed a mocking reenactment, Mook's fingers dancing maniacally on imaginary keys. To him, the farmer's son was an educated fool.

While Dad handled his children's amusements, Mom established dominion over our educational and cultural betterment. Most of the books in our house were acquired by her. On our shelves were the 14th Edition of the *Encyclopedia Britannica* and works by Saroyan, Dos Passos, Sinclair Lewis and Sholem Aleichem next to Book of the Month Club selections and editions of *Reader's Digest Condensed Books*. Affixed to the inside of the more high-brow tomes were stickers reading EX LIBRIS, FRIEDA AND MILTON. In Joel's and my room were *The Adventures of Robinson Crusoe* and *The Last of the Mohicans* with the classic Maxfield Parrish illustrations, and selections from the Hardy Boys series. There also was *The

Adventures of Little Black Sambo, containing images of Sambo's exaggerated pickaninny features. Mother bought that one too.

My parents were of a generation of white Americans too accepting of racial slights. When I was a boy, African Americans made up 10% of Benton Harbor's population, and their numbers were rapidly growing, but there were few Black students at Fair Plain School and none in my fifth-grade class. That's the year — 1950 — our parents congregated in the school auditorium to watch their little darlings put on a production evidently considered by our teachers to be of educational value: a minstrel show.

A photo shows 36 white children all in blackface except for a girl I don't recognize and me. The girl may have arrived too late to be painted or was the only one among us with the good sense to balk at the performance. I'm unblackened because I've been cast as the interlocutor. Wearing a top hat and floppy outsized bowtie, I sit front row center, egging on the zaniness of the "end men," Bones and Tambo, played by Elden Butzbaugh and Johnny Bridgham. Bones and Tambo are stock minstrel show characters whose jokes and actions are amalgams of racial stereotypes. Other classmates are darkies laughing at the supposed gaiety while I fill a role analogous, I now realize, to a plantation owner overseeing his slaves.

Preferred memory: On an earlier occasion, my mother, bless her, took me to see Paul Robeson, the son of a former slave, perform in the Benton Harbor High School auditorium before an audience both Black and white. Robeson's program consisted of Negro spirituals, Russian folk songs and labor anthems. His powerful voice made me a captivated eight-year-old. Afterwards I went backstage and timorously got an autograph from Robeson, who, I learned, had gone from football greatness at Rutgers to earn a law degree from Columbia and star as a singer and actor in Hollywood and on Broadway while fiercely fighting racial injustice.

Robeson's Benton Harbor appearance was peaceful, but soon, amid McCarthy-era hysteria, his concerts drew angry mobs protesting his Communist leanings. For Mrs. Ender's eighth-grade English class, I did a book report on a biography of Robeson, and at *Sports Illustrated* I would write a story about this giant of a man who had been "cheered as an All-America and reviled as un-American all within the same remarkable lifetime." I can thank my mother for sparking my interest in Robeson.

Mom also signed me up for piano lessons with the estimable Alice Baran Hatch, than whom there was no finer music pedagogue in the Twin Cities. As a piano prodigy, Alice Baran had played at Town Hall in New York City, delivering a performance that the *New York Times* critic said evinced "feeling and intelligence" and was, withal, "a delight." Marriage to a Whirlpool executive, Ad Hatch, brought her to Benton Harbor, where she played at Twin Cities events and taught piano.

I had stubby fingers, sweaty palms and no discernible talent. At recitals, while Mrs. Hatch's advanced pupils like Valerie Fisher, Joan Faber and the Woodford twins, Peggy and John, excelled late in the lineup playing Liszt, Mozart and Bartok, I appeared at the beginning, playing pieces that had pelicans and choo-choos in their titles. By the third year, audiences must have wondered what the big lug was doing performing with the tots. When I sat down and began to play, they had their answer.

One recital posed a scheduling conflict for my father. It was the same day as the start of a four-day men's Chamber of

Commerce Great Lakes cruise for Twin Cities business and civic leaders he had signed up for. The agenda for the voyage on the *S.S. City of Cleveland* promised on-board drinking and card-playing, with stops ashore for sightseeing and a Tigers-Yankees game in Detroit. In the end, Dad elected to skip the cruise, telling me, "I'd rather hear you tickle the ivories." He couldn't possibly have meant that, but there he was, seated with Mom in the Congregational Church's Sonner Hall for an evening of piano tickling by me and 20 others.

Two days later, the *City of Cleveland* collided in darkness and fog with a freighter on Lake Huron. Five men were killed — Benton Harbor chief of police Alvin Boyd, former mayor Mervyn Stouck, auto dealer Fred Skelley, salesman Richard Lybrook and a South Bend businessman, Louis Patitucci. Several other men were seriously injured. Discordant though my piano playing had been, it must have sounded better than the grinding together of two hulls that brought the Chamber of Commerce revelry to a tragic conclusion. Because it kept my father safely at home, I consider my performance a triumph.

Unexpectedly, Mook in time became the parent more the consumer of books. Mom stopped reading them, being too busy clipping grocery coupons, newspaper articles and recipes, pasting S&H green stamps into booklets to be exchanged for gifts at redemption centers, and watching television. "I keep my mind sharp watching game shows," she said, unconvincingly. Dad, on the other hand, usually had books on his nightstand, and if he wasn't too tired, he read a few pages before turning off the lights. The EX LIBRIS, FRIEDA AND MILTON stickers could have been replaced with EX LIBRIS for Dad and EX-READER for Mom.

My father read a few favorite books over and over. Biographies of George Burns and Jackie Gleason were well-thumbed, as was Irving Stone's *Clarence Darrow for the Defense*. Dad admired Darrow and spoke of the time he was having dinner at the Grande Vista restaurant and recognized the famed lawyer dining there with H.T. Dewhirst, a former California judge who had succeeded King Ben as head of the House of David. Dad was knowledgeable about Darrow. "Do you know that when he saved Leopold and Loeb from the electric chair, their parents beat him out of part of his fee? How do you like that?" he said, miffed on Darrow's behalf.

Another book Pop swore by was *Maxwell Street*, a chronicle of Chicago's once exuberant Maxwell Street outdoor market neighborhood. Maxwell Street was a block from Roosevelt Road, which the author, Ira Berkow, felicitously calls "the highway of the hegira." Ira, a retired *New York Times* sports columnist and one of my closest friends, gifted a signed copy of *Maxwell Street* to Mook, who every few years instructed me, "Tell Ira I read his book again."[1]

About his reading habits, my father explained, "You finish a book, and after a few years, all you remember is that you liked it. You read it again, and you enjoy it just like before."

Despite his lack of formal education, Dad was responsible for teachable moments. He imparted an important lesson on a trip to Chicago he and I took when I was 11 to see a Cubs game as guests of his friend David Ross, the owner of a Benton

---

1. In *Maxwell Street*, Ira profiles notables who came out of the West Side, including Hyman Rickover, bandleader Benny Goodman, U.S. Supreme Court Justice Arthur Goldberg and Jack Ruby, born Jacob Rubenstein, the killer of Lee Harvey Oswald. Another West Sider featured in *Maxwell Street* is CBS founder William S. Paley, whose cigarmaker father, Sam, created La Palinas, Mook's smoke of choice. La Palina translates as "the Paley woman" in honor of Sam's wife, Goldie, who was the model for the woman in the Spanish get-up on the cigar box. (John S. Minary, William Paley's chief financial advisor mentioned in the book, is a Benton Harbor native.)

Harbor lampshade company, Progressive Industries. Mr. Ross's sons, Mike and John, were with us, also Buddy and Jerry Alberts and their father, Harold. The four boys were all good friends of mine.

Before the ballgame Mr. Ross took us to lunch at the Standard Club, one of Chicago's two fancy Jewish men's clubs. The other, the Covenant Club, catered to Jews of Eastern European descent, while the Standard Club was a redoubt for those of German origin and therefore was either snootier than the Covenant Club or was presumed to be. In the Standard Club's dark-wooded Grill Room, the men ordered filet mignons. I was the first of the boys to order and told the waiter with formality befitting the surroundings, "I'll also have a filet mignon please, sir." The other boys followed my lead and ordered filets too. I thought Dad would be proud of how grown-up and polite I'd been, but he admonished me. He said it was my fault that all the boys ordered steak and that I'd taken advantage of Mr. Ross's generosity. "You should have had the hamburger," he said.

Misfortune stalked the Ross family. Two years earlier, Mr. Ross's wife, Gertrude, died of a heart attack at the age of 42. Less than a year after the Chicago trip, an early-morning fire destroyed the family's spacious house on Benton Harbor's North Shore Drive, where I'd had a sleepover two weeks before. Mr. Ross and his six-year-old daughter Ruth Ann died in the fire while Mike, John and an older sister, Naomi, survived. After Mike recovered from burns that briefly hospitalized him, he came for a reciprocal sleepover at my house. Upon arrival he went straight upstairs and stood at a window. "Pretty narrow if you had to jump," he said.

Mike's younger brother, John, became a highly successful lawyer in Phoenix. He was a Phoenix Suns season ticket holder, and when I was in Arizona on a *Sports Illustrated* assignment, he took me to a Suns game, which turned out to be the last time I saw him. On August 16, 1987, John was returning from playing golf in Scotland with his close friend, Bill Blakley, also a prominent Phoenix lawyer. On a stopover in Detroit, John and Bill boarded a connecting Phoenix-bound flight, Northwest Airlines 255, and were among 154 people killed when the plane crashed on takeoff and burst into flames. Having survived one fire in Michigan, John was fated to die in another.[2]

When I think of the Rosses, I have two inescapable feelings — sorrow about their snakebit lives and guilt that I didn't order the hamburger.

There was another lesson, one that my father surely would have made more entertaining for me but was delivered by my mother instead. A dialogue runs through my mind of how the assignment might have gone to her and not him:

"You're the father. This should be your responsibility."

"You'll tell me I handled it all wrong. You know the right words to use."

"You're right. I'll do it."

The Big Reveal: Mother and I are sitting on the edge of my bed. Afternoon sunlight floods the room, with further illumination provided by a slender book for young people she has placed in my hands. I learn about squiggly creatures journeying

---

[2]. The Arizona State University's law school's library was named in memory of John Ross and Bill Blakley. When the law collections were relocated, Ross-Blakley Law Library became Ross-Blakley Hall, home of the university's English department and Institute for Humanities Research.

down a tunnel like a bowling ball headed for the pins. The tunnel is in the woman's body. In the man's body is a launching apparatus whose tricky hydraulics are essential to the operation. When the lesson mercifully ends, the subject has been so thoroughly covered by my mother that I have only one question: "Even President Truman?"

Soon my knowledge of male-female relations deepened. In addition to the darkroom, our house's basement was fitted out with an auxiliary kitchen, bathroom, utility room and a knotty-pine recreation room. The rec room featured a wet bar, Ping-Pong table, jukebox and stacks of record albums, some featuring Jewish entertainers — the klezmer bandleader Mickey Katz, better known later as Joel Grey's father; the golden-voiced cantor Yossele Rosenblatt, hailed as the Jewish Caruso; and the bawdy, big-bodied nightclub comedienne Belle Barth. On the cover of Barth's album *If I Embarrass You Tell Your Friends*, she wags a warning finger. One of her jokes refers to her self-proclaimed anatomical capaciousness. Barth says she sat on a fire hydrant and slid to the ground. There also were *Pardon My Blooper* records, compilations of sometimes risqué radio gaffes such as a commercial in which an announcer blunderingly says, "Remember, it's Wonder Bread for the breast in bed."

Because my mother did the record buying in our household, I felt a frisson of excitement realizing that Belle Barth and *Pardon My Blooper* ribaldry was to her taste as well as to Dad's.

One day, craving a Snickers bar or to satisfy some other urgent need, I was rummaging through my parents' bedroom dresser drawer where I knew they kept loose change when a Christmas card caught my eye. Beneath the image of a woman hoeing in a garden were the words "From an old ho-er." The card was signed "Bertha." From the playground intelligentsia, I knew that Benton Harbor's most notorious madam was Bertha Russell. My finding the card in their shared dresser drawer suggested that both of my parents were acquainted with Bertha.

Bertha Russell had friends in high places. Her bordello on Territorial Road was frequently raided, and she was jailed only to be quickly back in business. She claimed she was running a boarding house for young women — a sorority house, you might say, in search of a university. Next door to Bertha's was Heath Company, a nationally known manufacturer of hobbyist electronics kits based at the time in Benton Harbor. An informal history penned by a Heath Company executive says that when the whorehouse was torn down, the company's boss, Howard Anthony, salvaged chunks of wood from the rubble and sent them to town officials and gentry with notes reading, "This is the last piece you'll get from Bertha's."

A friend of Joel's told him he saw our father entering Bertha's one afternoon. Maybe so, but I don't remember seeing any wood in our house that looked like it came from her place of business. Might Dad have kept a relic from Bertha's in his cluttered office?

Chapter 11

Laryngitis

My mother considered her family, the Goldbergs, superior in every way to my father's people, the Kirshenbaums. Nevertheless, she believed it important that children get to know all their grandparents, which for Roberta, Joel and me, meant Grandpa and Grandma Kirshenbaum in Benton Harbor as well as Mom's parents in Chicago. Without passing judgment on the relative merits of the two sides of the family, Mook agreed that visiting grandparents was, as a general rule, a good thing for children to do.

Accordingly, we were taken to see Mendel and Gittel on the farm on Sundays, but not, thank goodness, every Sunday. The visits were a duty for us, and our grandparents acted as though our presence was onerous for them as well. On our arrival, our cheeks weren't pinched, and we weren't hugged or clucked over and told how much we'd grown since the last time, even if the last time had been many inches and pounds ago. Our Kirshenbaum grandparents greeted us as strangers, and we viewed them the same way.

When Dad was with us, he was civil with his presumptive

father. He took the high road because, he said, "The Good Book says to respect your elders," to which Mom accurately rejoined, "He's always quoting The Good Book, but he's never read it." As we all knew, the real reason Dad maintained a semblance of peace with Mendel was that he didn't want to impair his relationship with Gitla, whom he loved unreservedly.

What made visits to the farm more bearable for me was the presence of Aunt Rose and her family. The youngest of the six Kirshenbaum siblings, Rose was the only one born not in Poland or Chicago but in Benton Harbor, also the only one who made it through high school. Rose grew up on the farm and when she married David Goldstein, he moved onto the farm with her. There Aunt Rose and Uncle Dave raised their three whip-smart children, Enid, Deana (the cousin who alerted Joel and me to Dad's transgressions in South Haven) and Gary. Because the children lived with their (our) grandparents, all spoke at least some Yiddish. When I was little, I thought it weird that there were children in the United States of America able to converse in Yiddish, but the time came when I envied them for that.

Never at the farm did we cross paths with Dad's enemy brothers, Hymie and Abe. For this Aunt Rose is to be thanked. Being in residence, she was the gatekeeper who made sure the coast was clear when Mook phoned to say he wanted to bring his children to visit. At the farm I did meet Mook's Chicago sisters, Dorothy and Freida, but never at the same time, because, in another bitter family conflict, they also didn't get along, requiring Rose to keep the two of them apart as well.

There came a moment, however, when a collision between the Chicago aunts couldn't be avoided. It happened when Grandma Kirshenbaum was taken to Memorial Hospital to die. Advised that the end for their mother was near, the aunts rushed separately to the Twin Cities. As the story goes, one of the sisters — Frieda, say — arrived first and was fluffing Grandma's pillow when Dorothy burst into the room. Elbowing Frieda aside, Dorothy removed the pillow from beneath her mother's head and replaced it with one that hadn't been sullied by contact with Frieda. When one sister took a water pitcher and began filling Grandma's glass, the other yanked it away. There was shoving and name-calling, followed by purses swung, hair pulled, and the pitcher emptied by one sister onto the other's head. Grandma screamed for a nurse, "Help! My daughters, they're killing me!"

The brouhaha may have awakened in Gitla life-affirming memories of scraps between the daughters when they were little. Rejuvenated, she went home, her demise put off for another day.

That, anyway, is the story.

The warring sisters both married well-to-do Chicago men. Aunt Frieda's husband, Sol Kirman, had a business liquidating unsold department store merchandise. Frieda and Sol struck me as standoffish, halfway to invisibility, but their only child, Ben, was personable and full of the dickens, a contrast for which there was a possible explanation: He was adopted.

Aunt Dorothy's husband, Zell Zwick, had a plumbing supplies company and real estate holdings, including a stake in the 12th Street Store on Roosevelt Road. I was tickled having an uncle whose initials were ZZ, and when I discovered that the Zwicks were on the last page of the Chicago telephone directory, it was something to brag to my friends about. Zell was a jaunty little man who talked fast and big, dropping the names of politicians, fat cats and mobsters of his acquaintance. In conversation, he waved his arms and raised and lowered his shoulders in the manner of a dance instructor teaching the mambo. Dorothy wore outlandish hats and too much jewelry and was cockamamie and cunning. She was younger on her driver's license than on her Social Security and her Medicare cards, her true age falling somewhere in the middle.

The Zwicks had a fractious marriage. To wheedle money out of Zell, Dorothy charged cashmere sweaters and expensive jewelry on his 12th Street Store account and returned them for cash. When they'd had enough of each other, Zell moved out of their Lake Shore Drive apartment and into the Grandeur, a 14-story residence hotel of which he was part owner on Granville Avenue on Chicago's North Side. By coincidence, my mother's hapless brother, Irving, after the breakup of his marriage, lived in a building on the same street. My father called Granville Avenue "the boulevard of broken dreams."

The Zwicks had two sons, Mort and his older brother, Bob. Mort was born at 11:30 p.m. on August 29, 1938, and I came along at 3:20 a.m. on the 30th. I think of Mort and Bob as quintessential Chicago wise guys. They were friendly with Cousin Ben Kirman but told him, "You're adopted — you're lucky we talk to you." Ben had some Chicago wisenheimer in him too. "What I'm lucky about," he countered, "is that I wasn't born a Kirshenbaum."

I've never forgiven Aunt Dorothy and Uncle Zell for recommending to my parents that they send me to Camp Flambeau, the sleepaway camp in northern Wisconsin they had chosen for Mort, nor have I pardoned Mom and Dad for going along with the recommendation. I don't know what possessed any of them to condemn their six-year-old sons to eight weeks in the Northwoods on the outskirts of nowhere, 330 miles from Chicago and 430 from Benton Harbor.

Camp Flambeau, set amid towering pines and birch trees

on the shore of Duck Lake in Eagle River, Wisconsin, was a camp for Jewish boys mostly from Chicago and Milwaukee. The camp was owned by Captain Daniel D. Glasser, a World War I Army officer who as an assistant U.S. District Attorney in Chicago had been found guilty of accepting bribes to fix bootlegging cases, a conviction overturned by the U.S Supreme Court on grounds that the lawyer representing Glasser had a conflict of interest. Prosecutors wanted to retry the case, but a judge ruled against it, raising suspicions that Glasser had gotten to the judge as bootleggers had allegedly gotten to Glasser. Employing his Army rank as an honorific, Captain Glasser ran ads for Camp Flambeau inviting boys to spend "idyllic summer months together in the great outdoors, cradled in the arms of Mother Nature."

Also in Eagle River, four miles away on Catfish Lake, was rival Camp Ojibwa, where Mom's cousin Sima Gebel was the camp nurse. The summer I was at Flambeau, a 20-year-old Ojibwa counselor, Alan Sherman, purportedly got the inspiration for his hit novelty song, "Hello Muddah, Hello Faddah," in which a camper at a fictional Camp Granada writes home complaining of rainy weather and food poisoning only to dash off a never-mind letter the next day saying that the sun had come out and all was well.

At Camp Flambeau, I metaphorically never saw the sun. I was homesick and worried I'd be eaten by bears, another peril mentioned in Sherman's ditty. Because the latrine was distant from the tent where we slept, I was afraid to go out in the dark and several times wet my bed. I was bullied by Cousin Mort, who showed off to his big-city friends by shoving and punching his younger-by-four-hours cousin. A couple of times Sima visited and tried to comfort me.

On parents' weekend, Mort began picking on me as usual.

That this was happening in front of his and my parents and other visitors sent me into uncharted territory. I for once retaliated, answering a Mort push with one of my own. There was more shoving, and we fell together to the ground, punching and wrestling. I was crying and waited for Dad to come to my rescue and was mortified to hear Mom tell him to let Mort and me fight it out. Then I realized that Mort was crying, too. Now he also was experiencing humiliation. My mother's instincts had been right. She knew my cousin had been making my life miserable and thought I needed to stand up to him. She could be wise that way, and on this occasion Dad was wise to defer to her.

The next few summers found me at sleepaway camps closer to home and more to my liking. I spent three summers at the Culver Military Academy's Woodcraft Camp for boys in Indiana, where the campers were of all faiths, the military trappings minimal and my complaints few — no bed-wetting or bullying, only sports, campfires, nature studies and canoeing on the Tippecanoe River. In time, Camp Flambeau went out of business, the property becoming a state-run facility for juvenile delinquents. I picture it as a place filled with scores of Mort Zwicks cradled in the arms of Mother Nature and the Wisconsin criminal justice system.

My father and Mort's father were good friends. Uncle Zell had business that took him to South Bend, and now and then he swung by Benton Harbor to visit Mook. Once I eavesdropped as they talked on our house's porch, me unseen sitting on the floor at the doorway. The conversation turned to their marriages, Uncle Zell's from the sound of it even more troubled than my father's. I was startled when I heard Zell say, "I can get Dorothy bumped off for 20 grand," all the more when he added, "I think they'd throw in Frieda for five more."

Imagine my hearing talk of a possible rubout of my mother and my aunt. Drawing on knowledge gleaned from my comic books and my radio crime shows, I doped it out that ZZ wanted his wife in cement boots because he had a chippy on the side. But I knew that Double Z wouldn't let the hits go down with him dropping 20 large and his compadre shelling out only five G's. I knew it didn't work that way, not with the boys in Chi-Town it didn't.

In the end, Mom and Aunt Dorothy weren't snuffed, whacked or offed. Zell had just been shooting his yap. My flight of fancy, thankfully, was just that.

———

BY THE TIME I visited the Kirshenbaum farm, the vineyards were withered, the pasture had reverted to wild and the only animals to be seen were a few scraggly chickens, who would be spared the fryer because the batter in fried chicken contains dairy, a verboten pairing of meat and milk in a kosher kitchen, but who would have no defense against being boiled or fricasseed. The house had been updated with indoor plumbing, but the decommissioned outhouse and outdoor water pump remained. The farm was like a museum stripped of all but those two objects of curiosity.

Unless you count Grandpa Kirshenbaum as a third. Cartoonishly scrawny, he had a thin face framed by outward- and upward-pointed ears ("on two distant planets," Cousin Enid said of those protuberances) that made him look poised for liftoff. He acted as if he had things to do but couldn't decide which to tackle first. There is only one time he addressed me that I remember. I was maybe nine. "Nu, Jerry, you know about sex?" he asked. I didn't have to answer because he'd posed the question only to see me squirm. He chuckled at my discomfort and shuffled away, perhaps to prepare for air traffic control to send him skyward.

With Grandma, there wasn't much give and take either. I thought her chief purpose in life was to shoo the flies off the bowl of fruit that rested on her lap. I sat across from her, and there were stretches of silence, each of us waiting the other out. When she spoke, it was softly. "*Vilstu* a banana?" she asked. Other times it might be a peach or a plum she was offering.

Grandma was Edith Bunker-like in her subservience to Grandpa. She was a bit player in a production for which only her husband's name was on the marquee. Uncle Abe had received kudos in the family for memorializing Mendel at Ellis Island, but nobody seemed bothered that he hadn't thought to do the same for Gitla, a slight all the greater considering that she came through Ellis Island and Mendel didn't.

I saw on Grandpa's naturalization application that he was 5'4". When I mentioned this to Enid, she said, "He may have been short, but he was a towering figure." Mendel was Eiffel-ish not only in Enid's eyes but also, it was evident, in the view of the rabbis and learned elders who journeyed from Chicago to bask in the glow of his company. I once saw several of these worthies gathered around him at the dining room table while Grandma brought them tea, which she served the old way, in water glasses instead of cups.

The men discussed politics and argued over the pros and cons of Zionism and pored over passages in holy texts. I heard English, Yiddish and snatches of what I took to be Russian and Polish. These were no dummies. Religious Jews regard a luxuriant beard as a sign of wisdom, and although Grandpa's growth was sparser than that of his hirsute visitors, they hung on his every word. Girth is something else said to signify wisdom. Girth he lacked altogether.

I honor the courage it took for Grandpa and Grandma Kirshenbaum, my other grandparents and millions more like them to travel from the only world they knew to a faraway land filled with promise but also uncertainty. Mendel feared for those who didn't get out in time. On May 20, 1936, the Benton Harbor *News-Palladium* ran a letter to the editor expressing concern about the endangered Jews in Nazi Germany signed M. H. Kershenbaum. Mendel took an expansive view of his name. The "H" here stands for Hersch, his middle name. He sometimes also employed Hersch and the variations Herszk or Gerszk as his first name, this with the randomness that moved him in this letter to the newspaper to spell the first syllable of his surname "Kersh" instead of "Kirsh." On his World War I draft card he was Mendel Herschel Kershenbaum. In the 1920 U.S. Census he was, unaccountably, John Kirshenbaum.

Grandpa's letter boiled over with incendiary imagery. "Think of the once aristocratic Germany, where for more than three years, a hell fire has been raging, the flames already reaching other countries, a fire as devastating as an earthquake, or an eruption of a volcano with its flowing lava, as conspicuous to the eye as if the sun had been darkened in broad daylight. Within this Germany and its Nazi flames, one half a million people are begging for help and crying, 'Save us.'"

M.H. Kershenbaum's prescient plea on behalf of German Jewry went unheeded as the flames he spoke of vaulted beyond the borders of Germany and consumed most of Europe.

As he got on in years, Mendel became less paterfamilias and more ponderer and putterer, ceding control of the farmhouse to his daughter, Aunt Rose. Visiting the farm, Dad liked to talk things over with Rose's genial husband, Uncle Dave, a scrap metal dealer and fellow poker player. He also chatted with Rose if he was in the mood for her, and she for him. Rose was spindly, energetic and quick with the lip. "Rose is an expert about everything — just ask her," Dad said. Her children agreed. They had a saying they whispered to one another: "Rose knows." They weren't surprised to discover that their mother's senior class entry in the Benton Harbor High School yearbook called her "a girl who is frank."

Mook and Rose squabbled as people do when they have more in common than they care to admit. As in tradition-steeped football rivalries, their clashes were recurring and often entertaining but with no trophy awarded the victor like the Jeweled Shillelagh (Notre Dame-Southern Cal) or the Bronze Boot (Colorado State-Wyoming), only the satisfaction one derived from gaining momentary advantage over the other. Each knew the buttons to push. When he thought Rose was talking too much, Dad asked, "Tell me, do you ever get laryngitis?" Rose complained to him, "Mook, sometimes you carry your jive too far." Her jive was to insist he was of legitimate birth, even though she knew he found the subject bothersome and of no account. She claimed that at Ellis Island, Grandma tried to hide Schmul's age by holding him tightly in her arms only to have him escape her clutches and run free, a boy clearly older than 1y 6m. Rose told him, "You know, you weren't born in 1906. You were born in 1904."

To which he replied, "What, were you at my *bris?*"

One day Rose mentioned that she wanted to visit their sister Frieda Kirman in Chicago. Dad was going to Chicago on business and offered to drive her. When he picked Rose up at her home, no sooner did she enter the car than she suggested they go by way of Galien. Dad had driven to Chicago often enough to make it there blindfolded and never by way of Galien, yet here was know-it-all Rose giving him directions.

"She was trying to cause trouble because that's what she is, a troublemaker," he said.

Galien (pop. 450) is a Berrien County farm community said to be the source of the cereal leaf beetle that in the 1960s spread across North America destroying vast fields of wheat and oats. Despite the damage to its reputation and a whole lot of grain, Galien is a pleasant enough little place, with silos punctuating the landscape and cows grazing, but going that way would have added six miles to the trip.

"Galien is out of the way," Dad said.

"But there's less traffic," Rose said.

"That's because nobody except you is fool enough to drive there to get to Chicago."

Mook didn't always get the last word with his sassy sister, but this time he did. He drove her to Chicago, but not, you may be sure, by way of Galien.

Chapter 12

Beware Of The Yarmulkes

When Uncle Irving called my father mentally strong and a man of infinite patience, he was speaking immutable truths. What others took hard, Mook took in stride. On the death of a friend or admired celebrity, he said with a shrug, "Nobody gets out of this world alive," and if the deceased's age warranted, he might add, "Well, he didn't die a young man." At word of a tax increase, he ho-hummed, "So what else is new?" and the same was heard if a politician was found to have been on the take. Rain in the forecast? "If it rains, you know what I'm gonna do? I'm gonna let it rain."

Coming home from work, he left business worries behind him. I see him in my mind's eye as he settles in for the evening. He removes his shoes, reads the newspaper on the couch and dozes off, pages open on his lap. Waking, he slices one or two pieces of an apple with a pen knife, never enough to spoil his appetite. Just before dinner, he tosses down a shot of whisky, one shot only. Dad wasn't a drinker. Dining out, he might allow himself a beer or cocktail, but usually not even that. He mostly stuck to water, and he shunned what half the nation calls soda and the other half calls pop. "Water is better for you than pop," said Pop.

His success at poker owed to his preternatural self-control. He was said to be a tight player, his face as unreadable as Buster Keaton's, his manner unruffled no matter the stakes or the cards dealt. A corollary to his imperturbability was his talent for getting under the skin of rival players. In a celebrated occurrence in the Pit, Sam Unger, a large, shambling man who spoke with the accent of his native Lithuania, was grumbling during a run of terrible luck. After losing several raise-after-raise hands and out a great deal of money, Unger raked in a pitifully small pot. "Glad to see you get even, Sam," Mook said. Enraged, Unger removed the dagger from his back and lifted himself to his feet, ready to take it outside. He had to be restrained while my father waited innocently for the next hand to be dealt.

Direct confrontation wasn't Mook's style, not even in the face of the irritants and incitements of his supposed father. Instead of responding overtly to Mendel's provocations, Dad found satisfaction knowing that the old man was aware of the beautiful house on Miami Road, the Cadillacs in the driveway and the fur coats and jewelry Mom was wearing. Mook also may have been getting back at Grandpa, if only in his own mind (and perhaps not even that, but subconsciously), with the patch of earth he tended at the side of our house. How else explain seeing my otherwise unfussy father remove the seeds from the little packet, plant them carefully in the ground, and nursemaid the tomatoes thus produced? Here was the onetime work-shirking farm boy proving as an adult that he could grow things better than Grandpa could.

Examples of my father's self-discipline abound. When a doctor suggested he might try to lose five pounds, he effortlessly lost 10. Not one to rush to catch trains or planes, he arrived at stations and airports hours early, content to people-watch until boarding time. He sidestepped arguments. Cornered in a discussion, he wriggled free, saying, "I rest my case," even if he never had a case. He hedged expressions of shaky opinions with "according to me." Noting the preponderance of widows in Mom's and his crowd, he said: "The wives are killers. They drive their husbands to their deaths, according to me." Advised that females outliving males was the natural order of things among humans and many other species of mammals, he said, "I rest my case."

He distrusted orthodoxies, trends and conventional wisdom and was alert to hypocrisy and insincerity. To friends going on vacation, he said, "Don't send me any of those wish-you-were here postcards. If you really meant that, you'd take me with you." Before his birthday, he instructed, "Just give me your good wishes. If you give me a gift, it only means I'll have to give you one on your birthday." He found folly where others found fun. At news of somebody crashing a private plane or killed in a scuba diving accident, he said, "Too much money," his spoilsport thesis being that if the victim hadn't been able to afford such a pricey activity, he would have been spared his misfortune.

During recessions, he believed his own eyes rather than the economists when he entered a restaurant and saw it filled with diners. "So where's the recession?" he asked, sounding as if he was about to crawl under a table to look for it. He rejected much of what, in the heady years after World War II, was extolled as "progress." He shunned credit cards and ATMs and refused to wear seatbelts. As evidence of what he thought was unthinking acceptance of seatbelts, he told of a horrendous car-train collision at a railroad crossing in Watervliet, a town near Benton Harbor, in which all five occupants of the car were killed instantly. He said a state trooper investigating the accident was quoted as saying, absurdly, "It would have been worse if they hadn't been wearing their seatbelts." I searched for an account of the accident containing the ridiculous comment. When I told Dad I couldn't find anything, he smiled at my gullibility. There'd been no car-train accident and no state trooper talking nonsense. He'd invented the whole thing.

About seatbelts, he rested his case.

MY FATHER SUCCEEDED in soothing a distressed Uncle Irving, but being a Frieda whisperer was many degrees more difficult. Mom required more understanding than Dad could summon. His lightheartedness was salt in her wounds, his otherworldly self-control a taunt. Over the years the labels pinned on Mother escalated from vivacious to high-strung to the psychiatric diagnosis of manic depression, later rebranded as bipolar disorder. My father didn't try to keep up with the evolving jargon. Of his wife's mood swings, he said simply, "She blows hot and cold."

I couldn't be as stoical as Dad was about Mom's outbursts. Her screaming pierced me like a hundred knife stabs. As a boy, I'd be on the phone with a friend, and when the shrieking started in the background, I'd make an excuse to quickly hang up, praying that my friend hadn't heard. After I left for college, Mom's hysteria worsened, and my brother bore the brunt. "I was ashamed to have friends over," Joel says. "I locked myself in my room, did my homework and listened to baseball on the radio. When the yelling got worse, I turned the ballgame on louder."

Anything could send Mom off the rails. The too little help

she received caring for Roberta. Her sons' failure to pick up their toys and clothes. Her husband's inability to perform difficult house repairs. Dad had his handyman friend Ken Peterson come over to tackle the more challenging items on her to-do list. "Thank God for Ken Peterson," she said.

My mother was an obsessive housekeeper. She went through a succession of cleaning women, some of whom she fired because they didn't vacuum or mop to her satisfaction, others who quit before she had a chance because they couldn't stand her hectoring. Most were "colored girls," a term applied by many whites of my parents' generation to Black women of any age, but there were enough Caucasians in the mix to make Mom an equal opportunity hired-help abuser. She also discomfited maids by oversharing her personal problems with them. When she wasn't excoriating cleaning women, she treated them as her confidantes.

Both of my parents could be off-putting, but with a fundamental difference. When my father ruffled feathers, it was often on purpose, for the fun of it. My mother had an astonishing lack of self-awareness and provoked unknowingly. My *Sports Illustrated* colleague Frank Deford wrote that Bob Feller, the flame-throwing Cleveland Indians pitcher, was so given to public gaucheries that his wife asked a doctor, "Really, is it medically possible to die of embarrassment?" My mother's indiscretions had us asking the same question Anne Feller did.

"My daughter has diabetes," she informed the waitress at the Green Cottage, the Lobster Lounge or any of the other Twin Cities restaurants where we ate out as a family. "I'll have to order for her. At home I weigh her food. She's also retarded. I have to do everything for her."

Indicating me, she volunteered, "This one's a picky eater.

He'll have a lettuce wedge, no dressing. I don't know how he can eat salad dry like that."

About Joel: "Do you have a children's menu? Ordering from the regular menu would be a waste. He'll leave everything on his plate."

Herself: "With my gallbladder, I better not overdo it."

When the waitress departed with our orders, Dad said, "Frieda, you didn't have to tell her all those things."

We joked about Mom's compulsions. When traveling, she packed Comet and a brush to scrub the sink in her hotel room, and we kidded that she cleaned the hotel's other bathrooms while she was at it. I told friends that I got up during the night to go to the bathroom and came back to find the bed made. That wasn't true, but I did once return and the wastebasket had been emptied. Often my mother's claimed illnesses were suspiciously the ones that Dr. Theodore R. Van Dellen wrote about in that day's syndicated column that the *News-Palladium* carried. We laughed about Mom's recuperative powers. Dad said, "She lies around all day moaning that she's dying, but shopping at the mall, you can't keep up with her."

She had faith in our family doctor, Charles Ozeran. She knew his office and home phone numbers by heart and felt free to call him at any hour, saying, "Charlie, I'm feeling such and such" or "Charlie, I need this or that medicine." Dr. Ozeran had a hangdog look and caring manner and was said to be a fine physician, but his hands were badly scarred from performing X-rays without wearing protective gloves, which suggested a certain carelessness on his part. He maintained an apothecary in a glass-enclosed area in his office where medicines were dispensed by a pharmacist in his employ. I don't know if this profit center gave him an incentive to write unnecessary prescriptions, but whether for appointments or to pick up pills, my mother spent a great deal of time in the office of Charles Ozeran, MD.

I was a guard on our Fair Plain eighth-grade basketball team. In the final minutes of a game against Stevensville in our boxy home gym, I was slammed into by a rival player in a scramble for a loose ball. My nose was broken, and I went to the bench holding a towel to my bloodied face while a seventh grader, Tommy Garland, came in to shoot the free throw I'd been awarded. After the game, a loss, our coach, Mr. Schneider, a Fair Plain math teacher, asked me who our family doctor was, and we headed to his car to get me medical attention.

"Oh my God," Mom said at the sight of me. Mr. Schneider must have thought that Mrs. Kirshenbaum, through some occult power possessed by Jewish mothers, had divined that calamity had smitten her first-born son and teleported herself in a puff of smoke to Dr. Ozeran's office. I knew better. She was in his office so often that I might have been surprised if she wasn't there.

MY MOTHER WAS capable of surpassing warmth. When I was six, I heard her crying in her bedroom. I entered and found her in bed. She pulled me under the covers with her, held me tight and said, "President Roosevelt died." I was sad that she had lost such a close friend, and I cried too. In her arms I felt protected.

I thanked the stars for the times she was "well." On Friday nights she said a blessing as she lit the candles, a cloth napkin covering her head. Sometimes she let me help prepare the chopped liver for the Sabbath meal. I didn't want to touch the slimy slab of liver, and she placed it in the grinder for me. I cranked the handle, watching the miniscule holes on the spout resembling showerhead openings as strands of liver emerged spaghetti-like and settled in a heap in the bowl, looking more squashed than chopped, if you want to know the truth. Mom said I did a good job, which made me happy.

I never doubted my mother's love for me. For years she had me believe that I'd won a "beautiful baby" contest. There was a photo of me with curly blond hair sitting in a highchair and holding a trophy. I later learned that the trophy was awarded because Mother had sold the most raffle tickets for a charity. When I was 10, I was admitted to Mercy Hospital with symptoms of spinal meningitis. In bed attended by a masked nurse, I asked why my parents hadn't visited. The nurse said she thought they would arrive soon. She left the room, and the door swung open just wide enough for me to catch a glimpse of Mom and Dad on a bench wearing grave expressions. I realized they weren't allowed to be near me for fear of contagion. I could see how difficult my death was going to be for them.

I didn't have spinal meningitis and returned home the same day.

Mother visited the sick and took meals to the grieving. She belonged to a women's singing group that entertained nursing home residents, many of them younger than herself. "I can't stop doing good," she said. That may have been true, but it would have been better if she'd been content to let others say it. That was the problem with her good deeds: she often came on too strong performing them. She sold Israel Bonds and raised money for United Jewish Appeal with a manner calling to mind the joke about Sonny Liston, the fearsome heavyweight boxing champion. Liston, it was said, should open a restaurant because even if the food was terrible, who would be brave enough to tell him? Likewise, who dared say no to Mom? On the phone soliciting a donation, she demanded of the woman at the other end, "What do you mean you can't afford it? What about the fur coat Morris bought you?" She knew the store where the coat had been purchased, its cost, even the size. Raising money, she also raised hackles. "She's like the cow that gives a full pail of milk, then kicks it over," Mook said.

Cows delivering milk and horses geeing and hawing weren't the only barnyard expressions Dad employed with Mom. When she carried on at length about her ailments, he told her, "On the farm we shot horses with fewer things wrong with them." When she spoke admiringly of a friend's expensive new necklace, he said, "I need to put blinders on you." He told of a heated argument she got into at a social event with a family friend, Harry Litowich, a silver-haired gladhander and Republican three-term Michigan state senator. "She was going at it with Harry like a banty rooster," Mook said. "You ever see banty roosters fight? They stand toe to toe pecking at each other until one of them dies. She was like a banty rooster." It sounded like Harry was also banty rooster-like, but it's my mother we're talking about here.

If only to lend them financial support, our family belonged to all three of Benton Harbor's Jewish congregations, but we mainly worshipped at the reform synagogue Temple Beth El, where, differing from the conservative Children of Israel synagogue and even more from the orthodox Ohava Sholem *shul*, men and women sat together, organ music was played, and as much English as Hebrew was heard. Another difference was that Temple Beth El held sabbath services only on Friday nights while the other two houses of worship conducted them on Saturday mornings as well.

My father embraced Judaism culturally but distanced himself from many of its doctrines and practices. This caused clashes with Mother. She kept kosher at home, which he complained was a nuisance and expensive, meat from the kosher butcher shop being pricier than the cuts at the supermarket. Dad had misgivings about organized religion of every kind. Although he didn't live long enough to learn of the 21st Century's widespread sex abuse scandals involving Catholic priests, televangelists and Southern Baptist ministers, there was enough clerical misbehavior during his lifetime to earn his scorn, including by rabbis who embezzled from their synagogues or seduced congregants' wives. He called these rabbis "fakers."

Mom didn't like hearing that. "There are many wonderful rabbis," she said.

"I'm talking about the ones who aren't wonderful," he said.

When Mook attended synagogue services, it was less to get right with the Lord than to schmooze with friends who might be present. One Sabbath service at Temple Beth El was conducted by a visiting rabbi he thought had faker written all over him. When, after the service, the rabbi reached out to shake hands with him and wish him good Shabbos, Dad brusquely said, "I don't know you and you don't know me," and turned away.

In his teen years, Susan's and my son, David, was a camper and then a counselor at Stagedoor Manor, a summer theater camp in the Catskills, which I called, to give it a proper American Indian-sounding name, Camp I-Wanna-Be-A-Star. Visiting David at Camp I-Wanna-Be-A-Star with my parents, we stayed at Brown's, one of the last of the great Borscht Belt resorts still in existence and itself soon to perish. Brown's remaining guests were few and mostly elderly. The hotel's Jerry Lewis Theater Club showroom was shuttered, guest room furnishings threadbare, and, in the dining room, if you were in your 50s or even early 60s, you might find yourself placed by the hostess at the young people's table. Mook was lobby sitting at Brown's one morning when two old men wearing prayer shawls and other regalia of Jewish orthodoxy tottered by. A kindred spirit seated next to Dad whispered, "Beware of the yarmulkes [skullcaps]."

This — "beware of the yarmulkes" — became a favorite saying of my father's.

But his reservations about traditional Judaism didn't stop him from posing as its protector when he felt like stirring up trouble. Performing theological jujitsu, he voiced objections to some of the reform movement's innovations as deviating too far from the faith in which he'd been raised and had rejected, but now — follow if you can — made a show of defending. To a woman who'd been married by a female rabbi, he said, "I don't recognize your marriage." To one who'd converted to Judaism, he said, "To me, you're not Jewish." Both women knew he was trying to get a rise out of them. The first laughed, and he laughed with her. The second wasn't amused, and he dismissed her as a sourpuss.

The yarmulke wearer he was wariest of was of course Grandpa Kirshenbaum, for whom he nevertheless once performed a good deed that produced a eureka moment for himself, spiritually speaking. The epiphany occurred when Mendel let it be known that he wanted to visit his brother Sam, who had retired from the Chicago bakery and was spending time in Arizona. Dad, also welcoming the chance to see Sam, offered to drive him. During the trip, adhering to Jewish dietary restrictions, Mendel subsisted on acceptable foods he brought with him such as sardines and cold soup. Out of consideration for his pious traveling companion, Dad ordered neutral items like eggs, fresh fruit and tomato soup until they stopped at a restaurant where a diner at another table was eating a steak that looked good and smelled better. He said he felt guilty ordering a *treif* [non-kosher] steak in front of Mendel but couldn't resist. As the old man looked on in silent disapproval, Dad took one bite of his steak and broke a denture. "Right then I knew there was a God," he said.

Pop had an ecumenical streak that confounded his Jewish friends. If someone was in a lather about an impending court appearance or upcoming major surgery, he urged "one day at a time, sweet Jesus," a line from "One Day at a Time," a Christian country song written by Marijohn Wilkin and Kris Kristofferson. The song is a plea to Jesus to grant the strength to get through one's daily struggles. The message squared with Mook's suck-it-up approach to life. He used the "one day at a time, sweet Jesus" line to tell people to cool their jets about whatever was bothering them.

He also drew inspiration from Mahalia Jackson's soaring "Peace in the Valley," a pop anthem with Christian overtones. When Mom said she wanted a new dishwasher with the latest features, Dad argued for her to hold off spending the money as long as their existing dishwasher still got the job done. "One day at a time, sweet Jesus," he told her. She replied by asking what about all the money he was spending on cigars? He proposed a deal: he would give up cigars if she forgot about a new dishwasher. She took the bet, certain that the grip his La Palinas had on him was unbreakable. Surprising Mom and the world, he quit cigars for good. She got the new dishwasher anyway, which Pop probably knew would be the result of the ridiculous wager, but he said triumphantly, "We have peace in the valley."

Listening to a recording of David and his grandfather in Benton Harbor, I feel vestigial pain hearing my mother raging in the background. She and Dad are getting ready for a bat mitzvah party, and she wants 13-year-old David to come with them, telling him that boys and girls his age will be there. David says he isn't feeling well, but she isn't buying it. Becoming more and more worked up, she yells at him, "You may fool your mother and father, but not me, kid!" She rages on, voice louder, "Other women show off their grandchildren at affairs like this, and I sit there eating my heart out!"

David asks, "Grandpa, when you married Grandma, what was she like?"

"What do you mean?"

"Was she the way she is now?"

He's asking if his grandmother has always been given to ranting, but Mook misunderstands, or pretends to. "Hell no, she was pretty," he says, redirecting the conversation. "You've seen our wedding picture, haven't you?"

"Yeah," David says, surrendering.

"Well, you don't expect somebody to look the same when they were young like they do now. I looked good then too, didn't I?"

"You still do."

"Oh, come on...."

At last Mom accepts that her grandson won't be attending the party and calms down. She's getting herself ready but can't find her makeup. She asks Dad if he has seen it.

"I saw it lying around and put it in the medicine cabinet," he says.

"There's a cover that goes with it. Don't you know it's supposed to be covered?"

"That's why I covered it."

"What did you cover it with?"

"With the cover."

As a boy, I enjoyed the radio program *The Bickersons*, on which a married (and childless) couple, John and Blanche Bickerson, played by Don Ameche and Frances Langford, had funny and acerbic rat-a-tat exchanges. My parents sometimes bantered the same way.

> *"Milt, Sam Levenson is on Johnny Carson tonight."*
> *"I don't like him."*
> *"Since when? He's one of your Borscht Belt comedians."*
> *"He laughs at his own jokes."*
> *"He used to be a schoolteacher. You don't like him because he's educated."*
> *"I don't like him because he laughs at his own jokes."*
> *"Bob Hope laughs at his own jokes."*
> *"I don't like him, either."*
> *"Who doesn't like Bob Hope? Only you."*
> *"How come with everybody else you're the defense attorney, and with me you're the prosecutor?"*

Some of my parents' badinage threaded the needle between playful and poisonous. Dad liked to see how far he could go with Mom with devilments that included intentionally misogynistic comments. He called her "my chattel." He said, "I'm in the bag business and I've got an old bag at home." Sometimes Mother tried giving it back to him. When he observed that one of her women friends was losing her looks, she riposted, "And who are you, Clark Gable?" And if she was an old bag, well, he was an old coot. When he was in his 70s and came home with a new overcoat, she told him, "You know, at your age, that's the last overcoat you'll ever buy." He thought he detected anticipatory glee in her voice. "I think you envy the widows," he told her.

On *The Bickersons* John is about to leave on a business trip. Worried about being left alone, Blanche asks, "Suppose a burglar breaks in the house and finds me?"

"It'll serve him right," John says.

It's axiomatic that radio fires the imagination as television doesn't. Listening to *The Bickersons*, I had no trouble imagining.[1]

---

1. In a column for the *Minneapolis Tribune*, I whimsically addressed the radio/imagination subject with a conversation between my fictional parents:
   We'd sit in front of the old Gothic receiver and Harry Von Zell or somebody would say, "And here's beautiful Betty Grable."
   "Hubba, hubba," my dad said.... "Listen to how beautiful she is."
   "Take your ears off her this instant," replied my mother.

Chapter 13

Three Boutonnieres

That the feud between Mook and his brothers ended was surprising, that it was my mother who brought it to an end, astonishing. After long fulminating against Hymie and Abe for their underhanded (and reciprocated) machinations against Dad, she found it not so much in her heart as in the exigencies of the moment to broker peace. The occasion for the burying of the hatchets was my bar mitzvah.

Nothing more reliably lifted Frieda Kirshenbaum out of a funk than throwing a party. She considered "entertaining" the solemn duty of the American housewife and kept at hand manuals of the hosting arts like *Esquire's Handbook for Hosts, Hoyle's Official Book of Games* and *Mr. Boston's Deluxe Bartending Guide* to consult when she needed guidance. Of course she seldom did, because hospitality — planning the menu, fussing over the guests, even the vacuuming and dishwashing afterwards — came naturally to her.

She hosted baby and wedding showers, March of Dimes events, mahjongg and Canasta parties and "eye saver" fundraisers to combat trachoma. My bar mitzvah was to be her biggest splash yet. Not the religious part, over which she had little say other than to ensure that an arrangement of mums, daisies, asters and other fall flowers be placed beneath the Temple Beth El *bema*, the platform on which stood the ark housing the Torah. It was the reception afterward, a steak and champagne blow-out for 300 guests at the Whitcomb Hotel, that showcased her event-planning acumen.

She was putting on the dog, and for once my father didn't object. Invitations flew out to the Temple Beth El membership, battalions of out-of-town friends, Mook's closest Chicago business associates, and the far-flung Goldberg clan, some of whom I'd never met. I especially wanted to make the acquaintance of "the red-headed cousins," two sisters always referred to only by the tint of their locks. They sounded like they belonged on *The Shadow* or one of the other radio mystery shows I listened to. *Tune in tomorrow for The Case of The Red Headed Cousins!*

But there was a hole in the wide net Mother was casting. She knew that if Dad's brothers weren't in attendance, it would remind everybody that the family celebrating this magnificent event was sadly fractured. To avoid tut-tutting and without informing Dad, she boldly invited his brothers to my bar mitzvah. Jaw-droppingly surprised, Hymie and Abe asked if the invitation was also coming from Mook. When she hemmed, hawed, dodged and ducked, they said they would attend only if they knew he wanted them to be there.

"Behind my back?" my father protested when she confessed what she had done. But he was on the spot. His wife had gone rogue on him, and what man in those antediluvian times wanted it known that he couldn't control his woman? And maybe, just maybe, Dad thought it time to give peace a chance. And so, hat in one hand and olive branch in the other, he crossed the Rubicon. He invited Hymie and Abe, and they accepted. He wasn't saying sorry about anything, and they weren't saying sorry either. What all were saying was *enough*.

A photo memorializes the historic reconciliation. The three Kirshenbaum brothers stand side by side by side at my bar mitzvah, each with a white boutonniere in his suit lapel, each looking not quite certain the moment is real. Another photo shows Grandpa and Grandma Kirshenbaum, who might have refused to attend if Hymie and Abe hadn't been invited, seated in the Temple Beth El sanctuary, orthodox elders preparing to witness a grandson's bar mitzvah in a reform Temple.

THE PATH to my bar mitzvah began with my taking Hebrew instruction at age six from Temple Beth El's then rabbi, Alfred Friedman, at his home on Cherry Street. A couple of times, when Mook picked me up after class and if he was in a truck, he gave my classmates rides home too. I was sure I was the envy of the other kids because I had a father who drove trucks. It must have amused onlookers to see four or five youngsters clinging to the side rails of the open bed of a Harbor Bag Company truck and squealing merrily as it rumbled from one child's home to another.

I juxtapose this image next to one of another truck transporting unusual human cargo on Benton Harbor streets during those World War II years. This truck carried a dozen or so German prisoners of war watched over by a lone GI smoking a cigarette and with a rifle slung indifferently over his shoulder. I was troubled seeing enemy soldiers in our midst and so loosely guarded at that, but Dad assured me that the Germans were no threat and were happier being in Benton Harbor than they would be still fighting overseas.

The prisoners, I learned, were among 400,000 German captives brought to the U.S. during the war for multiple reasons: It was easier to handle them in the U.S. than on the shifting front lines in Europe; the Liberty ships that transported troops and munitions to Europe had room for POWs when deadheading back to the U.S.; and the prisoners could fill in for American workers away in the war. In Benton Harbor, the Germans picked up trash in the parks and helped harvest crops on short-staffed area farms.[1]

There were other Germans who, as Jews, had even greater reason to be happy to be in Benton Harbor. When Rabbi Friedman left for a congregation in Chicago, I studied Hebrew at the conservative Children of Israel synagogue with an instructor, Immanuel Lubliner, who fled Nazi Germany as a teenager in 1936. Mr. Lubliner, who one day would be a rabbi in the New York State towns of Peekskill and Dobbs Ferry, was rail-thin and singularly odd. One day he took our class to the synagogue's basement, where the bodies of deceased community members were ritually prepared for burial. On this macabre field trip, I saw my first dead body and was terrified, though less so, I'm sure, than Mike Radom was when he was the same age I had been and was locked in the basement morgue by my scalawag cousins Ted and Ben. Finding himself alone with a corpse, Mike issued cries for help that could have raised the dead but didn't.

---

1. Heinz Kluetmeier, a gifted Berlin-born photographer and one of my closest colleagues at *Sports Illustrated*, was the son of a Luftwaffe officer who was captured by American troops during the war. Brought to a POW camp in Tennessee, Fred Kluetmeier, as the ranking German captive, was tasked with overseeing construction of the camp tennis court, and as a reward spent most of his incarceration playing tennis. Fred loved tennis and fell in love with America. After the war, he gathered up his wife, Ilsa, nine-year-old Heinz and his other son, Jorn, and emigrated to Milwaukee.

Rabbi Friedman's eventual successor at Temple Beth El was Rabbi Josef Schwarz, who, with his wife, Anneliese, escaped Hitler's Germany at a dangerously later date than Mr. Lubliner did. They found their way to the Philippines, where Rabbi Schwarz presided over a Jewish community in Manila comprised largely of fellow exiles from Germany and Austria. When the Philippines were conquered by Japan, Germany's Axis ally, Rabbi Schwarz was drawn into a harrowing situation. He is a key figure in a book *Escape to Manila: From Nazi Tyranny to Japanese Terror*, which tells of him conducting delicate negotiations with Japanese military leaders on behalf of his congregation. During the battles that raged when MacArthur returned to take back the Philippines, Japanese troops destroyed the synagogue and drove the rabbi, Anneliese and their young sons Michael and David from their home.

At war's end, the Schwarz family sailed on a Norwegian freighter to the United States, where the Hebrew Union College in Cincinnati helped Rabbi Schwarz land the vacant Temple Beth El position. The rabbinate is a transient profession — it's said that a rabbi who isn't run off by his congregation isn't really a rabbi — but Josef Schwarz served as Temple Beth El's spiritual leader and in an emeritus capacity at the successor B'nai Shalom synagogue for 36 years. Even Mook thought highly of him. He called Rabbi Schwarz "a good, decent man," complaining only that he wished his sermons were more interesting.

Rabbi Schwarz arrived at Temple Beth El in October 1949, and I celebrated my bar mitzvah under his tutelage two years later. After reading from the Torah and delivering the obligatory speech thanking my family for helping me through the wobbles of my first 13 years, I stood before the rabbi as he blessed me and, in accordance with the precepts of the Jewish faith, pronounced me a man. It was a wonder that the congregation, hearing this said of a 5'3" braces-wearing squirt in a suit purchased from a clothing store boy's department, didn't explode in laughter.

By holding the reception at the Whitcomb Hotel, my mother was making a statement. The Whitcomb stood on high ground in St. Joseph overlooking Silver Beach amusement park and the shimmering waters of Lake Michigan. The hotel boasted a 40-tub bathhouse, barber shop and, on the top floor, a solarium and a gymnasium. For nightlife, there was the nautically themed Marine Bar, which guests entered via a gangplank to dance to "Decca recording artist" Jane Turzy and her combo. Hugely popular with travelers, the Whitcomb also played a vital role in the Twin Cities' civic and social life, hosting men's clubs — Rotary Monday, Kiwanis Tuesday, Lions Thursday — and weddings, proms and cotillions. The Whitcomb also occupies a place in literature, fictionalized as the Merritt Hotel by Saul Bellow, who tells of Augie March — him again — traveling from Chicago to stay at the Merritt with his patroness, Mrs. Renling. The hotel, Bellow writes, "was vast, and it was brick construction, but went after the tone of old Saratoga Springs establishments."

On special nights out, our family dined in the Whitcomb's Calvin Britain room, where guests consumed planked Lake Michigan whitefish and prime ribs of beef baked in rock salt while an orchestra played. There were finger bowls and tiny cups of sherbet for cleansing the palate. After dinner, Joel, Bobbie and I conversed with Polly Whitcomb, the parrot that for nearly 30 years occupied a perch in the hotel's lobby. Polly once was kidnapped before being recovered 24 hours later in a cloak-and-dagger operation that kept police and the entire Twin Cities on edge. Polly's favorite expression was "Shut that door." Children coaxed her into saying dirty words. Next to her was a sign: "The opinions expressed by Polly are not necessarily those of the management."

The Whitcomb was owned by a Chicago financial firm headed by Edward Frieder, who installed his daughter Irma's husband, Leon Harris, as the hotel's managing director. My parents were friends with the Harrises, although Mom was perplexed by how a fine Jewish woman like Irma could have fallen under the spell of Christian Science. The Harrises lived in the Whitcomb in a large second-story suite. "Our living room had a beautiful view of the harbor and lighthouse," Irma wrote in a reminiscence of her family's life at the Whitcomb. "Sea gulls were seen hovering over the water and the sunsets were magnificent... the excursion boat, the *S.S. Roosevelt*, would go by, noiselessly, every day, as well as large lake freighters during the summer months. We knew they were coming by the ringing of the bridge bells."

The Harrises attended my bar mitzvah. At the reception, they were, in effect, guests in their own home.

In the Whitcomb's Tropical Room, tall candles on the tables cast a warm glow, steaks were served with wines red and white, and many magnums of champagne were drained, with hard drinks served in a side room. In addition to ice cream and a huge cake topped by the plastic figurine of a bar mitzvah boy who looked Gentile, there were pastries from Rahmig's House of Fine Chocolates in Chicago: punch-filled eclairs, profiteroles, coconut balls, Victoria boats, tartelettes, butter cookies, macaroons, fondant-dipped almonds and four kinds of petit fours.

Presiding over the reception was a family friend, Paul Price, the eldest of five brothers, one of them the prizefighter Sammy Price, whom we've met previously and will revisit in this chapter. As chairman of the Benton Harbor Fruit Market board and exalted ruler of the Elks Club, Paul earned a reputation as a man comfortable in front of a microphone. In the Tropical Room, he told jokes, most of them about Dad.

> *Times weren't always good for the Kirshenbaums. Remember when Milt came over on the boat? He only had one bag but my, how they've multiplied. It was pretty tough for him getting started. He had to run a poker game at his office every day to help pay the overhead.... As time went on, the boys realized that all they were doing was helping Milt start a business with their money, and they had no stock certificates to show for their investment...*

> *My understanding is that this outstanding event cost a lot of money. I think it only right that we help Milt defray the expenses, because he's been busy this week and couldn't get up a game to pay for everything. Waitresses, will you see that everyone gets a separate check?*

Only at the end did the bar mitzvah boy get a mention.

> *Between the poker and the bag business and climbing the social ladder, Milt and Frieda found time to raise Jerry.*

Attention then was directed to sheets of lyrics on the tables. To piano accompaniment, I was serenaded with a singalong that included:

We can't give you anything but love, Jerry.
We'd like to give you something nice, Jerry.
But all we have to give is free advice, Jerry.
Till we get as wealthy as your dad, Jerry,
We can't give you anything but love.

———

BARELY A YEAR after my bar mitzvah, the man I knew as my grandfather, Mendel Kirshenbaum, died at the age of 83. In the motorcade to the cemetery, I was sandwiched in the back seat of a car between Dorothy Zwick and my mother. Aunt Dorothy considered this an opportune time to ask me a question along the lines of the one once sprung on me by the man, her father, we were about to lay to rest. From Mendel it had been, "Nu, Jerry, you know about sex?" From Dorothy now came, "So, Jerry, have you been to a whorehouse?"

As I gasped for air, Mom rescued me. "Dorothy," she said, "he's only 14."

"What do you mean? Zell takes the boys all the time," said Aunt Dorothy, referring to my cousins Mort, my age almost exactly, and Robert, 16.

"Well, Jerry is a small-town boy. Chicago boys grow up faster."

Whereupon we arrived at the cemetery.

As I at last began to throw off the shackles of childhood, Mook thought it time for me to learn "the value of a dollar," which for him meant my finding summer work. A worthy goal but one, I informed him, that required a more robust mode of transportation than a bicycle. When I was 14, motor scooters were the rage among my friends, and I was unhappy not having one. Riding my bicycle past Saul Colef's Miami Road house where Dr. Ozeran now lived, I espied Buddy Alberts on his scooter talking to the doctor's pretty stepdaughter, Marion Slaughter, and looking like he was getting somewhere with her, each gunning of the engine suggesting to me further progress. No wonder Buddy hadn't called me lately, the bum. After pleas to Pop about my plight (without mentioning the Marion part), I came to own not just any scooter, but a top-of-the-line tomato-red Cushman Eagle with a range of 90 miles on a gallon of gas at a time when gas cost 27 cents a gallon. This restored me to Buddy's good graces and improved my standing with other friends like the basketball-playing stringbean Leroy Goff, who I took on the back of my scooter, his long legs nearly grazing the pavement, to go swimming at Paw Paw Lake, a 30-mile round trip accounting for no more than eight cents of my last fill-up at the pump.

Following Dad's advice to find summer work, I discovered that not all jobs are created equal. My friend Frank King III, the son and grandson of surgeons, also had an Eagle, and we decided to go stylin' together and pick strawberries. At the farm of Mook's friend Sam Braudo three miles out Empire Avenue, Kingie and I were assigned a row of berries parallel to a line worked by migrants, among the thousands who traveled from Arkansas, Louisiana and other Southern states to toil in summer months on Berrien County fields. Some migrant families lived all summer in their cars, which was cheaper and less dangerous, if no more hygienic, than the squalid migrant housing available to them. My father occasionally hired migrants to help load trucks. He said he once picked up a worker at the car in which half a dozen family members were living. He said that when the car door opened, the stench was unbearable.

Kingie and I couldn't keep up with pickers as young as

eight or nine, and after a couple of hours, punished by a merciless sun, our backs aching and knees bruised, and having damaged almost as many strawberries as we picked, we quit and turned in the meager and literal fruits of our labor. We had hoped to earn folding money but went home with no money that folded and little that jingled either.

When I got my driver's license, I graduated to jobs for which I was better suited. One summer I worked for Jim Shanahan, the taciturn sports editor of the *News-Palladium*. I reported on American Legion baseball and Little League championship games, wrote non-sports stories for the city desk and had a brush with the big time when Detroit Red Wings great Gordie Howe spoke at the Benton Harbor Lions Club. Sent by Shanahan to cover Howe's appearance, I took his photo with a cumbersome Speed Graphic camera, wrote up what he had to say and earned a $5 stringer's fee from the Detroit *News* for calling in quotes I extracted from Howe about the blockbuster trade that day of his Red Wings linemate Ted Lindsay to the Chicago Black Hawks.

The *News-Palladium* job was excellent preparation for my envisioned career in newspapering, but the summer employment best attuned to the rhythm of my life at the time was as a busboy at Win Shuler's, an upscale restaurant in St. Joseph. There I worked a split shift, lunch and dinner, with three hours in between, during which, weather permitting, I met friends at Benton Harbor's Jean Klock Park, a half-mile expanse of Lake Michigan beachfront that on summer weekends drew as many as 10,000 visitors a day.

But when I tried to follow the same routine with my parents, it went poorly. My mother's principal chore for me was to mow our lawn. Our property was almost an acre, and we had only a hand mower — better, Dad decreed, for exercise

— and after mowing the front lawn, pleased with the smell of freshly cut grass and with myself, off I sped to Jean Klock Park. On my return, Mom lit into me for not also mowing the back lawn, also for failing to pull dandelions after she'd gone to the trouble of laying out the bifurcated little tool designed for that purpose. On the infrequent occasions when I took the measure of lawns front and back and pulled a good many dandelions to boot, she complained that I hadn't swept the grass cuttings off the driveway. She hollered I was lazy. I hollered there was no satisfying her. We both were onto something.

I started another summer as a salesman at Ray's Cut Rate clothing store *cum* pawn shop on Territorial Road opposite the post office. For assuring Ray's mostly poor and Black customers that his merchandise was of highest quality, I thought my photo belonged on the wall across the street next to the mug shots of other hardened criminals. I quit Ray's, and Dad said I could finish the summer working at Harbor Bag Company. There I cleaned bags and helped move heavy bales, arduous labor that gave me reason, I thought, to cool off at the beach. When Dad returned one afternoon from out of town and learned that I'd stolen away to Jean Klock Park and had also done so at other times, he called me into his office and said I was setting a bad example for the regular help. I told him I was sure that Shorty, Willie and the others were impressed that the boss's son was putting in any hours at all, but the only time in my life I was fired from a job was when I was sacked that day by my father.

I experienced a jolt of a different kind in November of my freshman year at Benton Harbor High School when Miss Bean, ripping one more hole in the thoroughly Swiss-cheesed church-state curtain, gave our English class a writing assignment on "What Christmas Means to Me." I unflinchingly wrote that although I didn't personally celebrate the birth of Christ, I enjoyed the colors and customs of Yuletide, listening to the tra-la-las of the carolers and the songs about flying reindeer and boughs of holly, and hearing my friends tell of the baseball gloves and radios they found under their trees on Christmas morning. Miss Bean, who would leave at semester's end to be married in Illinois, read my story to the class and spoke flattering words about it. I was pleased by that but relieved that she didn't identify me as the author. Nevertheless, a classmate, C.G., smoked me out. Filing out of the classroom, he came up alongside me and hissed, "Christ Killer." I slinked away, hoping nobody had heard. I said nothing to school authorities or to my parents about C.G.'s remark, thinking that the fault wasn't his but mine for having made the mistake of being born Jewish.

As a freshman, I was in awe of seniors like the football star Gene Michael and his girlfriend with the malt shop-perfect name Roxy Collis who walked the halls holding hands like teen royalty. I felt privileged to be in their presence, like a child allowed to stay up late with the grownups. But Mother decided on scant evidence that I wasn't working up to my ability at Benton Harbor High and determined that I should attend a school at which students wore uniforms and greeted their superiors with salutes. Because I'd enjoyed Culver Woodcraft Camp, I allowed her to strongarm me into enrolling as a sophomore — third classman in military school parlance — at Culver Military Academy.

Culver Military Academy was to Culver Woodcraft Camp as a hurricane is to a zephyr. Cadets marched to mess hall in formation and fired M1 rifles with live ammunition, and plebes like me were required to compete in the academy's intramural boxing tournament. A disastrous draw matched me in my first and only bout with a brute who, as I assumed a turtle-like crouch and a strategy of back-pedaling retreat, TKO'd me in 30 seconds, throwing a dozen punches to my none. When my conqueror made it to the tournament's championship match before losing, I consoled myself knowing that I wasn't the only one pummeled by him.

Cadets at Culver were required to study in their barracks rooms for two hours each night, and I did well academically, tying in spring semester for second in the 189-member sophomore class despite sneaking listens to baseball (a heavy diet of St. Louis Cardinal games, which came in more clearly than those of the Cubs and White Sox) on earbuds connected to a transistor radio hidden under my desk. But I was unhappy at Culver and argued with my mother, who insisted that I stick it out. Dad enjoyed watching the cadets and Culver's famed Black Horse Troop pass in review on the parade grounds on the shore of Lake Maxinkuckee, but when I had my way and returned to Benton Harbor High School for my junior and senior years, he was happy no longer having to pay Culver's high tuition.

I didn't fare quite as well academically in public school as I did at Culver, but I had what I thought a richer experience. Culver was male-only, and Benton Harbor High was a place of greater diversity — girls as well as boys, poor and advantaged, Blacks and whites, 4H farm kids and townies, and a stew of Italians, Greeks, Irish, Jews and other ethnicities, even a few House of David members, one of them a girl who starred in school plays, another a boy who played on the football team. Many of my friends were non-Jews — Kingie, Bruce Conybeare and Steve Findley Methodist, Don Virkus Baptist, John Null Catholic, others Lutheran, Presbyterian and what have you. In elementary school I trick-or-treated and played softball with some of these boys and in the deeper-voice years, I double-dated with others of them, but funny thing: until my junior year, seldom did friends of other faiths enter my house, nor I theirs. Religion imposed limits.

So did race. I was friendly with Black classmates at Benton Harbor High, including Jim "Jellybean" Reynolds, all-state in football and basketball and a future star in the Canadian Football League. Everybody loved Jellybean. School officials knew when he'd been truant because of the spelling error he made in the excuse notes ostensibly written by his mother, Patsy. The notes read, "Jim was sick yesterday" signed, "*Pastry* Reynolds." In school hallways Jellybean gave me cheerful hellos, and once, when I ran into him on a downtown street, a well-remembered punch of friendly intent but painful result on a shoulder where I'd just been vaccinated. One night I drank beer in a car with another Black schoolmate, Pete Rhodes, a senior, and his 13-year-old girlfriend who whispered to me reassuringly about their age disparity, "I may be only a girl, but I knows what a woman knows."

These superficial interactions occurred in a town and at a school where racism was a constant. In Benton Harbor, Blacks suffered discrimination in housing, policing and employment, and at Benton Harbor High School there was racial insensitivity on the part of administrators and teachers. The actor Ernie Hudson (*Ghostbusters, Grace and Frankie, Oz*), a 1964 Benton Harbor High graduate, told the *Wall Street Journal* that he and other Black students were routinely and unthinkingly placed in classes of "unlearnables." Ernie said it wasn't until his senior year that teachers realized he could more than keep up and moved him into regular classes.

At Benton Harbor High School, I was elected senior class president, not a hottie-attracting role like that of Roxy Collis's football-playing boyfriend but one squarely in the nerd genus of student taxonomy.[2] I also was sports editor of the school newspaper, *The Tiger*, writing a column, "The Press Box," that I desultorily filled with idle musings. The school's former basketball coach Bill Perigo had gone from success at Benton Harbor High — winning the 1941 Class A state championship — to become head coach at Western Michigan College (now University) and then the University of Michigan, taking with him his son, Don, the best athlete in my fifth-grade class. The Perigo precedent led me to write, when his successor as the Benton Harbor coach, Don Farnum, also began enjoying success, "As [Farnum's] victory string grows, he will no doubt receive numerous bids from colleges." The day that column ran, coach Farnum passed me in the hall and said, without breaking stride, "If you hear of any of those job offers, you'll let me know, won't you?"

Farnum took the Benton Harbor High Tigers to the Michigan Class A title game six times, winning twice. His biggest star, Chet Walker, to whom I "loaned" $120 that he promised to pay back but didn't, forcing me to write it off as a

---

2. What a class! At our 50th reunion, attended by nearly half of the class's 330 members, the Saturday night dinner was upended by our class salutatorian Frank Zindler, editor of *American Atheist* magazine and soon to be interim president of American Atheists. When Ron Mayforth, pastor of Trinity Baptist Church in Kelowna, British Columbia, rose to deliver an invocation, Frank rushed forward, yelling, "No prayer!" As dueling chants of "Prayer!" and "No Prayer!" rang out from the crowd, Ron Carmichael, the Arizona Republican party stalwart emceeing the event, body-slammed the half-foot taller Zindler, who was escorted back to his seat by several fast-acting ex-Tiger football players. Rattled, Rev. Mayforth proceeded to deliver a prayer that failed to mention Jesus or even God. After dinner I noticed firebrand atheist Zindler and servant of God Mayforth in a corner chatting. Coming out of hiding as class president, I told them I was glad to see they were getting along. They said no problem: In school, they'd been chemistry lab partners.

gift per Mook's lesson about money-lending, became an NBA Hall of Famer starring for the Syracuse Nationals, Philadelphia 76ers and Chicago Bulls. Farnum's undefeated 1965 state champions were arguably the most accomplished team in Michigan basketball prep history, putting up men-against-boys numbers, averaging 97.1 points a game with a victory margin of 33.3 points in games played with only eight-minute quarters and no three-point line. When Farnum retired after 17 seasons as Benton Harbor's all-time winningest coach, the school gym was named after him. His "you'll let me know, won't you?" sarcasm still stings.

Some of my extracurricular activities during my high school years gave my father reason to think I was on the fast track to dissolution. One night at the Starlight Drive-in Theater, Jerry Light and I were drinking peppermint schnapps with beer chasers. I got out of Jerry's car to go to the refreshment stand, fell and crawled back. Jerry got me safely home, but I didn't make it upstairs to my bedroom and woke in the morning on the couch in the den with khakis torn and jacket dirt covered. Through a haze, I saw Mook looming over me. He didn't yell at me the way Mom would have if she'd found me there. "Rough night, huh, boy?" was all he said, and he left for work. His look was a combination of boys-will-be-boys acceptance and who-needs-this-crap annoyance. At dinner that night, I tried to hide my hangover. Dad said nothing of the matter and didn't have to.

In 1953 my mother took Roberta, then 21, to Johns Hopkins for a follow-up study that the hospital was conducting of its earliest blue baby surgery patients. From Baltimore Mother writes a letter to Dad in which she evinces surprising vulnerability. She apologizes for having talked recently about "going somewhere alone," writing, "I honestly am not happy without you. I need you these days for many reasons — your strong shoulder, sympathy and love and care. The Frieda of old with her strong will, stamina and courage is almost no more."

Making nice in another way, Mom also writes, "Try to get along with Jerry. Perhaps with [Roberta and her] away you can get closer to him — pals — try to go to a show after dinner & spend more time with him." Reading these words, written by my mother when I was 14, I'm reminded that my teen years were an interregnum during which Mook and I drifted somewhat apart. I'd become more difficult and he more disapproving of me, but he was too congenitally even-tempered and my misbehavior too small potatoes for father-son relations to spin out of control.

Although I lacked Pop's passion for poker, I played penny-ante games with friends. I was hosting a poker night in our basement rec room with Dick Lewis, Tom Edwards, Buzz Erikson and a couple of others when a voice from the stairway boomed, "Don't move, you're under arrest for illegal gambling!" Before us in street clothes appeared Sheriff Erwin Kubath, the most recognizable public figure in Berrien County, with my father a step behind and looking deeply concerned. As an FBI-trained deputy sheriff, Kubath had found the weapons in Killer Burke's house used in the St. Valentine's Day massacre, one of the feats of derring-do that helped catapult him to seven terms as sheriff. My friends and I quickly realized that Kubath was joking and that Mook had put him up to it. The sheriff chatted with us for a minute or two, then left, probably with the campaign contribution from Dad in his pocket that I imagine was the reason he was at our house.

My father had become friendly with Kubath while partnering with Sammy Price in Twin City Bonders. I don't know if the sheriff was aware of Dad's felony and incarceration, but he deputized both Sammy and him. Mook kept his deputy sheriff's badge No. 56 (six-pointed silver shield surmounted by a gold crest) in his office desk. The only time I know of that he wore it was when he and his ex-prizefighter partner drove to Missouri to apprehend a bail jumper. "I didn't have to do much," Pop said modestly. "Sammy made sure the guy came back with us."

My father eventually quit Twin City Bonders, leaving Sammy to run it alone. Sammy also had a beer distributorship — Blatz, Carlings Black Label and Edelweiss were his brands — and he trained young boxers and refereed wrestling matches, using his fists to subdue ersatz villains like Gorilla Grubmeyer and Ivan Kalmikoff when they acted up in the ring. One night Sammy came up against a real-life bad guy, James Martell, who robbed Buck's grocery store in Benton Harbor of $220, drove his car into a ditch making his getaway and, seeking a phone to call a wrecker, had the colossally bad luck to ring the doorbell at Sam and Josephine Price's house at 1567 Union Street. Opening the door and finding a Luger in his face, Sammy grabbed the weapon and knocked out Martell with the butt. The front-page story in the next day's *News-Palladium* was headlined EX-PUGILIST KO'S GUNMAN AFTER A HOLDUP HERE. A photo shows a groggy Martell, a prison sentence for armed robbery in his future and an encounter with Sam Price in his immediate past.

Like many other boys of my generation, I was drawn to the cartoon ads for Charles Atlas body-building equipment depicting a bully on a beach kicking sand in the face of a 97-pound weakling. I strongly identified with the 97-pounder but felt no need for Charles Atlas's assistance, confident that through my father's connections, I had Sammy Price and

Sheriff Kubath in my corner. I felt further protected when my cousin Fern, Uncle Hymie's middle daughter, married storied street brawler Marv Schultz, bringing into the family the hero of a Benton Harbor-vs.-St. Joseph beach rumble and several celebrated one-on-one clock cleanings. Marv is also remembered as the seldom-played benchwarmer on the Benton Harbor High School basketball team who inspired the cheer WE MAY LOSE THE GAME, BUT WE'LL WIN THE FIGHT AFTERWARD.

AFTER THEIR RECONCILIATION, Dad and his brothers made up for lost time, meeting for coffee or lunch, old slights forgotten, new ones overlooked. It helped that Mook had long since moved Harbor Bag Company from the Flats to Riford Street, away from Hymie and Abe's United Bag Company and the awkwardness of proximity. The brothers were still competitors but now friendly ones. They were "the boys" again, a triumvirate triumphant.

As I got to know my uncles, I found that they weren't such bad eggs after all. They were characters. With Hymie, food was paramount. He still had to eat at noon and six, and he was persnickety in restaurants, arriving with jars of his home-made salad dressing and bottles of Foster's catsup, which he preferred to the dressings and catsup, usually Heinz, the restaurants offered.

My father asked, "Foster's, Heinz, what's the difference?"

"There's a difference," Hymie said adamantly.

Hymie was a steak and baked potato man but was open to other culinary delights. One day the three brothers and Aunt

Rose were having lunch together when Hymie ordered a cheese sandwich.

"This is a great cheese sandwich," he announced after the first bite.

A moment later, "I'm really enjoying this cheese sandwich"

Next: "You ought to try this cheese sandwich."

Mook, Abie and Rose were trying to have a conversation, but Hymie kept interrupting.

"Gotta tell you, this cheese sandwich — "

Rose had heard enough. "Hymie," she said, "it's only a cheese sandwich."

Uncle Abe was wily and a bit of a fabulist. Although he never served in the Armed Forces, he acquired an Army colonel's uniform and marched in Veterans Day parades, sharing the adulation of spectators with the real veterans. Depending on one's tolerance for outrageousness, Abe could be entertaining. Invited by a friend to the St. Patrick's Day banquet of the Benton Harbor Knights of Columbus in a room decorated with images of shamrocks and leprechauns, he showed off his blarney by hammily leading the crowd in a rousing "When Irish Eyes Are Smiling," then engaging in an exchange with the event's guest of honor, Michigan Supreme Court Chief Justice Thomas M. Cavanagh. To laughter and cheers, Abe assured the jurist that life in the Old Sod had greatly improved "since one of my boys took over," a reference to Robert Briscoe, Dublin's first Jewish Lord Mayor.

My father was as accepting of his brothers' peccadillos as they were of his. In wonderment, he said, "We started life as dear brothers, and we're ending as dear brothers."

I don't know if he ever thanked Mom for inviting my uncles to my bar mitzvah. If he didn't, he should have.

Chapter 14

Master Class

Northwestern University, sophomore year. To help me furnish the off-campus apartment I was moving into with my friend Ron Yonover, Dad came into Chicago by truck to take me shopping. Joining him in the truck, I was reacquainted with the thick, musty smell of burlap that I've always associated with Mook and manliness.

Except when buying his Cadillacs (powder blue or metallic gray), my father wasn't a shopper. In stores he followed Mom through the aisles as she said, "we'll take this," which meant, usually, *"I'll* take this." On our way home from a visit to Roberta in Texas, we stayed one night in the resort town of Hot Springs, Arkansas, where my parents attended an auction. Minors weren't allowed in the auction hall, and I waited on a bench outside swatting at mosquitoes and listening to the auctioneer's machine-gun volley of words. When they emerged, Dad was carrying a silver tea serving set that Mom had him bid on. Both of them were smiling, she more than he.

But now, in the Polk Bros furniture and appliance store on North Central Avenue in Chicago, my father came into his own as a shopper, helping me select a bed, wastebasket, lamp and other necessities. We also bought a desk, but that was more aspirational than necessity. Desks, after all, were meant for studying, which I hadn't done enough of as a freshman, resulting in the scrapping after only one year of what was meant to be a four-year, $200-a-year scholarship. This was a greater loss than you might think because tuition at Northwestern, then the only private school in the Big Ten and the costliest, was an are-you-kidding-me $795 a year, which nowadays wouldn't get you through the first half-hour of new-student orientation. To keep the scholarship, I was required to maintain a 3.00, or B average, but I landed somewhere around 2.7.

I'd won the scholarship while attending Northwestern's National High School Institute "Cherub" journalism program the summer between my junior and senior years of high school. For six weeks on Northwestern's verdant Lake Michigan-hugging campus in the Chicago suburb of Evanston, I joined 78 other teenagers from 23 states, most of them the editors of their school papers. At the closing banquet, trophies were awarded to the best performers in six categories: reporting, feature writing, editorial writing, editing, contemporary affairs and creative writing. I took first place in reporting while crew-cut Terry McNally from Corpus Christi, Texas, who as Terrence McNally would become one of the most honored playwrights in Broadway history, was tops in two categories, contemporary affairs and creative writing.[1] Scholarships were

---

1. In a PBS documentary about McNally, *Every Act of Life*, a photo appears of Terry and me — he has a hand on my shoulder — and three other Cherubs as he tells in a voiceover of having had sex with boys growing up in Corpus Christi. Because it's not specified that the photo was taken in Evanston, viewers might assume that I and others in the photo were some of Terry's Texas

given to the four top overall performers. I won mine as an alternate when not all of the scholarship winners ended up attending Northwestern — McNally, for one, opting for Columbia, closer to the bright lights of the Broadway he already had in his sights.

Doing well against super-bright kids from around the country was a confidence boost for me, losing the scholarship a comedown. Thankfully, my father didn't seem to notice that my partial free ride had vanished. He unquestioningly paid the bills coming from Northwestern, trusting that a great university wouldn't shortchange him. But I'd shortchanged him, and myself as well.

I blame my academic shortcomings on too many hours spent as a freshman in student government folderol and hanging out at the Hut, a louche coffee shop operated by Hank and Irv, brothers-in-law who intensely disliked each other. The Hut was as Bohemian as things got in WASPy, old-line Evanston, which besides being a college town was the home of the Women's Christian Temperance Union, whose blue-nosed ladies kept the city undefiled by the sale of alcohol. In this

---

boyhood sex partners. I wrote Terry that I was honored to be seen in the film. Replying, he said, "Good to hear from you, Jerry. I truly hope you don't mind being part of the documentary." He said he was receiving immunotherapy in New York City for his COPD and was trying to arrange having it done closer to his home in the Hamptons. He died less than a year later, a casualty of the COVID-19 pandemic.

Another Cherub with fame in his future was Jerry Rubin, a bow tie-wearing preppie on the Northwestern campus who in a vertiginous transformation became the wild-haired activist of "Chicago Seven" renown. As a Cherub, Jerry received no more than honorable mention in one category, but an *Esquire* profile of him, "The Making of a Yippie," claims he was the program's top student. Jerry must have been the source of the misinformation, a counterculture icon feeling the need to puff himself up as a high school hotshot. Neither *Esquire* nor the article's author, famed journalist J. Anthony Lukas, fact-checked the assertion.

bastion of teetotaling propriety, the Hut stood out as if it was a brewery. Marijuana use and mixed-race dating weren't unknown on the Hut's grungy premises, prompting more than a few Northwestern sororities to declare the "Beat retreat" off limits to their members, prohibitions so widely and enthusiastically ignored that the Hut's menu could make the plausible claim, "Through These Portals Pass The Big Ten's Most Beautiful Girls." When, in 1959, several members of the visiting Oklahoma football team came down with food poisoning before a 45-13 Northwestern victory, there were suspicions that gamblers with money on underdog Northwestern had poisoned the Oklahoma players. Another theory was that the Sooners must have had a team meal at the Hut.

I was so attached to the Hut, roommate Ron no less so, that the apartment we rented was, strategically, in the same building, one flight up. This made it even easier than before to join friends in the booths below, drink gallons of bad coffee and listen to the excellent jukebox (to this day, I can't hear Dave Brubeck's "Take Five" or anything by Edith Piaf without thinking of the Hut) while neglecting our housekeeping duties upstairs. When Dad brought Mom to see the apartment for the first time, she entered the bathroom, took one look and said, "Milt, take me to a gas station."

Weeks into my sophomore year, I was bowled over by a freshman theater major, Xenia Gratsos, a born-in-Europe, raised-in-Canada head-turner who was smart, talented and contradictorily worldly yet so open to romance with a Michigan bumpkin that I was able to whisk her off the dating market in a preemptive strike. A year into our relationship, Xenia was crowned Northwestern's homecoming queen, chosen in a campus-wide election over four other finalists, one of them the reigning Miss Illinois. Photos in the Chicago papers from the pep rally on the eve of the 1958 Homecoming game against defending Big Ten champion Ohio State show Northwestern president J. Roscoe Miller placing a tiara on Xenia's dark tresses as both flash megawatt smiles, hers warm enough to melt glaciers, his the one he customarily displayed when accepting huge checks from alumni donors.

The next day Xenia was introduced at halftime of Northwestern's seismic 21-0 upset victory that snapped Ohio State's record 15-game Big Ten winning streak. The game showcased Wildcat running back Ron Burton, with whom I was friends from our having lived a few doors apart on the first floor of the freshman dorm, McCulloch Hall. In its next issue, the campus magazine *Profile* ran a photo spread on Xenia anointing her "Miss Wildcat," while Burton went on to win first-team All-America honors and, as the No. 1 overall draft choice of the new American Football League, become the first player in the history of the New England (originally Boston) Patriots. In future years Ron and I got together for lunch and dinner in New York and at Northwestern alumni reunions, and he never failed to ask, with a glint in his eye, about Xenia, who shone as he did on a special football Saturday in Evanston.[2]

Xenia was the positive influence I needed in my life. Besotted with her, I quit student government — my election as

---

2. Ron died of multiple myeloma at 67, leaving a legacy of good works. He used earnings from his six seasons with the Patriots and his career as a John Hancock community relations spokesman to establish the Ron Burton Training Village, a summer camp in Hubbardston, Massachusetts, for disadvantaged youths. The camp is in its 40th year, supported by Boston corporate leaders and operated by Ron's wife, JoAnn, and their five children, all Northwestern graduates. I attended Ron's funeral in 2003 in Boston's Tremont Temple Baptist Church at which Patriots owner Robert Kraft delivered a eulogy and a choir of Ron Burton Training Village campers sang the Mook favorite, "One Day at a Time (Sweet Jesus)."

sophomore class vice-president was my last hurrah — and moved as a junior to an apartment many blocks from the Hut. Often Xenia and I could be found in the reading room of Northwestern's monumental Charles Deering Memorial Library or deep in our books and the easy chairs of the campus Jewish center, Hillel, in the hushed company of pre-med majors and other serious students. At Hillel Xenia drew what's-the-*shiksa*-goddess-doing-here looks (I of course was proud to be seen with the *shiksa* goddess), but soon we were accepted as regulars, and my grades greatly improved. (The Hut also underwent change. Hank and Irv spruced up the place with new linoleum and a fresh paint job, causing the *Daily Northwestern* to report, "The Hut is no longer The Hut. It's clean.")

Xenia came along barely a decade after a distressing moment of my formative years. I was five or six, and the kids at Fair Plain School, from seeing me sometimes dropped off in a Cadillac, were calling me rich. I didn't want to be rich. I wanted to be normal. Tearfully, I begged my father, "Why do we have to have Cadillacs? Why can't we have some other kind of car?" To calm me, he said that the fathers of some of my schoolmates were lawyers, doctors and businessmen who were as well-off as he was, regardless of the cars they drove. He said that rich people didn't make their livings driving trucks or come home in dirty work clothes as he did. He said there were gradations of wealth and that even in Benton Harbor, we were nowhere near the top.

In our den was a phonograph with a record player that dropped platters one atop another so you could listen to Al Jolson one minute and the Andrews Sisters the next without leaving your chair. This remarkable contraption was manufactured in Benton Harbor by the V-M Corporation, owned by one of the local families whose wealth, Dad said, dwarfed ours. When I saw that the nabob running V-M was named Victor Miller, I brightly deduced that he'd used his initials to christen the company only to find out I had it wrong, that the company was founded by Victor's father, Walter Miller, and what V-M stood for was "Voice of Music." Still, lesson learned: relatively, we weren't so darn rich.

Xenia's background drove the lesson home with a sledgehammer. She was born in Athens into a Greek family with holdings in banking, mining, real estate and shipping. Her father, Panos Gratsos, a Swiss-educated collector of rare books, Picasso etchings and attractive women, owned a line of freighters with two of his brothers, Dimitri and Alkimos. Another brother, Constantine Gratsos, partnered with Aristotle Onassis. Costa Gratsos and Ari Onassis were said to be as close as brothers and even were lookalikes. Costa oversaw the Onassis empire's North American operations, and, upon Onassis's death, helped run the whole shebang. I met Uncle Costa when Xenia and I were in New York on a school vacation and stopped by his Park Avenue apartment to pick up theater tickets he'd bought for us. During the decades that I've since lived in New York, I've seen hundreds of Broadway shows, none from seats better than those that Xenia and I had, courtesy of Costa Gratsos, for the musical *Jamaica* starring Lena Horne and Ricardo Montalbán.

Xenia's mother, the former Danae Antonopoulos, was a Hellenic beauty who'd been pursued by Onassis before marrying Panos. She was related by marriage to the Greek actress Katina Paxinou, who won the Best Supporting Actress Oscar playing Pilar the gypsy woman in *For Whom the Bell Tolls* and was married to the Greek tragedian Alexis Minotis.

Xenia was encouraged by Paxinou in her thespian ambitions and referred to the actress as her great-aunt.

The Gratsos shipping line had offices in Athens, London and New York. When it opened an outpost in Vancouver to handle the transport of British Columbia timber to the Far East, Panos headed it up, moving to Vancouver with Danae and eight-year-old Xenia. Panos and Danae soon divorced, but neither remained single for long. Panos "took off with," as a Vancouver columnist put it, Beatrice Koerner, the daughter of Otto Koerner, a Czechoslovakian Jewish émigre and Canadian forestry baron, while Danae wed Hugh Martin, a Vancouver construction magnate whose company built tunnels, bridges and Empire Stadium, the site of the Roger Bannister-John Landy "Miracle Mile" race that was the lead story in the inaugural August 16, 1954 issue of my future employer *Sports Illustrated*.

Some people on our sheltered Midwestern campus didn't know what to make of Xenia. During sorority rush week, a hostess at one of the houses, hearing that Xenia was from Canada, asked her if she lived in an igloo. There were wildly exaggerated rumors that Xenia was the daughter of the world's richest man. "I wish they'd stop talking about how rich they think I am," she complained, sounding as I had about Mook's Cadillacs. It was true, however, that Xenia had spent Christmas vacations as a schoolgirl skiing in Zermatt, was as much at home in the grand hotels of Europe as Eloise was at the Plaza, and recently had been given the honor of christening the Gratsos line's newest freighter, *Polyxene G,* which was named after her paternal grandmother, as she herself was.

So that we could be together during summer vacations, Xenia pulled strings. The first summer, she persuaded her father to allow Ron Yonover and me to travel to Europe on the *Polyxene G,* set to carry 13,000 tons of coal from Newport News, Virginia, to Copenhagen. Furthermore, thinking it only right that she be given the opportunity to sail on a vessel over whose bow she had smashed a bottle of perfectly good champagne, she arranged to join us on the crossing, with her mother along less as chaperone than as delightful traveling companion. Humble collier though the *Polyxene G* was, a shipping journalist had called its owners' suite "just about the last word in luxury." The suite was where Xenia and Danae stayed on the journey, and where Ron and I, while bunking belowdecks with the crew, joined them in the evenings for wine, cheese and bites of steak.

Panos allowed that if I bought a car in Europe, I could bring it back to the U.S. on the ship. At a dealership in Copenhagen, with funds from Dad, I paid $900 in American Express travelers checks for a new Renault Dauphine, a tin can of a car then challenging the Volkswagen Beetle in the lower reaches of the U.S. auto marketplace. After Xenia and her mother flew off to Greece, the plucky Renault carried Ron and me through Denmark, Germany, the Netherlands, Belgium, France and Italy, not eating up the road but nicely nibbling at it, with time out for an English Channel crossing that gave us three days in London. Late in the trip, I heard from Xenia in Greece saying she could meet me on the Riviera. She and I spent two days together in Nice, after which Ron and I were reunited with the *Polyxene G* in La Spezia, Italy. The Renault was hoisted aboard, and he and I sailed to the U.S., minus Xenia and Danae.

The next summer, at Xenia's bidding, her stepfather, Hugh Martin, wrangled a reporter's job for me at the *Vancouver Sun* through his friendship with the paper's publisher, Don Cromie. Hugh Martin was a man of patrician bearing whose closeness to a Vancouverite named Isy Walters made me think he would have gotten along well with my father. Born Isadore Waltuck, Isy was a Russian Jewish immigrant who went from junk dealer and popcorn salesman to running carnivals and burlesque shows and was now operating Isy's, a Vancouver nightclub that presented current stars like Sarah Vaughan and Little Richard as well as performers from bygone days with nostalgic appeal.

One night Xenia and I went with Hugh and Danae to Isy's to see the vocalist Gene Austin, whose 1927 recording of "My Blue Heaven" had been the all-time bestselling single until overtaken in the 1940s by Bing Crosby's "White Christmas." Treating Hugh as a personage one mustn't leave town without meeting, Isy brought Austin to our table, and soon we were joined by the singer-comedian Phil Harris, a friend of Austin's who was passing through Vancouver and wanted to say hello. Harris and Bing Crosby were leaving in the morning on a fishing trip to northern British Columbia, but Crosby had stayed back at the hotel, depriving us of a face-to-face meeting of the "My Blue Heaven" and "White Christmas" record-making record breakers.

Another evening at Isy's the headliner was the singer-actor Alan Jones. As he did with Austin, Isy had Jones join us between sets. With Jones was his wife the shoe heiress and Thoroughbred owner Mary Florsheim. Jones had been a heart-throb of 1930s and '40s movies. In the 1937 film *Firefly*, he performs his signature song "Donkey Serenade," which scales the heights of love-ballad ridiculousness. Bouncing on a horse like a bobblehead doll, he sings to Jeanette MacDonald, who rides alongside in a carriage drawn by mules. When MacDonald gives him the hi-de-ho, Jones sings to the mules instead. His "Donkey Serenade" was the well-received highlight of his appearance at Isy's.

Days later Hugh and Danae had Jones and Florsheim to their house for dinner, and Xenia and I were included. After appetizers, Jones, a well-mannered guest in every way, collected an armful of dishes and took them to the kitchen, which was my cue to do the same. Plates in hand, I entered the kitchen as Jones was swigging from a whiskey bottle. Hurriedly returning the bottle to its hiding place under the sink, he held a finger to his lips and said, "Don't tell Mary." I was Alan Jones's new best friend.

Mom would have been pleased that I helped clear the table, Dad that I kept another man's confidence, but Jones's alcoholism was no secret, and Mary and he would divorce. He had four marriages, eclipsed by his son, the crooner Jack Jones, who had six.

My stories for the *Sun* included bylined interviews with figures from polar ends of the music world — the maestro Bruno Walter, in town to conduct an all-Mozart program with the Vancouver Festival Orchestra, and the country singer Tennessee Ernie Ford, vacationing in Vancouver with his family. An assignment to cover the opening of the circus at the Pacific National Exhibition normally would have merited a few uncredited paragraphs deep inside the paper but instead landed me with the lead story on Page One, which I was instructed to write first-person. The *Sun* was a broadsheet, but my story screamed tabloid.

3,500 See Trainer Mauled
By Lion at PNE Circus
By JERRY KIRSHENBAUM
Sun Staff Reporter

I watched in horror Monday while a lion mauled its trainer at the PNE's Shrine Circus.

For a moment I sat there stunned like most of the other 3,500 spectators, wondering if it was all part of the act.

It wasn't.

Prince El Kigorda the trainer was carried blood soaked from the ring, savagely mauled by three-year-old Caesar...."

With that, another outing with my father bursts through the fog of memory. I am nine years old and Pop and I are in the Benton Harbor Naval Reserve Armory, an unlovely barn of a building where Sammy Price thrilled fight fans, where the German POWs were billeted during World War II, where Benton Harbor's junior college and high school basketball teams once played their home games and where, on this magical night, November 10, 1947, Dad and I are watching the Harlem Globetrotters making a must-see Twin Cities appearance.

The Globetrotters' patented antics fill the Armory with gales of laughter, and when Goose Tatum, their "Clown Prince," jostles with a player on the rival "stooge" team, new jollity seems in the offing. But it becomes apparent that Tatum and the other player are throwing punches for real. They're quickly separated, but the air goes out of the building, and few laughs are heard the rest of the evening. Funnyman Goose Tatum in a fistfight is a crowd-deflating sight, as the goring of Prince El Kigorda will be in Vancouver.

At the end of the summer, I was told that a job awaited me at the *Sun* after college if I was interested, and I was called to the publisher's office. Don Cromie was a fun-loving man known for wearing loud sweaters and for spinning yo-yos during directors' meetings. As a model train zipped around the office overhead, Cromie told me that he'd taken a chance on me as a favor to Hugh and hadn't known what to expect and was glad it had worked out. I felt good knowing I hadn't let Xenia's stepfather down.

I brought Xenia to Benton Harbor two or three times. On a snowy Christmas Eve, we went to the Annunciation Greek Orthodox church on Broadway with my high school friend Buzz Erikson and his younger brother, George, who'd been raised in Eastern Orthodoxy through their Ukrainian American maternal grandfather, Basil Kocaka. At the church, Xenia lit candles in memory of departed family members, and Buzz and I ran into a classmate, John Andrews, and his older brother, Andy. Andy Andrews was the man in town to see about joining a junket to Las Vegas or laying bets on the football games. A raid on Andy's house turned up a cache of loaded dice, marked cards and an electronic device for secretly moving dice. Andy was assistant manager of the Michigan Hotel, where my father bought cigars. "Andy Andrews is a perfect gentleman," Dad said, excusing Andy's waywardness as he had Benny Adler's in Chicago.

John and Andy were the sons of Greek immigrants, George and Stavroula Andrews. George, a Benton Harbor businessman, wed Stavroula in Paris as a favor to her father to gain her admission to the U.S. George's brother Zacharias, known as Charley, had been a chauffeur and bodyguard for King Constantine I of Greece. Members of one colorful Greek family, John and Andy were surprised that I had acquired a serious girlfriend from another.

In fall of my senior year at Northwestern, I told my father I wanted to see him the next time he was in Chicago. In early

December, I drove my Renault from Evanston to Chicago's South Side and met Dad at the Stockyard Inn next to the Union Stockyards, where cattlemen brought their herds in from the Great Plains. Over steaks in the Inn's Matador Room, I nervously said what I had to say.

"Xenia and I are getting married."

"Xenia's a very nice young woman," Dad said. "I wish you a lot of happiness."

I was relieved but puzzled. "Thanks. I was afraid you were going to try to talk me out of it."

"You told me you were getting married — you didn't ask me?"

"Yeah...."

"And whatever I said, you're still going to marry her?"

"Yeah...."

"Like I said, I wish you a lot of happiness."

It was a master class of a father allowing a son to make his own mistakes.

Xenia and I were wed in Chicago's Federal Building by U.S. District Court Judge Julius Miner, whose son, Judd, was a Northwestern friend of mine. My parents were there, and Xenia's mother came from Vancouver, but her father was in Europe. After the ceremony, Dad left $100 with a secretary as a thank-you to the judge.

Xenia's parents were remarkably accepting of the marriage. At dinner on Rush Street after the wedding, Danae took me aside to say that she hoped I'd quickly get Xenia pregnant, thinking that her having a baby would help her "settle down." Xenia was 20, a month out of her teens, and I was all of 21, and we truthfully weren't ready for marriage, much less for parenthood, and it would have been crazy to do as Danae wished. I tried to guess what concerned her. Xenia was young when her parents divorced, and she was shunted off to Annie Wright Seminary, a private girls' school in Tacoma, Washington, where the writer Mary McCarthy, orphaned when both of her parents died in the 1918 Spanish flu epidemic, had also been parked as a girl. At Annie Wright, Xenia missed her father, who was often traveling on business, helicopter skiing in the Canadian Rockies or living the high life in the Greek Isles.

A story in the Vancouver *Province* tells of trauma Xenia experienced in childhood. In 1944, as Hitler's grip on Greece was slipping and the country edged toward civil war, the large Gratsos house in Athens had come under artillery fire and bombing. Panos is quoted as saying that the family fled, crawling through the streets with him pushing Danae, Xenia and their belongings before them. Four-year-old Xenia, the story says, experienced a nervous breakdown and was taken to the U.S. for treatment. I separately learned that in May 1946, with the Communist uprising against the Greek government intensifying, Danae and Xenia left Greece, sailing on the *SS Themistocles* from Piraeus to New York, where, records show, they were met by Costa Gratsos, who may have helped arrange Xenia's treatment.

Amazingly, Xenia's father offered me a job with his shipping line. He felt Xenia was becoming too Americanized and probably calculated that having me in his employ would put her in Europe where he could keep an eye on both of us. A dashing figure with aquiline features and darting movements, Panos hobnobbed with European cultural nobility. When the prima ballerina Dame Margot Fonteyn was appearing in Chicago with the Royal Ballet, she caused a stir in the Northwestern dorm, the Pembridge, when she phoned Xenia, said she was a friend of her father's, and took her to lunch. I once told Panos I enjoyed Dvořák's *New World Symphony,* and he put me in my place, calling it "bourgeois." I thought I'd be smothered working for him and wondered what role in the shipping business he could possibly think I was suited for. Even hiding me in landlocked Switzerland might have been too risky. He probably would have had to station me in Liechtenstein, which is *double* landlocked, surrounded entirely by other countries that like itself have no access to the sea. I thanked him but said self-importantly, "I plan to go into journalism."

He had never heard such poppycock. "You'll never get another opportunity like this," he said, and he was right. Not in all the years since have I been offered a position in the shipping industry.

In London, Panos had bought the boyhood home of the 19th Century author Anthony Trollope called Orley Farm, a name Trollope used as the title of one of his novels. While Panos and Beatrice were away, Xenia and I stayed at the house with Hayter, the family butler, who was less formal than I'd imagined an English butler to be. One evening when Xenia wasn't feeling well, I went to the movies with Hayter, with whom I realized I had more in common than I did with Panos — possibly more, truth be told, than I did with Xenia.

The house was within walking distance of the 400-year-old Harrow School, whose alumni include Lord Byron, Nehru, King Faisal of Iraq and Winston Churchill. To feel at home in such rarefied surroundings, I reminded myself that this wasn't the first time I had breathed the same air as men of distinction. Was I not from the Benton Harbor that produced the wrestler Bobo Brazil?

Regarding one of the above-mentioned Harrovians....

On a warm Athens evening, Xenia and I have taken our seats with Panos and Beatrice in a chic open-air taverna. Panos is friends with Onassis, who has alerted him that he will be at the restaurant with Winston Churchill, who has been vacationing in Aegean waters aboard Onassis's 325-foot yacht *Christina O*. Onassis enters with Churchill and the opera diva Maria Callas, and the diners stand and applaud Churchill, who flashes his V for victory sign while the orchestra breaks into the overture to *My Fair Lady*, said to be a Churchill favorite. While Xenia and I stay put, Panos and Beatrice go to the Onassis table to be introduced to the great man.

I didn't smoke cigars or sip brandy with Churchill. Seeing him a few tables away was special enough.

Xenia and I kept splitting up and reuniting. I was with her in San Francisco when she landed the lead role in a musical, *Ticket to the World*. The *San Francisco Examiner* Sunday magazine ran a cover story on Xenia in which she mentions me as her husband but equivocates, "The girl I'm playing [in the musical] is a lot like me. She wants to travel and see life before marrying... I'm married now, but feel tied down in some ways, and I couldn't stand not being able to travel." She mentions her pink bedroom having been shot up by bullets in Athens. "Ever since then, I've been moody and nervous."

I learned a good bit of Greek from Xenia, including several colorful swear words. We proved to be geographically incompatible, I bound for graduate school at the University of Michigan and journalism jobs in Minneapolis and New York, she destined for Los Angeles and the world of film, television and valet parking. She starred in several movies. In a Yugoslav film *Hell River*, under the name Brioni Farrell, she was the hypotenuse of a love triangle with a Nazi officer and a partisan played by Adam West and Rod Taylor, respectively. She played a lead in *The Student Nurses*, a sexploitation box-office success for which she was dispatched to the world premiere at a drive-in theater in Lafayette, Indiana, where the mayor presented her with flowers and the key to the city. She had roles on popular TV shows including *Mission: Impossible, The Man from U.N.C.L.E., Dallas, Bonanza* and *Columbo*.

Xenia was the center of my life for five years and never stopped being part of it. Through the years we talked by phone and had dinner together when work took me to Los Angeles. She always asked about "Daddy" and laughingly recalled the time my mother took her to task for wrongly using a milk fork with a meat meal in her kosher kitchen. The last of Xenia's three husbands, the actor Eugene Robert Glazer, lovingly cared for her during her Alzheimer's years. After Xenia's death from that mind-sapping disease, I wrote a remembrance that a mutual Northwestern friend, the veteran Hollywood actor Lawrence Pressman, read for me at the memorial dinner in Beverly Hills. "Xenia was unforgettable," I wrote, "and if I'm remembered by Northwestern people, often as not it's because of my being associated with her. Many times somebody hearing my name will say, 'Aren't you the guy who went with Xenia Gratsos?' A woman who didn't attend Northwestern but had heard glowing things about Xenia said to me, pulling no punches, 'She sounds amazing. What did she see in you?' I could only reply, 'Excellent question.'"

My Copenhagen car died around the same time that my marriage to Miss Wildcat did. In Benton Harbor Mook and my brother enjoyed taking the Renault for spins until Joel, shot full of Novocain from a dentist's visit, blacked out at the wheel and wrapped the Renault around a tree, leaving him unhurt but the car totaled. As for my scrapped marriage, I didn't get any I-told-you-so's from my father, who, after all, hadn't told me so. Moving on with my life, I began graduate studies in political science at Michigan.

In the Twin Cities on Christmas break from Ann Arbor, I

went with my father to the Whitcomb Hotel for a dinner of the Economic Club of Southwestern Michigan, of which he was a charter member. Dad wasn't a clubman by nature. His Masons and Elks attendance was spotty, and an improbably swanky dinner of the Chicago District Bag Dealers Association was almost certainly a one-off. A photo shows Mook and two dozen other dressed-to-kill burlap bag merchants in front of waiting shrimp cocktails in Chicago's Congress Hotel at a long table that seems to stretch to infinity. An inscription identifies the occasion as "Lou Danziger Night." A gentleman at the head of the table who must be Lou Danziger is getting a pat on the back from the fellow next to him.

As a member of the Economic Club, Dad rubbed shoulders with Twin Cities movers and shakers and enjoyed hearing the newsmakers brought in as speakers. Ours in the Whitcomb's Tropicana Room, the site of my bar mitzvah reception, was Senate Majority Leader Mike Mansfield, a Montana Democrat, who began his remarks by noting lightly that he was in enemy territory, Benton Harbor and St. Joseph in those days being solidly Republican. Mook may have leaned Democrat but so distrusted politicians of all stripes that I can't be sure.

The Economic Club was originally men only. When Eleanor Roosevelt was the speaker in 1954, several local women donned waitress uniforms and stood in the back of the room so they could hear her. In time the club opened its doors to women, outgrew the Whitcomb and moved to larger quarters at Lake Michigan College in Benton Harbor. My mother attended a dinner there with a friend and came home with an autograph, "Frieda, thanks for saying hello! Mario Cuomo." Mom, a Democrat, admired Cuomo, at the time the liberal governor of New York.

By then, however, Dad had quit the club, feeling it had

grown too big and lost its chumminess. Pinpointing the moment when chumminess went out the window, he said, "When they let women in, the club went to hell."

None of the celebrated figures whose names I've dropped here — Bruno Walter! Trollope! Onassis! Churchill! — would have impressed my father more than the writer of a letter he received a few days after Xenia's and my wedding. It read, "My dear Mr. Kirshenbaum. I am grateful for your thoughtfulness. I was happy to serve you without any consideration and I am herewith returning your generous remuneration...."

My father couldn't get over the letter from the judge who married Xenia and me. "I sure as hell didn't expect him to return my hundred dollars," he said. He called Julius Miner "a great man."

Chapter 15

Two Bobbies

GRANDMA KIRSHENBAUM DIED at age 90, 10 months after the dust-up at her hospital bedside between Aunts Dorothy and Frieda. In our immediate family, I was the only one who could have been with Dad at the funeral. Joel couldn't be there because he was in finals week as a freshman at the University of Michigan, and our mother and sister were absent for reasons that threw a blanket of heavy new gloom over our family. Both were institutionalized, Mom voluntarily in the psychiatric ward of Chicago's Billings Hospital, Bobbie by court order in the Kalamazoo Psychiatric Hospital, the largest public mental facility in Michigan.

After receiving a master's degree from Michigan, where I overlapped for one semester with my brother, I'd been greenlighted to go on for a Ph.D., but I had no interest in continuing with my studies and took a job as a reporter at the *Minneapolis Tribune*. Although I'd been at the *Tribune* only two weeks, I wouldn't have hesitated to ask for time off for my grandmother's funeral, but when Dad phoned, it was too late.

"We buried Grandma today."

I said I was sorry about Grandma and asked why he hadn't let me know in time for me to come in for the funeral. "You just started your new job," he said. "I didn't think you should be taking time off."

The decision of whether to attend my grandmother's funeral should have been mine to make, but my father had taken it out of my hands. It saddened me to think that after saying goodbye to his mother, he came home to an empty house. I tried to picture him there. Was there something in the refrigerator for him to eat? Did he turn on the television or leaf through a magazine? Or did he go straight to bed, exhausted after what must have been a trying day?

The one positive note in all this was that my mother and sister were separated and no longer at each other's throats as they had been from the day Roberta returned from Texas for good four years earlier. Back in Benton Harbor, Bobbie was again reliant on Mother, who was less able to care for an incapacitated adult daughter. Mom and Roberta found themselves in a downward spiral, each resentful of the other, neither feeling she had a life of her own.

These problems were playing out under a new roof. For several years my mother had been complaining that the large house at 1530 Miami Road, with its three flights of stairs and many nooks and crannies, had become a housekeeping burden for her, a gilded cage from which she needed to take flight. She believed her life would be easier in a contemporary single-level dwelling like those she saw in the home design magazines she was buying in bunches. My father loved our existing house, which I once heard him refer to, with rare grandiosity, as "the mansion," but when Mom wouldn't take no for an answer, he reluctantly consented to her building her dream house on a lot he bought for the purpose at 1390 Miami Road. At least they'd be moving only two blocks away, still on the same beautiful street, still on the side overlooking the St. Joseph River.

Because Mother kept changing her mind with the architect about details of the new house, it took longer to complete and cost much more than it should have. She claimed to have found a way to defray the extra expenses: she said that at lunch with her women friends, she skipped dessert.

Making the change in her life as sweeping as possible, she replaced the traditional furnishings of the old house with a turquoise-and-salmon-hued palette in the new one more suited to the tropics than to Michigan. In haste she sold a cabinet from the old dining room for $70 only to remember that she'd left $100 in one of the drawers. There went some of the savings from the skipped desserts.

But finally it was finished, a mid-century modern showplace featuring radiant-heated floors, central vacuum cleaning and every other up-to-date amenity except air-conditioning. Only there did my father draw the line, maintaining that the house would be sufficiently cooled by its brick construction and the property's abundant shade trees. On that one point he wouldn't budge.

In the new house Mook is heard on tape again enumerating for his grandson the deprivations he experienced on the farm, this time adding, "And, you know we didn't have air conditioning."

"You still don't," David says knowingly.

"Never have, never will, as far as I'm concerned," says Mook, who considered fresh air superior to air conditioning with the same conviction with which he proclaimed water preferable to pop.

It's a late-summer day and apparently a warm one, and Dad asks David, "You're comfortable here, aren't you?"

"Yeah, but in New York — "

"Oh, New York, that's different. It gets plenty hot in a New York apartment," he says, a rare concession from a man who, first thing he did upon entering a hotel room, was to turn off the A/C and open the windows. If the windows were permanently sealed, he never stayed at that hotel again. He was so opposed to air-conditioning that until Cadillac made it standard on all its models, he declined it as an option. He joked that on hot days, he rolled up his car windows and sweated it out because "I didn't want people to think I was too cheap to buy air-conditioning."

Unfortunately, the change in residences did little to buoy my mother's spirits. The new house had an open layout, with living room, dining area and kitchen all leading into one another. That left fewer doors for her to slam when she was angry, but because of the openness, the doors she did slam reverberated all the louder. Coming home from work one night, Dad was greeted by Bobbie, in tears from having suffered Mom's wrath all day. "Why did you let Mother build this house?" she asked.

"I was trying to make her happy."

"Mother will never be happy."

Of that exchange, Dad said, "Bobbie was plenty sharp, don't kid yourself."

Perhaps too sharp. My handicapped sister was alert enough to know that women her age had husbands and children and she didn't, which created a longing in her that she may not have fully understood. At Brown School, she'd been friends with a fellow student named Maynard, a sweet-natured, horn-rimmed-glasses-wearing man several years older than she. They considered themselves boyfriend and girlfriend. Maynard was Jewish, and Mom and Dad, wanting to give their daughter whatever pleasure in life they could, conferred with Maynard's parents and counselors of all kinds about whether it was feasible for the two of them to live in a supervised setting as husband and wife.

The issue likely came up during the follow-up visit for blue baby patients that Roberta made to Johns Hopkins with Mom when she was 21. A Johns Hopkins memo says that while in Baltimore, our mother discussed with Dr. Taussig "matters of a personal nature." Afterward Taussig wrote to Dr. Ozeran expressing her "strong recommendation" that Bobbie be sterilized. "This seems to me extremely important as she is suffering from severe mental retardation, diabetes and congenital heart disease," Taussig wrote. "In view of these facts, I believe it would be extremely detrimental for her ever to become pregnant."

I don't believe my sister was sterilized, but I understand Taussig's reasons for recommending it. I'm surprised, though, by her characterization of Bobbie's retardation as "severe." I would think that "moderate" better fits someone who could read and write, follow the plot of a Doris Day movie and play simple card games. Bobbie also could be playful. There was a bit of doggerel she recited because she enjoyed the rhyme, perhaps without realizing its perfect relevance to her situation: "Dear, dear, bread and beer, if I were married, I wouldn't be here."

In the end, it was decided that it was inadvisable for my sister and Maynard to marry. Bobbie had been aware of the deliberations about the possibility and now, believing her one chance at happiness gone, she was crying and slamming doors the same as Mother. Several times she was caught sneaking candy or cookies.

"You can't do that with your diabetes or you're going to die," Mom said.

"I want to die," Bobbie replied.

Much as she loved her daughter, Mother could be casually cruel to her. Some nights, after warning Bobbie not to sneak sweets, she herself would sit on the couch in front of her and spoon in ice cream from a carton on her lap. Taking Bobbie to a lunch with her women friends, Mom made a thoughtless remark that got back to Dad. Complaining about her health problems, she pointed to her daughter and said, "And look what else I have to put up with." Bobbie enjoyed attending the women's lunches with Mother, but hearing that, she frowned and looked away. Mom couldn't help herself. At home she many times complained in Bobbie's presence about "the sick child God gave me."

One day my father brought home a dog, thinking it would be a distraction for his wife and daughter. The dog was mostly mongrel, and he named it "Mostly." But Mom and Roberta didn't feed or clean up after Mostly, and those became Dad's chores. During an electrical storm, the dog tore holes in the screens on the porch, and Mook gave him away. Finding gallows humor at one of our family's lowest points, he said, "Everybody else in the house has gone crazy. Why shouldn't Mostly?"

When Roberta was in her late 20s, Johns Hopkins requested that she return to Baltimore for another study. It fell to Dr. Ozeran to reply that a visit this time was impossible. Mrs. Kirshenbaum, the doctor wrote, had "severe depression & guilt complex" and "refused to accept the fact that she needed help for her mental state." About Roberta: "[Patient] was in Texas for several years in a private school. Cardiac condition was good but had diabetes that was hard to control. Came home in 1959. Mental condition deteriorated."

As Bobbie's depression deepened, fears grew that she might hurt herself. On Dr. Ozeran's recommendation and with my parents' sorrowful consent, Berrien County Probate Judge Julian Hughes issued an order committing my sister to the state hospital in Kalamazoo. When Mom, Dad or Dr. Ozeran tried to talk to Roberta about the decision, she lashed out at them and turned for support to another physician she'd been seeing, Dr. Robert Gould. It didn't seem strange in the least that the doctor in whom my unhappy woman-child sister now was placing her trust was a pediatrician.

The turmoil in Bobbie's mind was reflected in notes she left around the house. In the past her handwriting had been clear, but now it was often unintelligible, words running off the margins of the paper, sentences left unfinished, thoughts scrambled and anguished.

> *"Please make Juge [sic] Huges [sic] cross that out on the paper you sing [sic]..."*
> *"If you and everybody try to keep me away from Gould I wont ever [unintelligible]"*
> *"Dr. Gould is my heart...."*
> *"Did you really make Dr. Ozeran sing papers to keep me from marrying...."*
> *"Please write to Maynard and tell him he will come up here...."*

I was in Benton Harbor in March 1963, finished with Ann Arbor and about to start my job in Minneapolis when the day came for Dad to take Roberta to Kalamazoo. I was to accompany them. In the morning Dr. Michael Faber came to the house to sedate her with an injection. She didn't resist, perhaps thinking she was receiving another of her insulin shots. Mother had packed a bag of Bobbie's medicines for us to take with us. She didn't come out of her bedroom to say goodbye to her daughter, and we could hear her sobbing behind a closed door. When Bobbie fell asleep, Dad and I carried her to the car and laid her in the back seat, covered her with a light blanket and set out on the 50-mile drive to Kalamazoo. At the wheel, Dad said softly, more to himself than to me, "We're taking the wrong one."

The Kalamazoo facility was founded in 1894 as the Michigan State Asylum for the Insane and was renamed the Kalamazoo Psychiatric Hospital. Located on a quiet stretch of Oakland Avenue, the brown-brick building was right-angled, straight-lined and bordered by clipped hedges and well-pruned trees — an orderly place for disorderly minds. Bobbie walked unsteadily as Dad and I helped her along the walkway into the hospital. An attendant took her by the arm and led her toward an inner door. Roberta disappeared, not looking back.

Reading *The Autobiography of Malcolm X*, I learned that Malcom X's widowed mother, Louise Little, was released from the Kalamazoo facility the same year my sister was admitted. Mrs. Little spent an unthinkable quarter century inside those walls. Her son, born Malcolm Little, writes that his mother had suffered a nervous breakdown when the family was living near Lansing, Michigan. Malcolm says that when he first visited her in Kalamazoo, she was in a "pitiful state" and didn't recognize him, but that she recovered enough for him and his brother Philbert to secure her release. I wondered if Roberta might have been assigned Malcolm X's mother's bed.

With her daughter in Kalamazoo, my mother was free to concentrate on her own needs, and she checked herself into

Billings for a workup, arriving with a list of physical complaints. It didn't take doctors at the Chicago hospital long to suggest that she might benefit from psychiatric care. Perhaps surprisingly, Mom agreed. More than her neglectful husband, her unfeeling children or busy Dr. Ozeran, who better to listen to her grievances than psychiatrists?

What followed with both mother and daughter was a testament to psychiatry's dark arts and magic potions. In July I visited Benton Harbor from Minneapolis and went with Dad to see Bobbie in Kalamazoo. He'd told me she was doing well, but I wasn't prepared for how well. This wasn't the incorrigible Roberta we dropped off at the hospital three months earlier. She greeted me with a hug and showed me around, whispering about other women patients — this one endlessly talking aloud to her dead husband, another always eating pieces of paper, a third staring vacantly into space. My sister could have been a staff member discussing with visiting mental health professionals the cases before her of delirium, hallucination and extreme apathy. Not once did she mention Maynard.

That summer Bobbie wrote Mom from Kalamazoo, her handwriting again legible:

Dear Mother,
How are you. I am feeling fine. Dad and Sam Unger came to see me and Dad brought me a radio a Philco. Uncle Hymie and the rabbi came to see me. How long do you have to be in the hospital...?

Mother was the first to come home. She was on lithium, a mood-stabilizing drug for bipolarism. Although lithium hadn't officially been approved for use in the U.S., psychiatrists at Billings and elsewhere were dispensing it experimentally. Mom went with Dad to visit Aunt Gere and Uncle Jack in Madison, and I drove down from Minneapolis to join them. Aunt Mirian and Uncle Sam were also there. During the visit Frieda sat quietly and let others do the talking. Her placidity was noted. *She's not herself.... Strange to see her like this.... It must be the medicine.*

Then Roberta also returned home. She had spent less than a year in Kalamazoo. Together again, she and Mom settled into a less stormy relationship. Forgetting Maynard, Bobbie developed a pen pal relationship with Brooks, another man she'd known at Brown School and who in her mind was now her boyfriend. The son of a Texas businessman who bred cattle, Brooks sent Bobbie typed letters that told of calves born on the ranch and of his helping at his father's office. Bobbie wrote back about a new dress Mom bought her or a television show she watched with her parents.

In April 1966, I left Minneapolis and joined *Time* in New York as a writer in the Nation section and took an apartment on East 69th Street. On one of Dad's visits to New York, I introduced him to a woman I'd begun seeing, Susan White. When he teased Susan with an expression that wouldn't have met with Gloria Steinem's approval, "long hair, short sense," she teased back that his hair at the time was almost as long as hers. Susan's feistiness and sense of humor scored points with him.

We had dinner one night at Lou G. Siegel's, a kosher restaurant in the Garment District. Our waiter looked at Susan and said something in Yiddish, and my father nodded. Susan wasn't Jewish and didn't understand, and neither did I. Dad translated. He said the waiter called Susan "pretty as the world." In English, the world can be strange, small, wide or wonderful, but who ever heard it referred to as pretty? As we have seen, Yiddish is odd that way.

Another time we dined at Pete's Tavern, the tin-ceilinged eatery on Irving Place where William Sydney Porter, the writer known as O. Henry, is said to have penned his short story "The Gift of the Magi." At another table were New York Senator Robert F. Kennedy, historian Arthur Schlesinger Jr. and Roosevelt Grier, the ex-football player and Kennedy bodyguard and friend. My father kept staring at them. Sophisticated New Yorkers though Susan and I thought ourselves to be, we kept looking their way, too.

We were all admirers of the Kennedys. On October 14, 1960, during his presidential campaign against Richard Nixon, while I was in school in Ann Arbor, John F. Kennedy delivered a speech well past midnight on the steps of the Michigan Union. Women's hours were suspended for his late-arriving appearance, and thousands of students were in a celebratory state. In his speech, Harvard man Kennedy got roars from a surefire applause line — "I'm proud to say that I attended the Michigan of the East" — and proposed formation of what would be known as the Peace Corps. I was far back in the throng, but earlier in the evening, I had gone with two friends, Michigan Law School students David Finkelman and Ashley Ross, to Willow Run Airport near Ypsilanti to see if we could catch a glimpse of Kennedy's arrival. We got there just in time. As JFK exited his plane and walked toward a waiting limousine, I impulsively jumped out of David's car and ran toward the limousine. Kennedy was in the back seat. I reached through the open window and shook his hand. David and Ashley remained in the car, content to bear witness to my fanboy exuberance.

My father's favorite Kennedy was the family matriarch, Rose, whose deep Catholic faith sustained her through incalculable losses — the deaths in airplane crashes of two of her children, JFK's assassination and the institutionalization of a mentally incapacitated daughter. Dad likened Rose Kennedy's trust in God to the refusal of orthodox Jews to question His unknowable ways regardless of misfortunes suffered. On June 6, 1968, a few weeks after we saw Bobby Kennedy at Pete's Tavern, Rose Kennedy's strength was again tested when RFK, now a candidate for president, was slain at close range in a Los Angeles hotel kitchen as his older brother had been from afar on a Dallas street.

Meanwhile, my sister's health was failing. The operation at Johns Hopkins had improved and probably extended her life, but her heart never completely mended. On digitalis for arrhythmia and Esidrex for high blood pressure, Roberta was admitted to Mercy Hospital in Benton Harbor twice in 1967 and three times in 1968 — January 24, February 4 and July 10. On the evening of July 11, a Thursday, I phoned her at her hospital room. She was upbeat and said she'd be going home the next day. On Friday night, after closing my last story of the week at *Time* — I now was writing in the Business section — I was in my New York apartment preparing to leave for the weekend in the Hamptons with Susan when my brother called.

"Do you have an extra black suit?"

What was he was talking about?

On vacation from law school in Berkeley, Joel was visiting our Aunt Edna and Uncle Harry in Los Angeles when Mother phoned to tell them that our 36-year-old sister had died. The funeral was set for Sunday. Joel was hoping to go directly to Benton Harbor for the funeral without having to return to the Bay Area to pick up a suit.

Roberta had died in her sleep of heart failure a few hours after I'd spoken to her. When I phoned home, I was grieving and uncomprehending why my parents hadn't called to inform me of my sister's death. Mother explained that she knew Friday was my closing night at *Time* and that she intended to phone me first thing Saturday morning. Trying to control my anger, I told her that Saturday morning would have been too late. By then I would have left for the weekend with Susan and been unreachable.

Because of the importance my father attached to my job in Minneapolis, I missed my grandmother's funeral. Now, because of the deference shown by my mother to my work schedule at *Time*, I nearly missed my sister's. Maybe if I hadn't gotten myself fired at Harbor Bag Company by him and had picked more dandelions for her, they would have better trusted me to make employment-related decisions for myself.

I arrived home with suits for Joel and me. After the funeral, Mom asked me to write Bobbie's Texas boyfriend with our heartbreaking news. I wrote Brooks and told him how much his letters had meant to my sister. A return letter came from his mother expressing sympathies and revealing a secret. She said that Brooks couldn't read or write and that she had typed the letters to Roberta and signed her son's name to them. She said she read Roberta's letters to Brooks, and he enjoyed hearing her news. She had kept the correspondence going for his sake.

For several years after that, my mother and Brooks's mother exchanged Christmas and Chanukah cards and letters, two women who did all they could for their handicapped adult children.

Roberta died on July 12, 1968, little more than a month after RFK was murdered. Mook's thoughts turned again to Rose Kennedy. "We've both lost our Bobbies," he said.

Chapter 16

Loose Lips

EIGHT YEARS after rolling the dice with Xenia, I married Susan. "Another *shiksa?*" my father faux-fumed. "I want my money back from your bar mitzvah." Susan was smart-alecky too. Of our prospects for marital success, she told me, "You've made your mistake. Now it's my turn to make one."

Susan is further evidence that I have excellent taste in wives. I knew she'd been a model upon arrival in New York, but it wasn't until years later when I was rearranging cartons in our attic that I came across her modeling portfolio, which she'd never shown me. And that was only after we'd bought a house in Stockbridge in the Berkshire hills of Massachusetts and even had an attic. The photos show Susan honey-haired, high-cheekboned, pert-nosed and with eyes lustrously blue. When I saw pictures of her modeling Foster Grant sunglasses in which those peepers were covered by the sponsor's product, I called foul. Much better seeing them unsheathed in ads for Sheer-Mist carbon paper, an Old Town office products brand.

I also found clippings from the New York tabloids with photos showing Susan and five other knockouts swooning over

Bob Hope on his arrival at Idlewild Airport. The women are wrongly described as "pretty fans" (*Daily News*) and "M-G-M players" (*Daily Mirror*), with only the *Journal-American* calling them what they were — models hired to promote the U.S. premiere of the movie *Bachelor in Paradise*, not one of Hope's best. "We were paid $100 each," Susan said. "Unfortunately, we had to sit through the movie."[1]

It's to my regret that Susan and my sister never met, because I know how much they would have loved each other, but it wasn't until shortly after Roberta died that I had become serious enough about Susan to bring her to Benton Harbor. My mother was cordial to Susan but was preoccupied sorting Bobbie's clothes to give away and answering sympathy notes. Bobbie was on my father's mind too. He complained that the funeral director had tried to sell him the most expensive casket, saying, "Milt, don't you think your beautiful daughter deserves the best?"

Dad thought the pitch craven. "The guy knew Jews are supposed to be buried in simple caskets, but all he cared about was the money. Where's the mercy?"

One day Mook took Susan and me to see his friend Herb Mendel, who'd offered to show him the house he and his wife, Audre, were building on Rocky Gap Road on the Lake

---

1. After her modeling days, Susan worked as a legal secretary at the giant New York law firm Finley, Kumble. A client of the firm, construction magnate/playboy Richard Cohen, hired her away to be his personal secretary. Richard dated Dinah Shore, Barbra Streisand and Linda Evans and married, among others, Tina Sinatra, Frank's daughter, and Barbara Grant, Cary's widow. Richard suffered a freakish death. At a Beverly Hills dinner party, he choked on a piece of steak. A doctor at the party performed the Heimlich maneuver, breaking one of Richard's ribs, which in turn punctured a lung. The doctor then administered CPR. He had been eating peanuts, to which Richard was allergic. Richard survived the choking, broken rib and punctured lung but died of peanut breath.

Michigan shore. Herb was one of the Twin Cities' richest men. Round-faced and goggle-eyed, he was known in his youth as Froggie. His British-born father, Arthur Mendel, had founded a Benton Harbor smelting firm, Michigan Standard Alloys, which Herb built into an industrial giant that refined tin, aluminum and other non-ferrous metals for the automotive and home appliance industries. Herb and Audre, a former dancer with the American Ballet Theater, donated millions to Lake Michigan College, formerly Benton Harbor Junior College. One of their gifts, an entertainment and educational complex at the college, the Mendel Center for Arts and Technology, became the home of the Southwest Michigan Economic Club after it outgrew the Whitcomb Hotel.

The house Herb and Audre were building sat on 17 sun-dappled acres. When finished, it would give them another place to rest their heads when they weren't in their art-filled apartment on Central Park South in New York or their manse on the Intracoastal Waterway in Miami Beach. Herb chatted with helmeted workmen putting the finishing touches on an 8,000-square-foot house that we were told would have seven-and-a-half bathrooms. On the drive home, my father said, "People don't call him Froggie anymore."

Another day Susan and I went horseback riding with my cousin Ben, Uncle Hymie's son. When Susan pulled half a furlong ahead of us, Ben leaned forward in the saddle and asked in what sounded very much like a John Wayne drawl. "Ya got it bad?" Such an odd expression, but, yes, about Susan, I had it bad.

Susan was from a long-established family in Woodstock, New York, a funky art and music colony populated by headband-wearing survivors of half-forgotten culture wars who refuse to let tie-dye die. Woodstock is famous for an event not held there, the 1969 Woodstock Festival. Because town elders wanted no part of the festival's feared (and realized) madness, the event took place on a muddy dairy farm 50 miles distant, but the festival organizers borrowed Woodstock's name to capitalize on the village's rock music associations.

Susan's mother's people were the Cashdollars, a name of Germanic origin. As a girl on the family dairy farm, Susan's grandmother, Sarah Cashdollar, drove a milk wagon on icy mountain roads, once battling a black bear trying to get at the milk. Sarah later ran a boarding house, The Homestead, which served chicken dinners with mashed potatoes and hot biscuits to Woodstock artists and the actors appearing in summer productions at the Woodstock Playhouse. As a young girl, Susan helped out at the boarding house.

Susan grew up as dollar poor as Xenia did drachma rich. Her father, John White, a worker on government construction projects, was killed in a car crash when he was 38, leaving Susan's mother, Ethel Cashdollar White, to raise Susan, her sister, Jean, and brother, Buddy, on her own. Susan went to New York straight after high school. Her mother warned her about men slipping her Mickey Finns and safety-pinned a pink cotton pouch in her bra inside of which she placed a $20 bill. "I've tried to think of a situation when that would have come in handy," Susan says.

In New York Susan was pursued by men wearing bespoke suits and expensive watches. Not all of the men were married, only most of them. I dine out vicariously on Susan's stories of dining out for real at fabled Manhattan watering spots like El Morocco, Latin Quarter and Copacabana. One night a music publisher Susan was dating took her to the Copa, where a singer he worked with was headlining. Between sets, the star joined them at their table and whispered an invitation for

Susan to meet him later in his hotel room. When she declined, he wrote her a note in case she changed her mind: "OK? Nat King Cole."

Other men who passed through the revolving door of Susan's single-girl New York existence included future Hollywood filmmaking heavyweights Jerry Weintraub and Frank Oz, who were a talent agent and a Muppets puppeteer, respectively, when she dated them, and the singer Vic Damone, with whom she was fixed up after the collapse of his marriage to the actress Pier Angeli. Over dinner at the East Side steakhouse Danny's Hide-A-Way, Damone, drinking heavily, pining for Angeli and craving attention, began singing loudly enough to be heard throughout the restaurant. When Susan brought a breadstick to her mouth, Damone absently went to light it. There would be no second date.

Susan's first love was a man many years her senior, Charles Randolph Grean, with whom I became friendly as she did with Xenia, all very civilized, we told ourselves. Charlie was a bandleader, RCA Victor record executive and composer of novelty songs including "Sweet Violets" and "The Thing," the latter, in a recording by my Vancouver tablemate Phil Harris, reaching the top of *Billboard's* pop chart. More than that, Charlie did the string arrangements for Nat King Cole's imperishable recording of Mel Tormé's "The Christmas Song." I'd been a fan of Cole's since seeing him as a boy with my father and Joel at the Oriental Theater in Chicago. His hitting on my wife-to-be helped fill me in on what he'd been up to lately.

Susan and I were introduced by a Northwestern friend, Larry Grossman, and his wife, Jill Kollmar. Larry, a Broadway composer, worked with Charlie Grean in the music department of television's *The Jimmy Dean Show*, and while waiting for their men at rehearsals and in the green room during performances, Susan and Jill became friendly. I was involved at the time with Elizabeth Tweedy, who I'd begun seeing in Minneapolis, where she was a graduate student in art history at the University of Minnesota. Liz and I came to New York more or less together. She became associate director of the Museum of Modern Art's international exhibit program and at other times curated the art collections of David Rockefeller and the architect Philip Johnson. After Susan's relationship with Charlie ended and during a lull in mine with Liz, Larry and Jill invited Susan and me on a Sunday afternoon to their apartment on East 63rd Street so we could meet.

Larry and Jill told me that Susan was a model and had been seen most recently — a hand of hers, anyway — on a television commercial holding a Spring cigarette, a brand of the Lorillard Tobacco Company. Upon meeting her, I checked her hands, which were nicely tapered, as was the rest of her, but we didn't click. After two hours of conversational ducking and parrying, I walked her to her apartment eight blocks away. To this day she tells people that I tried to kiss her, but why, I object, would I have tried to kiss her when our blind date had been a dud?

O.K., I tried to kiss her.

And was rebuffed.

A full year later my friend Buddy Alberts was in New York and lined up a date with a woman who happened to know Susan. I was to join them, and the gods of fate moved me to incautiously call Susan and ask her to dinner. Either she didn't remember me or she was famished because she said yes. At the helpfully romantic Theater District restaurant Barbetta, this time we hit it off, and we began seeing each other. After a year-long courtship nourished by trips to Paris, Lisbon and Barcelona, we decided to take the plunge. Successful matchmakers after all, Larry and Jill insisted on hosting the wedding in their apartment, the scene of the now happy couple's unsuccessful introduction two years earlier. Our news brought from my mother a doozy of an expression of contrition. Recalling Susan's visit to Benton Harbor, she said, "If I knew you were going to marry her, I would have been nicer to her."

Susan had been raised in Christian Science, and my mother wanted her to convert to Judaism, but I told her it was too late, that she'd already converted — from Christian Science to hypochondria. Mom said enough with the jokes, that at minimum we'd better be married by a rabbi. It wasn't easy in those days to find a rabbi willing to perform a mixed-faith wedding, but after a few false leads we were steered to David Max Eichhorn, a rabbi with the National Jewish Welfare Board in Manhattan. In his office overlooking Madison Square Park, Rabbi Eichhorn, a chipper fellow with a ready smile set off by a Groucho mustache, agreed to marry us. Only years later did we learn that Eichhorn had been the Jewish chaplain with the U.S. troops who liberated Dachau, the Nazi concentration camp outside Munich. Eichhorn's letters home during World War II are collected in a book, *The GI's Rabbi*, which tells of his having conducted a poignant Sabbath service in Dachau's main square for the handful of Jewish prisoners who had survived the camp's terrors. He writes that Polish men also imprisoned at Dachau threatened to violently disrupt the service, presaging that antisemitism would survive the Holocaust even as six million Jews didn't.

The night before the wedding, Susan took flowers to my parents at the St. Moritz Hotel. There were hugs and warm words, but afterward, while waiting for the elevator, which was across from their room, Susan overheard Frieda, bemoaning that I was again marrying out of the faith, complain loudly, "How can he do this to us again?" to which Milton answered,

"We'll just have to make the best of it." Susan called Jill, then me, in tears. "They hate me," she said.

The next evening, in front of 30 guests in Larry and Jill's living room, Rabbi Eichhorn pronounced Susan and me man and wife. Afterward, my father inquisitorially asked Susan's mother of his new daughter-in-law, "How many credit cards does she have?"

Dad came to love Susan dearly. In her he found an inexperienced but enthusiastic gin rummy player who kept him off balance with her unorthodox discards. "What did you do that for?" he would ask, flummoxed by moves he'd never seen in games played with his sharpie pals. Susan didn't have a driver's license, and living in New York City, with its subways, buses and taxis, she hadn't needed one, but that changed when we bought our house in Massachusetts. My father told her that if she got a driver's license, he'd buy her a car, which is how she found herself in possession of a new Ford Taurus. "When I made that promise, I never thought you'd pass your driver's test," he zinged her, before adding, "but I was glad to do it for you, sweetie." Dad was measured in his compliments, so when he told me one day, "Jerry, you did good when you married Susan," it had the import of the Magna Carta.

Soon Mother also was won over by Susan and announced that she wanted to introduce her new daughter-in-law to her friends. A lunch in Susan's honor took place at my parents' house the next time we were in Benton Harbor. Susan said it was a very nice affair until she was sitting after lunch with several women in the living room and heard Frieda Ravitch, helping Mom clear the table in the dining area, say, "Susan seems nice, and she's very pretty."

"Oh, she's nothing, kid," Mother exclaimed. "You should have seen his first wife. She's an actress in Hollywood."

Susan told me, "You know how open their house is. I knew all the women heard. It was hurtful, but mostly it was very awkward."

Throwing a lunch in Susan's honor only to call her "nothing" was another instance of Frieda delivering a full pail of milk only to kick it over. In time Susan came to accept that her mother-in-law's verbal intemperance was part of the married-to-Jerry bargain. One of Mom's acts of kindness was to regularly visit an elderly and frail Benton Harbor widow, Fannie Weinhouse. One day she took Susan to meet Fannie. In the living room, Mom pointed to a framed wedding photo on a table and said, "Such a beautiful bride...." Turning to the shrunken woman leaning on a walker, she said, pityingly, "Look what happens to a person." Instead of objecting as she had every reason to do, Fannie nodded in agreement.

Susan would witness others get the squirm-inducing treatment from my mother, including me, excruciatingly, during a visit to Ann Arbor when our son David was attending Michigan. Mom, Susan and I were in the crowded lobby of the Bell Tower Hotel waiting for Mook to bring the car around when Mother caught a view of me that alarmed her.

"Jerry, you're getting a belly!" she loudly cried out. "Jerry, I didn't know you were getting a belly." I sucked in my stomach and looked around the lobby trying to locate this Jerry with the unfortunate mid-section. "Jerry, you don't want to get a belly!" she persisted. "When men get bellies, they're hard to get rid of!"

"Jerry, your *belly!*"

Frequent Mook lament: "You know the saying in the war, 'Loose lips sink ships?' Well, my wife has sunk a lot of ships."

Yet there was something about bellies that also loosened Dad's lips. As he himself related, he was having lunch with friends at Ashkenaz, a renowned Jewish delicatessen in the Rogers Park area of Chicago, when he noticed a man with an enormous stomach at the door about to leave. To his companions Dad said in Yiddish, "Look at the belly on that guy!" The man, blessed with excellent hearing to go with his ample breadbasket, shot my father a fiery look. "How was I supposed to know he spoke Yiddish?" Mook asked. At Ashkenaz, where diners' checks were inscribed, "Better than this, there isn't," it would have been difficult to find a customer who *didn't* speak Yiddish.

Mom may have sunk an armada in her lifetime, but on this occasion, Pop got himself a battleship.

Susan became privy to my mother's confidences. On a visit to Benton Harbor, she was listening to her mother-in-law talk non-stop, dispensing gossip, advice, opinions and complaints. When she at last paused to take a breath, Susan excused herself for a bathroom break. In the bathroom she heard a scratching noise outside the window. She looked out and saw Mother raking an area that didn't need raking. Having won back Susan's attention, Mom resumed talking.

Susan had won prizes in school for her short stories, and when she saw that I was earning a living as a writer, she probably figured how hard could it be? She heard of a job opening for an outline writer for the ABC-TV soap opera *All My Children*. She applied, was hired and in quick order became an editor and then a script writer. She would go on to have a 25-year career in daytime TV, winning two Emmys on *All My Children* and completing a network trifecta by also writing for *As the World Turns* on CBS and *Days of Our Lives* on NBC. No longer did my mother need to crow about a former daughter-in-law doing something or other in Hollywood. She now had one whose name scrolled across television screens in soap-opera credits five days a week.[2]

The apartment on East 63rd Street where Susan and I both met and married continued to be a welcoming place for us. For several years Jill and Larry included us in their family Christmas dinners. Jill's celebrity parents — Dorothy Kilgallen, the syndicated newspaper columnist and *What's My Line* television game show panelist, and Richard Kollmar, a Broadway producer who had played Boston Blackie on the eponymous radio detective show — had died, but Jill's aunt Eleanor Kilgallen and grandparents James and Mae Kilgallen were present at the dinners.

Eleanor, a talent agent who helped guide the careers of Warren Beatty and Grace Kelly among others, had delightful affectations. When something amused her, she exclaimed, "Ho, ho, ho, Henry Higgins," the movies and Broadway shows she praised were "devoon," and when she said, "Be still my heart," bluebirds fluttered, and bougainvillea rustled. If Eleanor stepped out of *Auntie Mame*, her father came gift-wrapped from Damon Runyon. A dapper little Irishman, Jimmy Kilgallen had a 75-year career as a reporter during which he introduced daughter Dorothy to the newspaper game and was the only journalist I know of who interviewed both Hitler and Babe Ruth. At the dinners, while Susan made sure to sit next

---

2. Keeping my wives straight tripped up John Lavine, dean of Northwestern's Medill School of Journalism, when Susan and I were in Evanston in 2011 for my induction into Medill's Hall of Achievement. Introducing me before an audience of faculty, alumni and guests, Lavine said, "...and while carrying a full load of courses, Jerry had time to woo and wed Susan, the Homecoming queen." Susan called out, "Wrong wife!" and the crowd howled at the dean's expense. A journalism educator who'd gotten his facts wrong presumably because of unreliable sources, Lavine knelt, kissed Susan's hand and apologized profusely.

to Eleanor, I positioned myself by Jimmy to hear his war stories, told in an argot that suggested late nights in gin joints with bartenders who knew about life and hatcheck girls who knew even more. When Jimmy said that Mae, in her 90s like himself, still had "great gams," I saw that he was right.

On visits to Benton Harbor when David was little, we went with my father to the House of David. The colony was near extinction, the practice of celibacy having exacted its membership-shrinking toll (Silver Beach amusement park was gone altogether), but it still had the little train putt-putting around the grounds, steam billowing and whistle blowing, and all of us, not just David, enjoyed riding it.

There also was a new attraction in town that Mook introduced us to, the Sarett Nature Center, a wildlife preserve with 120 acres of hiking trails lacing through woodlands and marshes. The center was named for Lew Sarett, born Lewis Saretsky into an early Benton Harbor Jewish family. Sarett was a poet, college professor, park ranger and lecturer on the Chautauqua circuit. He was the son of Rudolph Saretsky, a cutter at a Benton Harbor garment company, Western Pants, and Rudolph's wife, Jennie. Lewis was a star debater and athlete at Benton Harbor High School. He also was a hero, honored at age 17 in a ceremony in the mayor's office for having saved from drowning an 11-year-old boy who would play a key role at my bar mitzvah. If Lewis Saretsky hadn't pulled a flailing Paul Price from a section of the Paw Paw River known as "Devil's Hole," it would have fallen to somebody else to emcee the Whitcomb Hotel reception.[3]

---

3. Sarett's wife, the former Margaret Husted, was a sister of Jeannette Husted Rumsfeld, the mother of Secretary of Defense Donald Rumsfeld, who quoted Sarett when defending his actions as architect of the U.S.'s disastrous Iraq war. "I had an uncle, Lew Sarett, who taught speech and persuasion at North-

When my mother didn't feel up to making the trip to New York, Dad came by himself. "I go to New York to see my people," he said. He enjoyed being in a city where Jewish food was readily available and where theaters on the Lower East Side still showed Yiddish plays and films, although now with English translations. He also liked the bargain breakfasts that the signboards on sidewalks throughout Manhattan said were available as long as you ordered by 11 a.m. Something that bothered him, though, was the fruit displayed at New York's 24-hour minimarkets, apples and pears wrapped in tissue paper, strawberries tucked carefully in crates, grapes plump and unblemished. "Beautiful to look at but the damn prices — where's the mercy?" said this man accustomed to Farm Belt plenitude and low prices. To spare him sticker shock, Susan and I got in the practice of hiding our grocery receipts from him.

Dad was a walker. In Benton Harbor he sometimes hiked from Miami Road to the Harbor Bag Company building three miles away. In New York, where every block offered new sights for him to see and tell us about later, he liked walking even more. He thought nothing of hoofing from our apartment building on West 12th Street to pick up David at Trinity School on West 91st Street, then walking with his grandson back downtown.

During a visit to New York, perhaps feeling guilty that Mom wasn't with him to share the city's pleasures (she might have enjoyed the Yiddish plays, not the walking), Dad said he wanted to bring a gift back for her and asked Susan to help him find something. She thought of a quirky shop she had often

---

western University," Rumsfeld said. "He used to say that persuasion was a two-edged sword. Reason and emotion — plunge it deep."

passed on East 57th Street, Rita Ford's, which specialized in music boxes of all sizes and kinds. She went there with her father-in-law, who picked out a handcrafted inlaid box that Mother kept on the bedroom dresser the rest of her life, using it to hold pieces of jewelry. When the lid opened, the box emitted, apropos of nothing, the tinkly strains of "Isla di Capri."

Pioneering Michigan farm couple Mendel and Gittel. He was memorialized at Ellis Island. She wasn't. (Family Photo)

Young Mook couldn't swim but was drawn to the Lake Michigan shore, where wrongdoing resulted in headlines. (Family Photo/Collage by Lisa Schwebke)

Mom and Dad spiffy with me in Benton Harbor and with Roberta on a big-girl night out at the Clover Club in Miami. (Family Photos)

The Benton Harbor Fruit Market. Besides burlap bags, Pop trafficked in bushel baskets and cartons. (Benton Harbor Public Library)

Mook (dark vest, closest to camera) ready for poker at the Vincent Hotel, where prison-bound Al Capone had a going-away party. (Family Photo)

Revelers at a festive New Year's Eve party include my beaming mother (foreground, sleeveless dress) and, in back, Joey Kamin blowing up a balloon. Joey would be taken out gangland-style in Miami. (Family Photo)

Mom, Dad, Joel and me when Roberta was at school in Texas. Her returns home made our lives richer. (Family Photo)

Our Miami Road home until Mother fled the gilded cage and…

…built a modern dwelling down the street that didn't bring happiness. (Family Photos)

After two decades of hijinks-filled but dead-serious warfare, "the boys" (left to right) Abe, Mook and Hymie, made peace at my bar mitzvah. (Family Photo)

Terrence McNally (dark shirt) with me at his side and three other Cherub "toughs" on the Northwestern campus. Viewers of a PBS documentary may wrongly think the photo was taken in Corpus Christi. (Author's Photo)

Xenia modeled sweaters for an Evanston clothing store ad in the *Daily Northwestern* (I was a throw-in) and acquired a nickname at Homecoming. (Students Publishing Company)

Susan with me on our wedding day and with football hero Ron Burton at a Northwestern reunion. (Family Photos)

With Susan in the Yucatan for a *Sports Illustrated* swimsuit shoot. People asked, "You mean you took your wife along on an assignment with Cheryl Tiegs and Christie Brinkley? Well, why wouldn't I? (Family Photo)

Muhammad Ali held all the cards (left hand) when he KO'd Mook in Berrien Springs. (Family Photo)

Joel and I thought our father's life was an open book, but there was a chapter he'd kept secret. (Family Photo)

Chapter 17

Molotovs and Von Ribbentrops

"This used to be the best town in the country — now it's the worst," my father got to saying as the 1970s gave way to the '80s. He wasn't overstating the depths to which Benton Harbor had sunk. "Benton Harbor is rotting," began an Associated Press story that appeared in the *Los Angeles Times, St Louis Post-Dispatch* and scores of other papers. *The New York Times* ran a story on Benton Harbor's troubles headlined ONCE-VIBRANT MICHIGAN TOWN IS PARALYZED BY DEBT, DESERTION AND PERVASIVE POVERTY. A Chicago *Sun-Times* article on Benton Harbor quoted the town's former city manager as echoing Mook exactly, calling it "the worst town in America." Really, the *worst?* "I think that's pretty close to being correct," conceded an official of the Benton Harbor Chamber of Commerce. Ordinarily chambers of commerce are cheerleaders for their cities, but Benton Harbor now had little to cheer about.

Money magazine made it unanimous. In its annual ranking of 300 U.S. metropolitan areas based on such factors as safety, housing, finances and the arts, *Money* placed Benton Harbor

298th ahead of only Jackson, Mich. (299), and Atlantic City, N.J. (300). Benton Harbor officials objected to the low ranking and invited *Money* to come out for an in-person inspection instead of relying solely on data. The magazine complied and sent a reporter for a first-hand look. The next year Benton Harbor was 300th.

Even more shatteringly than in other Rust Belt communities, Benton Harbor saw its manufacturing plants shut down or move away. The town was hollowed out by an urban renewal plan that leveled the Flats, forcing 200 families, most of them Black, from their homes and resulting in the relocation of the Fruit Market to the far reaches of town. This left a void in the heart of the town where new investment was promised but never materialized. Benton Harbor's tax base was destroyed, and jobs vanished. With its economy destroyed, much of the city's middle-class African American population departed, leaving the poorest behind. Several leased Benton Harbor police cars and a snowplow were repossessed when the town defaulted on payments. Benton Harbor became a ghost town, buildings razed, storefronts boarded up, neighborhoods blighted. The *Sun-Times* reporter wrote that the only restaurant he could find in the downtown area was a soup kitchen.

As conditions worsened — 30% unemployment, 40% of the population on welfare, murder rate higher than in the most crime-ridden big cities — Benton Harbor's banks and businesses relocated to St. Joseph, as did the hospital, the YMCA and the paper where I worked one summer, the Benton Harbor *News-Palladium*, which merged with the St. Joseph *Herald-Press* to be rebranded as the *Herald-Palladium*, "the newspaper for Southwestern Michigan." Whirlpool Corporation remained but on Benton Harbor's outer edge — a lone survivor of a civic hurricane. Benton Harbor's population, which topped out at 19,000 in 1960, began a steady decline that would cut that number in half.

While Benton Harbor nosedived, St. Joseph, heretofore its tag-along little brother, prospered as a tourist mecca, with boutiques and restaurants on streets filled with shoppers and vacationers. Racially, the Twin Cities became opposites: Benton Harbor more than 80% Black, St. Joseph roughly the same percentage white. Wags called the Blossomland Bridge, which spanned the St. Joseph River between the two cities, the longest bridge in the world because, the joke went, it linked St. Joseph to Harlem. St. Joseph whites felt unsafe in Benton Harbor, and Benton Harbor Blacks felt the same in St. Joseph. The Twin Cities had become a microcosm of the racial divide in America.

As for the other part of Dad's assertion, that Benton Harbor was once the best town in America, well, you have my word for that too. As a boy, I knew there was no finer place on Planet Earth than Benton Harbor, Michigan, USA. I chanted to myself "We're Number One" whenever I discovered that somebody from Benton Harbor had achieved even a modicum of national recognition — when, for instance, Ruth Terry, the former Ruth Mae McMahon, made the leap from winning Twin Cities talent shows as a student at St. John's Catholic elementary school to singing in Roy Rogers and Gene Autry films and playing the title role in the 1943 movie *Pistol Packin' Mama*. I was certain that the Mardi Gras and Rose Bowl parades were poor imitations of the Blossomtime parade that in spring wended through Twin Cities streets lined with crowds cheering the floats from which waved the prettiest girls you could hope to see — Miss Coloma, Miss Buchanan, Miss Dowagiac, and, of course, Miss Benton Harbor.

Today I find further validation of Benton Harbor's former

greatness when learning of the notables once drawn to the town — not just thugs like Capone and pugs like Dempsey, but literati of highest rank. I noted previously that Berrien County native Ring Lardner wrote humorously about a visit he made to the House of David. That was in 1917. I can also report that earlier, in 1899, a teenaged Ring played tackle on a heavily favored Niles High School football team that traveled to Benton Harbor and was held to a no-joke 6-6 tie by a gallant Benton Harbor High eleven. And before Saul Bellow had the fictional Augie March visit the Twin Cities, Saul's mother, Liza, vacationed with him and the other Bellow children on one of the Benton Harbor farms that took in boarders, with husband and father Abraham Bellow joining the family on weekends. A Tuley High School friend and authorial rival of Saul Bellow, Isaac "Ike" Rosenfeld (who wrote an acclaimed novel, *Passage From Home,* but died at 38 without fully realizing his literary promise), vacationed as a boy with an uncle on a Benton Harbor farm called "Schwartz's." Whether that's where the Bellows also stayed is unrecorded.

Schwartz's likely was poultry farmer Joseph Schwartz's Flo-Ruth resort (named for daughters Florence and Ruth) on North Euclid Avenue, where the pastimes were simple — pinochle in the parlor, croquet on the lawn — and the *schmaltz* (rendered chicken fat) on the tables plentiful. In 1940, a gas tank at Flo-Ruth exploded while 80 guests were having lunch in the dining room, killing three people, including Schwartz's wife, Clara.

The literary figure who knew Benton Harbor best was the poet, journalist and Lincoln biographer Carl Sandburg, who lived for many years in the Lake Michigan village of Harbert south of the Twin Cities. If Chicago was Sandburg's "city of big shoulders," Benton Harbor was his town of out-of-whack arteries. "I like Benton Harbor," Sandburg wrote. "It hasn't the smug, checkerboard pattern of most towns. And I like its streets that amble off at tangents and end suddenly here and there as if tired of going on." Sandburg may have been thinking of Territorial Road, which starts out parallel to Main Street before taking a direction all its own, or of Five Corners, where Wall, Elm and Michigan Streets and Pipestone Avenue riotously converged, challenging motorists with 66 overhead lights, which, the *News-Palladium* boasted, may have set a national record for the number of traffic signals at one intersection. Crazy-quilt streets — no end of the things that made Benton Harbor the best.[1]

The changes that came over Benton Harbor after its halcyon days were profound. In 1951, the year before I entered Benton Harbor High School, police were called to break up BHHS students doing battle on a city bus with paper wads. By the 1980s, guns and knives, not balled-up paper, were the weapons favored by school troublemakers. Bullets were fired at Benton Harbor High dances and basketball games, and in 1988, two 17-year-old girls got in a fight on a school bus, and one stabbed the other to death.

Crime and decay were rampant in Benton Harbor, but Miami Road was at a remove from the worst of the worst, and my parents stayed put at 1390. So did the couple in the white frame house at 1398, Harry Diffenderfer, and his wife, Marie,

---

[1]. Another literary lion, James T. Farrell, mentions Benton Harbor in his urban trilogy, *Studs Lonigan*. In the trilogy's first book, *Young Lonigan*, Studs is checking out the girls on a Chicago beach with his pal Kenny Killarney, who's wearing a swimsuit he has stolen for the occasion. Kenny says, "A good lifeguard could swim all the way to Michigan City or Benton Harbor." Michigan City, Indiana, is 30 nautical miles from Chicago, and Benton Harbor is twice as far, but swimming to The Best Town in America, I submit, would have been worth the extra effort.

who in a fine neighborly gesture invited Mom and Dad to dinner at the Berrien Hills Country Club, where Harry, a stockbroker by day, moonlighted as the "King of Swing" conductor of the club's house orchestra. My parents said they had a good time at dinner with Harry and Marie and ran into other people they knew, none of whom seemed surprised to see them there. The club still banned Blacks and Jews as members, but in a humbled Benton Harbor, perhaps the high and mighty had lost some of their height and might.

With my father's contemporaries dying off or moving away, his poker games, including those at the Pit, ended. As when he quit cigars, Dad shrugged off the loss of something that had been a huge part of his life. "I played a lot of poker in my day," he said, unnecessarily. At the same time, the Harbor Bag Company's fortunes were in decline, with burlap bags for the storage of produce increasingly replaced by refrigeration and packaging innovations such as shrink-wrapping and synthetics like polyethylene and polypropylene polymer. Despite the business downturn, my father continued to build inventory. It's said that old habits die hard. For Mook, the hoarding of bags didn't die at all. Because he had enough stock to last several lifetimes, I suggested to him that if he stopped buying bags and concentrated on reducing his inventory, he'd be working less and his operation would be virtually all profit, but he set me straight, saying firmly, "When you're in business, you buy and sell. You don't just sell."

Meanwhile, Hymie and Abe were unaffected by the fall-off in the bag business for a simple reason: They'd gotten out of it. They had a new calling, real estate, to which they were first exposed in the late 1930s when Grandpa Kirshenbaum, all but giving up on farming, deputized the two of them, his de facto partners in matters great and small, to sell or rent the family farm either piecemeal or as a whole.

When Grandpa and Grandma Kirshenbaum purchased the farm in 1912, it was bordered by little-traveled Napier Avenue on one side and horizon on the other three. In 1931, a 3½-mile extension of highway M-139 was built, part of which skirted the farm's western edge, giving Mendel hope that this would increase the value of the property. Hymie and Abe packaged pieces of the farm in various configurations. Five hundred feet of frontage by the highway. A roadside parcel with a fruit stand thrown in. "Build to Suit" signs appeared. But there were no takers. According to a story in the journal *Michigan Jewish History* about Jewish farmers in the Benton Harbor area, the entire Kirshenbaum farm was put up for sale for $20,000. "After a while," the story said, "when [Mendel] saw he had no buyers, he compromised at sixteen thousand. Still, he could find no buyers."

Slowly a franchise row formed on the M-139 extension. This greatly inconvenienced a disabled man named Jack Mills, owner of a garage next to the Kirshenbaum farm, who had to dodge ever heavier traffic in his wheelchair to get to Louie's Tavern across M-139, but as Grandpa wished, his property became more valuable, and upon his death, the *Michigan Jewish History* story said, "the land passed to his children."

But not all the children. The property was bequeathed to three of the four siblings who lived in Benton Harbor — Hymie, Abe and Rose. The fourth, my father, was odd man out with Mendel as always. Also passed over were the Chicago sisters, Dorothy and Frieda.

Dorothy, for one, reacted angrily. She proposed to my father that they join forces to sue, but Mook, having made peace with his brothers, had no appetite for poking the hornet's nest. Besides, he wasn't the suing sort. He believed Americans were too litigious, and when he came across a quote by former Colorado Governor Richard Lamm that "no country has ever sued its way to greatness," he appropriated the statement as his own. His lawyer was Elizabeth Forhan, an Irishwoman who was Michigan's first female justice of the peace and a long-serving Benton Harbor municipal judge (and who, I've been told by a confidante of hers, had an affair as a young woman with the House of David's King Ben.) My father admired the trailblazing Lizzie Forhan and dropped by her office to chew the fat or have her prepare documents but never to sue anybody.

Dad was determined to stay out of court and made sure I did too. One day I was giving Tommy Tonnelier a ride home on the back of my Cushman Eagle and when I turned onto the Tonnelier driveway I was tail-ended by a car driven by a woman who missed my hand signal. The Eagle landed, and Tommy and I did too. We were thrown onto the lawn and suffered only scrapes and bruises, but the scooter was mangled. The woman was at fault, and we could have sued, but Pop said nothing doing, be thankful that Tommy and I weren't seriously injured. He was similarly dismissive of Aunt Dorothy's plea that they challenge the distribution of Mendel's property. "You go ahead and sue if you want," he told her, "but leave me out of it."

The Kirshenbaum farmland and surrounding area underwent a sweeping transformation. Aunt Rose, Uncle Dave and their children moved with Grandma to a house in Fair Plain, and the farmhouse was razed. On M-139 across Napier Avenue, a shopping center opened with a Woolworth's, Kroger's and an offshoot of the Chicago department store, Goldblatt's. Where the farmhouse stood, a hamburger stand appeared that introduced itself as something new in the way of fast food, offering "15-cent burgers" and "fast, cheerful, service... plenty of parking...no car hops...no tipping." On land where Mendel long struggled to make ends meet, Southwestern Michigan had its first McDonald's. For Hymie, Abe and Rose, the children's song "Old MacDonald Had a Farm" morphed into good old McDonald's has *our* farm.

The one who profited most from the M-139 windfall was Uncle Abe, who used his dealings over the sale of the Kirshenbaum property as a springboard to creation of a real estate company, South Shore Development, which constructed and leased warehouses in Michigan and neighboring states. Abie had always played the big shot and now he was one, a business leader and philanthropist who with his sons, my cousins David and Ted, donated $100,000 to Memorial Hospital in St. Joseph and many times that amount to the Mayo Clinic in Minnesota.

Far from begrudging Abe his success, my father seemed liberated by it, as if his having been the family moneybags was a weight lifted from his shoulders. Having advocated blinders for Mom, he now wore them himself. He talked about his financial success in the past tense, making it sound like another lifetime when he beat others to the check; easily covered the expenses for Roberta's care and Joel's and my education; gave generously to charities; was a soft touch for friends down on their luck and employees needing something extra in their paychecks — who, in short, saw the money go out as fast as it came in. "When I had it, everybody had it." he said. He also said, "I used to be the richest Kirshenbaum, now I'm the poorest." This suggested a parallelism: Milton Kirshenbaum and Benton Harbor had gone from top to bottom together.

But he was drinking black coffee by the mailbox. He'd been taken down a notch, but he and Mom were still living in their handsome if air-conditioning-less Miami Road house and still dining out when they felt like it, and he was still driving expensive cars, only now they were Mercedes instead of Cadillacs, a change for which he offered a jokey explanation that became part of his stockpile of oft-told stories.

> *I was in my Cadillac, which wasn't much more than a year old, and this Black fellow who used to work for me pulled up alongside me at a stoplight in a brand-new Coupe de Ville. He gave me a big smile and said, 'Mook, what are you doing driving that beat-up old thing for?' Well, that killed Cock Robin. Time was, you drove a Cadillac, people tipped their hats to you. Right then and there I said no more Cadillacs.*[2]

MY FATHER, having made peace with his brothers, was now an avowed pacifist as rifts old and new roiled his side of the family. His Chicago sisters, Dorothy and Frieda, remained enemy combatants, but Pop was non-allied, as he was when the friendship between Aunt Rose and Uncle Abe's wife, Lucille, frayed, reportedly over Lucille having undergone a nose job

---

2. Apparently I'd gotten over my aversion to Cadillacs. At Benton Harbor High School, I was one of many boys dopey over a lissome cheerleader, Karen Gobiel, the daughter of Bob and Pat Gobiel, the operators of the Market Diner. Alas, Karen preferred older men, and at 18, in the First Methodist Church in South Bend, she married a 25-year-old codger against whom the panting horde never stood a chance. Karen and I stayed in touch. That first marriage ended, and years later Susan and I visited Karen and a later husband, Roger Slater, at their home outside Seattle. Over dinner Karen told me I had let her drive my father's Cadillac, which I didn't remember doing. I must have been trying to impress her.

without clearing it with Rose. He also stayed out of the disputes embroiling my Camp Flambeau nemesis, Mort Zwick.

Cousin Mort became a lawyer and got rich trading pork bellies on the Chicago Mercantile Exchange. Mort was high-spirited, big-hearted and filled with bravado. To remind his children and grandchildren how blessed they were having him as head of the family, he gave them caps and sweaters bearing "Lucky Sperm Club" logos. Mort's wife, Jill, was a Republican member of the Illinois House of Representatives. They divorced (Mort won custody of their pet turkey), and when Jill was running for re-election, he entered the primary against her. A husband challenging an ex-wife for public office became a national story, which Mort took pains to make bigger. Calling a press conference, he trotted out Jill's and his four children and asked them which parent they would "vote" for. All answered on cue, "Daddy" or "Father."

To bring an end to this circus, Jill dropped out of the race. She would later change parties and become a top aide to Democratic U.S. Senator Carol Mosely Braun, with whom she had bonded when they were young mothers together in the Illinois legislature. Mort remained on the ballot and lost. He became an appellate court judge and ran for the Illinois Supreme Court, reportedly spending a million dollars of his own money on his campaign. He stood an excellent chance of winning, but after making truth-stretching accusations against his leading opponent and when questionable actions he had taken as an appellate judge surfaced, the Chicago papers rebuked him and the Illinois Bar Association withdrew its approval of him. After losing in a landslide big enough to wipe out an Alpine village, Mort retired in Las Vegas.

Mort fought other battles on other fronts. He and his brother, Bob, didn't get along. They saw eye to eye only in their shared hatred — not too strong a word — of their mother, my zany Aunt Dorothy. I once told Mort I got a kick out of his mother, and he replied, "That's because you don't know her. She's a bad mother, a bad wife and a terrible human being. If I saw her lying in the middle of the street, I wouldn't help her."

Coming to their sister's defense, Hymie and Abe reproached Bob and Mort for their callousness toward her, with Abe calling them "the Menendez brothers," a reference to Lyle and Eric Menendez, the California brothers famously convicted of murdering their parents. Mook refused to join in the condemnation of the nephews, saying, "It's between a mother and her sons. We don't know the facts." Consequently, Bob and Mort shunned Hymie and Abe but felt kindly toward my father. "Your dad is a straight shooter," Mort told me.

Then came another rupture in the Kirshenbaum ranks, this one unimaginable. Hymie and Abe, long partnered in business against my father and allied in every other aspect of their lives, became enemies. The rupture in their relationship occurred when Abe's son Ted and Hymie's son Ben launched a business together trading in cartons. The fathers had been United Bag Company, and the sons became United Container. They advertised, "Cartons: Need 'em in a hurry? Want to unload some? Call us." Before long, however, Abe, who had financed the venture, decided that Ben was a drag on the business and conspired with Ted to oust him. That left United Container no longer united and Hymie so furious that he never spoke to Abe again.

Accused of wrongdoing in the past, Abe defended himself with twaddle, saying things like, "When I look in the mirror, I like what I see," or "You'd understand why I did it if you walked in my moccasins." When Mook asked why he kicked

Ben to the curb, Abe came up with new hokum, claiming, "I consulted the best minds from coast to coast who said I did the right thing." To which Dad said, "I don't want to call you a liar, Abe. Let's just say you're careless with the truth."

But neither of them took the matter further. Abe said, "I can't be mad at you, Mook. Who else can I talk Yiddish with?" For his part, my father had spoken his piece.

In 1983 Hymie died. At the funeral, Mook sat with his sisters and Hymie's children and grandchildren in the family section at the front of the synagogue. Abe was seen slipping into the rear of the sanctuary. He paid his respects to Hymie seated alone in the last row.

In families, alliances form and fracture. One minute the Molotovs make peace with the von Ribbentrops, the next they're at war. My father, once the family pariah, ended up on good terms with all the Kirshenbaums while Hymie and Abe spent their final years on the outs. Yet who could have foreseen that there would be another severance of family ties, the ones Dad, Joel and I had with Mom's people, and that this break-up would happen as a consequence of her death?

Chapter 18

Taphephobia

Dr. Ozeran died in 1974, forcing Mom to go doctor shopping. She settled eventually on John Carter, a cardiologist and internist at the Cedarwood Medical Center in St. Joseph, who was treating her for diabetes and a heart arrhythmia, both thought to be under control. Dad's and her marriage, by contrast, was in extremis.

The boost my mother received from lithium hadn't lasted. Weaned off the drug, she crashed several times. The most troubling episode occurred in broad daylight outside 1150 Miami Road, where Uncle Abe and Aunt Lucille were now living, a Frank Lloyd Wright house that had been built for Heath Company founder Howard Anthony. Abe heard screams, looked out the window and saw his sister-in-law lying in the driveway in nightgown and slippers, having walked the three blocks from home. Abe phoned my father, who came to pick her up. The scene Mom created went unexplained. Dad tried to talk to her, but she wouldn't answer and didn't stop crying until she fell asleep for the night at home.

After Mother's death, notes she'd written to herself were

found that were a mélange of hurt feelings. "I'm a failure," she wrote. "Everything I knocked myself out for was believed by my family unnecessary, wrong, vicious, rotten. I haven't one redeeming quality." On another note, she listed complaints Dad supposedly had leveled against her: "I've been crying wolf all these years. I don't have any pain, so he says. I'm a lousy housekeeper...don't serve gourmet meals."

It's true that Dad didn't take Mom's complaints of physical ills as seriously as he should have, but nobody could have called her housekeeping lousy, and it's impossible to think that he asked for gourmet meals from her. The word *gourmet* wasn't in his vocabulary. At dinner at L'Escoffier, a French restaurant in Ann Arbor, he studied the menu, with its *carrée d'agneau, cassoulet* and *foie de veau Lyonnaise,* and concluded, "There's nothing to eat here." When the tuxedoed waiter began reciting the day's specials, Dad spoke over him, asking, "What's he talking about?" Only when it was explained that *boeuf Bourguignon* was a kind of stew did he consent to place an order.

My mother had two late-in-life automobile accidents that I know of. She was at fault in both. One was a hit and run. She backed into a car in a beauty parlor parking lot in St. Joseph without realizing it and drove off. Somebody caught her license plate number, and the police came calling. In the other, she ran a stop sign at Miami Road and Napier Avenue and rammed another vehicle. Dad thought it time to take away her car keys but was reluctant to try. "That's the worst thing you can do to an old person. It destroys their independence," he said.

My mother's erratic driving became a non-issue. On July 29, 1991, she died at the age of 82.

Here I need to get out in front of a false narrative about events surrounding my mother's death that swept through her side of the family, opening wounds that have never healed. The narrative consists of what can charitably be called misunderstandings.

On Frieda Goldberg Kirshenbaum's last day alive, a Monday, she had a morning appointment with Dr. Carter. She'd arranged for her friend Bertha Mindel to drive her. They planned to have lunch afterward. When Bertha arrived to pick her up, she found Mom lying on the living room couch and struggling to breathe. Bertha drove her to Memorial Hospital a mile away. In the emergency room, my mother was pronounced dead of a heart attack. Dad, at work, was called. He was sobbing when he phoned Susan and me with the news. Because of their rocky marriage and his usual stoicism about death, the tears surprised us.

When Susan, David and I arrived in Benton Harbor for the funeral, David was puzzled to hear his grandfather say, "I wonder if she's really dead." I think I can explain. Mook had told me that Grandpa Kirshenbaum had put family members on notice that "if they put me in a coffin, make sure I'm dead." An inordinate fear of being buried alive, a condition called taphephobia, is common in many cultures, including Judaism, which mandates burial within 24 hours of death, creating a time squeeze that presumably increases the risk of declaring somebody a goner who isn't gone. But reform Jews often deviate from the 24-hour requirement, and my mother's funeral wasn't scheduled until 10 a.m. Wednesday, giving my father an extra day to allay whatever doubts he may have had about her death.

Besides Joel and me and our families, the only out-of-town relative to arrive in advance of the funeral was Aunt Edna, who came from California. The youngest of Mom's three sisters, Edna was always on the go. I remember her having red smudges on her teeth, which I thought was from her being too rushed applying her makeup to properly blot her lipstick. I have the same recollection about Mom. The sisters shared the smudged-lipstick chromosome.

In Los Angeles, Edna Rappaport chaired the English department at Mira Costa High School before moving to the larger Redondo Union High School. She and Uncle Harry, also a high school teacher, had two children, Josh and Rachel. When Edna Goldberg and Henry Rappaport married in Chicago on February 13, 1946, Dad drew the assignment of driving the bridesmaids to the synagogue. The weather was worse than any he had experienced as a Chicago taxi driver. The front-page story in the next day's Chicago *Tribune* was headlined CHICAGO BATTLES BLIZZARD and told of high snow drifts whipped by 45-mile-an-hour winds, the closing of Lake Shore Drive and snarled traffic everywhere. "Imagine driving all over Chicago in a storm like that," Dad said. "And every bridesmaid I picked up was homelier than the last."

Edna was 10 when my sister was born. Thrilled to have a niece, Edna came from Chicago to Benton Harbor over her next Christmas vacation to visit her sister Frieda, brother-in-law Milt and nine-month-old Roberta. Years later Edna told me that she babysat Bobbie, who fell down the basement stairs. Bobbie, she said, was screaming terribly, but "thank God she was all right."

My sister was never all right. She was almost a year old when it was determined that she was mentally impaired, which doctors said was caused by her damaged heart cutting off oxygen to her brain. Edna's story made me wonder if Bobbie's fall down the stairs, not her heart, might have been to blame. I don't know if she told my parents about the accident, but I thought my saying anything to them so many years later might cause unnecessary pain, and I kept what Edna told me to myself.

Edna was my favorite aunt. She encouraged me and her other nephews and nieces to read, and she commented favorably on our writings. Five dollars came to me from her on my birthday every year until I turned 13. She sent me a Redondo Union student literary magazine she thought I'd be interested in because it contained poems by a prize student of hers who achieved ignominy: Lynnette "Squeaky" Fromme, the Charles Manson cult member imprisoned for trying to kill President Ford. Lynette's poems were about Dylan Thomas and were excellent.

In 1952 Edna arranged for Joel, our Chicago cousin Ron and me to spend Christmas vacation with Uncle Harry and her in the Bronx, where they then were teaching school. For three boys from the midlands, New York City was a Christmastime wonderland, with Salvation Army and Santa Claus bells ringing from the street corners and Patti Page's "How Much is that Doggie in the Window" blaring from speakers above record store doorways. Edna took us to see Helen Hayes in *Mrs. McThing* on Broadway and to the Empire State Building and the Statue of Liberty. On Christmas Day, Joel, Ron and I watched from the rafters in the old Madison Square Garden as the Knicks defeated the Celtics. On the court below were future Hall of Famers Bob Cousy, Easy Ed Macauley, Carl Braun and Harry Gallatin, but it was Number 10 of the Knicks — Max Zaslofsky! — we cheered for the loudest.

As the eldest of the boys, I explored Gotham on my own. In a scrum pushing onto a subway car, I saw a hand reach into the back pocket of a man in front of me and remove a wallet. As the door closed, the pickpocket exited the car and was swallowed up in the crowd on the station's platform. Danny the

Dip in the *Dick Tracy* comics was fictional; I saw a real-life Danny, part of an educational experience in New York for which I could thank my schoolteacher Aunt Edna.

Of Mom's saved folders of family correspondence, the thickest is the one containing letters from Edna. They're handwritten, some many pages long, often speaking of financial strain. "I don't ever buy a roast except maybe one every few months," Edna writes. "I'm making as many meals as possible with leftovers. I wonder what big families do today!" Mom worried about Edna's money struggles and sent her clothes, household goods, cash, even furniture. Edna was effusive in her thanks and didn't shy from asking for more.

> *"How I do appreciate all the clothes you gave me!..."*
> *"If you clean closets again, think of me..."*
> *"We thank you so much for your huge check..."*
> *"If you are planning to get rid of any of your clothes, I think now [because of weight loss] I can wear your things easily, especially summer clothes..."*

Mother and Edna spoke often by phone, sometimes at length. After a call Edna made that lasted two hours and 10 minutes, she wrote Mom asking her to help pay for it by money order "so Milt and Harry won't know." Some of their conversations ended with the slamming of receivers. "You should talk for a couple of minutes, say what you have to say and hang up," Dad said. "The longer you talk, the greater the chance one of you will say something hurtful." A life lesson that fell on deaf ears.

My mother's generosity to Edna was at the root of some of their arguments. With Mom's largesse came lectures that her sister should do a better job of managing her money. Edna took umbrage. "Your mother has never had to work for a living," she told me. "She doesn't know what it's like to live paycheck to paycheck."

Upon arriving in Benton Harbor for the funeral, Edna began going through Mom's clothes, purses and other possessions. Distracted, Joel and I at first thought she was only helping Dad get a jump on sorting our mother's belongings. What she actually was up to became clearer when she told Joel and me that she'd been searching everywhere for our mother's diamond-banded wristwatch, couldn't find it and would like to have it. There was clothing and other jewelry she said she also wanted. When she asked if she could have Mother's Judaica books, Dad didn't object, and I took two boxes of them to UPS and shipped them to California for her.

As Joel, Dad and I visited in the living room with friends paying condolence calls, Edna could be seen inspecting silverware and serving pieces from the cabinets in the dining area. People asked, "What's that woman doing?" Dad asked Joel and me to speak to Edna. When we told her she was causing a disturbance, she started to cry and said, "You don't want me here." We said of course we did. We told her to make a list of Mom's things she wanted, and we'd work it out with our father later. She agreed and dried her tears.

The next day Mook asked me to type a Harbor Bag Company invoice for him, a task that since the death of his accountant, Chuck Marshall, Mother had sometimes performed for him. The typewriter was in the bedroom where Edna was staying. Entering, I noticed her open suitcase on the floor brimming with jewelry. Edna walked in, saw me and, rushing her words, said, "It's costume jewelry. Your father said I could take it." Dad was walking by in the hallway and overheard. Voice controlled but eyes cold, he said, "Edna, that's a fucking lie" and walked away. He'd had enough of Edna. Joel and I had had our fill of her too.

Edna returned the jewelry. That night she kept to herself. In the morning, I drove her to the bus, and we exchanged muted goodbyes.

I know that Edna came to Mom's funeral out of love, but my father thought there was an additional reason. "She was afraid the gravy train had derailed," he said.

Besides resulting in the troubles with Edna, Mother's death laid bare an animus that her other sisters, Gere and Mirian, had toward my father. Aunt Gere didn't attend the funeral and didn't get around to phoning Dad until five days after Mom's death. Aunt Mirian, widowed since Uncle Sam's death eight years earlier, did attend but churlishly left without speaking a word to my father or, for that matter, to Joel or me either.

Then came a letter to me from Uncle Jack, Gere's husband, that made unmistakable the sisters' feelings about Dad, and Jack's feelings too.

Jack Netboy was an intelligent, affable man but who sometimes seemed to be spoiling for a fight. He had a brother, Anthony, a professor at Portland State College (now University) who wrote books on salmon — an apt topic for a writer named Netboy. Jack also was a writer, his authorship including letters to his hometown newspapers both civic-minded and peevish. When his two-year-old granddaughter was hospitalized after drinking from a bottle of toilet bowl cleaner, Jack wrote the Madison *Capital Times* calling for clearer signage in supermarket household-chemical aisles, a non sequitur since the accident occurred at home and involved a bottle clearly marked as dangerous. All the letter accomplished — besides getting Jack's name in the paper — was to embarrass the family member who left the open bottle within the child's reach.

After retiring to Florida with Aunt Gere, Jack complained to the *Miami Herald* that the local library didn't have a biography of Harry Truman he wanted. The paper ran a photo of him in the library in front of an empty shelf and looking as if his world had collapsed. It must have been a slow news day.

Jack's letter to me, unedited:

Dear Jerry:

Aunt Gerry [Gere] and I think it is time to allow our feelings to be known in the aftermath of your mothers death. A phone call from Aunt Edna after her return from the funeral filled in your reactions and those of your father and of Joel once your mother was buried. Unfortunately Aunt Gerry could not come to see her oldest sister depart much as she would have wanted to. If she had been able she too would have been shocked to hear you denigrate her accomplishments, as told by Aunt Edna who came out of love and grief to be with Frieda. We all knew your mother as a wonderfully warm, caring person, who spent a lifetime...almost 60 years...with a man who almost always cared so little about her and her wants. She devoted her life, contrary to what you may believe, to your fathers welfare. What pleasures there were to relish during her lifetime that she failed to partake of, much as we have done with much fewer resources. When she wanted to spend a winter here in Florida, he would not allow it! Thank G-d she was able to enjoy a few weeks with us some years ago. What a wasted life with a man who really didn't care. Where did all that hatred for our family come from, after all, did he not enjoy all those times when Aunt Mirian and Uncle Sam invited them to their home be it a holiday or otherwise! Why didn't you encourage your father who is so close to your small family, to notice that your mother was such an unhappy person. Jerry think back when Bobby was alive and the many times it was Aunt Gerry and Aunt Mirian who cared for her so lovingly.

I am positive your father did not appreciate that considering his ill manners whenever he could display them for us and that was too many time to recall. Aunt Gerry and I share our life at this point as caring people neither wanting to hurt the other no matter the problem. Why could not your mother and father shared their lives when they grew old. Life will not go on forever for us. It is for shame that Frieda did not live her life to the fullest stranded in such a small environment. She should have broken out of it long, long ago and you and your brother should have been the instigators. Despite what you may believe Gerrys sister Frieda was a highly literate lady. Our "kids" Sharon, Francine and Madie and Rob have always desired us to live our lives at the fullest. With the massive resources at your fathers disposal that would have been easily accomplished.

It will surprise you to know that your mothers sisters are of one mind... that your mother's death was needless. Had she not devoted so much of her energy to pleasing Milton her life might have gone on...maybe. She was out of contact with us except for birthdays and anniversaries and that was because she was so ill, so ill we never knew.

Where was your father the night Frieda was taken to the hospital dying, Where was he when she died.

We are very angry and all the above had to be told.
Uncle Jack

From Jack's letter, it was obvious that Edna had covered up her actions at Mom's funeral by giving the rest of the family a load of hooey. In the Nikos Kazantzakis novel *Zorba the Greek*, two peasant women rummage a dead woman's trunk and steal handkerchiefs, towels, a pair of silk stockings and a garter, but they have the grace to pause before the woman's body and cross themselves, and they plunder in plain view. Edna looted sneakily and lied to Dad, Joel and me, then lied to others when she got home.

I can't imagine what fiction she concocted that made Jack ask about my father's whereabouts the night before Mom died, but I can guess how she came up with the falsity about Joel and me denigrating our mother. Benton Harbor had a new rabbi, Amy Zwieback Levenson, who didn't know Mom well and asked if she could come to the house the night before the funeral to talk to Joel and me for help preparing her eulogy. As we sat with the rabbi on the porch, in burst Edna, taking command as if this were one of her English classes. With the enthusiasm she might have exhibited expounding on the joys of *Tess of the D'Urbervilles*, she began telling Rabbi Levenson that her sister was a revered figure in Benton Harbor's Jewish community and beloved in town generally. Joel and I applied the brakes. Knowing that our mother had made enemies and was viewed warily even by some of her friends, we advised the rabbi that she'd be on safer ground speaking of the deceased's devotion to her sick daughter, her religious convictions and her charitable work without presuming to tell funeral attendees what they thought of her. And that, in her admiring, malarkey-free eulogy the next day, is what Rabbi Levenson did.

Mom's other sisters also spun fairy tales. As Jack makes clear, Gere and Mirian blamed my father for Mom's woes. They should have turned the mirror on themselves. Whatever his shortcomings as a husband, Dad stuck with his wife to the end ("when you take those vows...."), but Gere and Mirian gave up on her as they evidently did on their other troubled sibling, Uncle Irving. In one of his letters to my parents, Irving wrote, "Gere and Jack do not wish to be bothered with my problems." In another, he said, cryptically, "I am unable to spend time with Mirian and Sam for obvious reasons." Gere and Mirian couldn't take Irving with his baggage, and it was the same with Frieda and hers. When Mom's emotional problems worsened, their phone calls to her were infrequent and their visits nonexistent. On their travels from Florida to see their children in Wisconsin, Jack and Gere never detoured to Michigan to see Mom, nor did Aunt Mirian ever come to Benton Harbor simply for a sisterly visit. Mirian's son, Ron, who drove his mother from Chicago to Mom's funeral, complained on arrival about the directions Joel had given him. Directions were needed because Mirian didn't know the way to the town where her sister had lived for six decades.

In his letter, Jack mentions a trip my mother made to Florida at what must have been a better time in her life. He and Gere knew she was no longer up to traveling, and their claiming that my father stood in her way was nonsense. Dad would have been only too willing to have her to travel to Florida. Henny Youngman quipped, "I just got back from a pleasure trip. I took my mother-in-law to the airport." Mook would have amended the joke to make it about taking his wife to the airport. Jack and Gere's supposed invitations for my mother to visit served no purpose other than to allow them to boast about their good fortune to be living where, Jack wrote, "there never is a dawn when the sun doesn't shine. Where else will you see bathing suits advertised in December?"

Jack's broadsides against my father were fueled by grudges

and by seeming envy of his "massive resources." The complaints about Dad's "ill manners" overlooked the loans he made to Jack and other family members, his kindnesses to his nephews and nieces, his affection for Grandma Goldberg and her *bubbe-mayses*, his bucking up a depressed Irving, and, if I may say so, the humor he injected into an often mirthless lot. The only member of the Goldberg clan my father may have been intentionally ill-mannered with was Jack, whom he considered to be self-righteous, thin-skinned and a bit of a fancy Dan. Jack once showed up at a family gathering proudly driving a new Cadillac. "I see you have yourself a Jew canoe," Mook said, using an expression antisemitic if spoken by non-Jews and objectionable even when uttered within the tribe but perhaps could have been taken as the poor joke it was since he at the time was himself driving a Cadillac. Instead, Jack stormed off. "Was he ever hot," Dad said, delightedly.

Mook's life was bookended by estrangements, first with the family he was born into, then with the one he married into. Of the latter schism, he said with customary levity, "I'd rather be with the icebergs in Alaska than with the Goldbergs in Chicago."

Not long after the arrival of Jack's letter, I received a kinder one from his daughter Francine asking what went awry at her Aunt Frieda's funeral. Francine, a cousin four months older than I, was the one relative who seemed to think there might be a story other than the one Edna told. She deserved a reply, and I didn't give her one. I have no good excuse for that, only that I wanted to put the unpleasantness with the Goldbergs behind me and move on.

AT WORK AT *SPORTS ILLUSTRATED*, I received a phone call from a man who said he'd been a student of Edna's at Redondo Union High. He told me that Edna had bragged in class that she had a nephew who worked at *Sports Illustrated* and after that, when reading the magazine, he watched for my byline. "Mrs. Rappaport was a wonderful teacher," he said. I said I was sure she was and thanked him for his sympathies. I didn't tell him I hadn't spoken to Edna since my mother's funeral 11 years earlier and that his call was the first I heard of her death.

I don't know which hit me harder — that my favorite aunt had died or that she bragged about me.

Chapter 19

Punchlines

I had a Black fellow working for me named Hog Eye who disappeared, you hear? I was afraid he died. One day I was in Port Huron, and damned if I didn't run into him. "Hog Eye!" I said, "where you been?" He shushed me. He said, "Mook, I'm not Hog Eye here." I said, "You're not?" He looked around and whispered, "No, here I'm Moon Dog..."

In Saginaw, this fellow, when he heard where I was from, said, "You know, years ago I played poker in Benton Harbor. There was a fellow there, Kirshenbaum — helluva poker player. I heard he died." I said, "You heard he died, huh?" "Yeah. I was sorry about that. Nice fellow, too." I stuck my hand out and said, "Say hello to the ghost..."

Al Hatosky was a good friend, but he had strange ways about him. He took three or four showers a day, and when he wasn't showering, he was talking. He was always bumping his gums. When he got sick, I went to see him. He was in bed and after a while, he said, "Mook, I can't talk anymore." When Al Hatosky couldn't talk anymore, I knew it was curtains.

DAD'S STORIES stick in memory thanks to repetition. "We've heard that one," somebody would interject, but he would press on, unspooling his yarn almost word for word from the last time it left his lips. He could have been the Bard of Benton Harbor preparing for a speaking tour — today Fort Wayne, tomorrow Grand Rapids — and going over his material to keep it sharp.

A Benton Harbor old-timer said to me, "Do you know your father is responsible for half the nicknames in town?" That Dad was a conjurer of nicknames as well as a teller of stories speaks to his prankish nature and powers of invention. One nickname he meted out was Gotta Go Moe, this the man who was always rushing off to transact urgent and unspecified business elsewhere. There also was Meter Man, here the skinflint who never picked up a check with the boys at lunch but unfailingly offered to drop a penny or two in the parking meter. Poopsie? This was the fellow famed for his room-clearing farts.

There was one moniker Mook issued with the gnashing of teeth. This was Gentle Ben, the man who doted excessively on his wheelchair-bound wife. "Unbelievable the way he fusses over her," Dad said. "'Do you need this, sweetie pie?' 'Can I get you that, lovey-dovey?' 'Are you comfortable, honey bun?' It makes us other husbands look bad. Our wives ask us, 'Why can't you be like Gentle Ben?'"

It transpired that Gentle Ben died before his wife did, which surprised many people but not my father, who sagely observed, "A lot of times, the sick bury the well."[1] Nor was he surprised when Mrs. Gentle Ben rose from her wheelchair, restored to good health as if by miracle. "She was like all the other widows," Mook said. "As soon as their husbands die, they go looking for the next one."

Dad's point about widows seeking new mates lost some of its observational edge from the fact that after Mom died, he was open to doing the same. To be sure, he set the highest standards for himself when on the prowl. "I don't want to be with some wrinkled up old thing," he said. He also specified, attaching as much importance to the olfactory as to the dermatological, "I'd rather smell perfume than liniment." Besides the sexism and ageism inherent in those statements, he was guilty of their partner in crime, body shaming. Informed that the matronly movie star Shelley Winters had once been a model, he asked, "What did she model, tents?" When some people generously suggested that a woman of his acquaintance resembled Elizabeth Taylor because, like the film beauty, she had lavender eyes and lustrous black hair, he couldn't let the compliment go unchallenged. "You know where she looks like Elizabeth Taylor?" he said. "Under her arms." To friends of other races and ethnicities, he made cracks he wouldn't have gotten away with as easily if spoken to strangers. Greeting Benny Forestieri, a friend of my brother's, he unfailingly said, "How does your day go, dago?" And he asked a Chinese American woman Joel was dating if she'd do his laundry for him.

But there were also from him displays of unexpected empathy and open-mindedness. Positioning himself as pro-

---

1. Unwittingly echoing Nietzsche's aphorism that "the sick are the greatest danger for the healthy," while at the same time anticipating future studies finding that 40% of caregivers, worn down by their ministrations, die before their charges do.

choice on abortion, he said, "What business is it of mine what a woman does with her body?" Whether others agreed or disagreed with him on this or any other issue didn't concern him. As long as he was treated fairly, he wasn't interested in what political leanings or prejudices were hidden below the surface. "I don't x-ray people," he said.

It's possible to blame some of my father's impolitic and plainspoken statements on the endemic injudiciousness of his generation. When he turned 80, a list of some of his favorite sayings was compiled titled THE WIT AND WISDOM OF MILTON KIRSHENBAUM. Copies were distributed at a birthday celebration at Carriage House, a restaurant on the road to South Bend. As attendees pored over the three typewritten, single-spaced pages required to do justice to Mook's wit and wisdom, there were nods of recognition and sighs of acceptance.

Some entries could have been put more elegantly. *Not all the nuts are in the nuthouse.... Some people who wear shorts shouldn't wear shorts.... There's such a thing as being too damn polite.*

Other expressions would have been at home on fortune cookies. *Don't carry hate in your heart.... May all your troubles be bubbles.... Spend where you must, save where you can....*

For Dad, few subjects were off limits if there was a laugh to be had. Mom's death didn't stop him from joking about her. He told of the two of them driving back to Benton Harbor from visiting Roberta in Texas: "My wife talked non-stop for 1,200 miles and I listened. When we turned onto our driveway, I said, 'Frieda, we're home.' She said, 'Stop interrupting me.'"

No tomfoolery was too timeworn for him. He was sharpest in the evening, he said, because "I only went to night school." The college he attended was, of course, Hard Knox. With his grandsons, he engaged in silliness that had given cavemen and cavechildren giggles. As adults, my David or Joel's Joseph had only to deliver the first line of some years-ago bit of business for Dad to join in as when the boys were little.

Grandpa, is that Hortense?
I don't know — what do you think?
She doesn't look tense to me.

Grandpa, I think you're stupid.
I want a second opinion.
I think you're ugly, too.

If something struck Mook as funny, he didn't guffaw or slap his thigh but emitted a chuckle or at most a couple of chuckles. These were expressions of respect, bestowed on the worthy, withheld from the undeserving. He was a fan of the insult comedian Jack E. Leonard (born Leonard Lebitsky in Chicago) but had no use for the Rat Pack hanger-on Don Rickles, not to be forgiven for usurping Leonard's role as king of the putdowns. He got a kick out of *Grand Ole Opry* cornball comedienne Minnie Pearl, an example of how far afield he was prepared to go if it tickled his funny bone.

He was a devotee of the Black comedian and civil rights activist Dick Gregory. In June 1972 Gregory was working a three-week engagement at the New York cabaret Upstairs at the Downstairs. Dad was visiting Susan and me in the city at the time, and he and I went to see Gregory. In the mostly young, racially diverse audience, my white-haired father stood out. Walking on stage, Gregory noticed him and had himself an icebreaker.

"Good to see you, sir. Where're you from?"

"Benton Harbor, Michigan," Dad said.

"Benton Harbor? I heard they elected a Black dude mayor."

"Yeah, that's why I left."

That brought down the house. Nobody laughed more than Gregory. His show was off to a good start.

Gregory knew Benton Harbor had a Black mayor because it had made national news the previous November when Charles F. Joseph, the 36-year-old manager of a Whirlpool-sponsored counseling center, defeated the seven-term white incumbent, Wilbert Smith. Five years earlier Carl Stokes in Cleveland had become the first African American to be elected mayor of a major U.S. city, and there still were few Black mayors in the U.S., especially in towns as small as Benton Harbor. A few years after Joseph's tenure, Benton Harbor elected as mayor a Mercy Hospital orderly named Wilce (pronounced "Will-see") Cooke. Mook had fun with Hizzoner's name. When Cooke went to Washington seeking financial aid for Benton Harbor but returned with nothing more than an autographed photo of him shaking hands with President Reagan, Mook punned, "Wilce asked Reagan for money, and Reagan told him, 'We'll see, Wilce.'" Dad said of Cooke, "Our town has a mayor who empties bedpans."

Years after beating Dick Gregory to the punchline, my father was KO'd by no less a figure than Muhammad Ali. For a planned *Sports Illustrated* story on sportsmanship, I arranged to interview Ali at his Berrien Springs home, the spread once owned by Louis "Little New York" Campagna. The combination of Ali's humanitarianism on the one hand and his trash-talking and cruel taunting of opponents on the other made him, it was thought, an exemplar of sportsmanship both good and bad. With my father living close by, I took him along, knowing he'd get a kick out of meeting The Champ.

When we arrived, Muhammad Ali was in his living room, finishing up with an aide handling merchandising for him. Ali autographed a pair of boxing gloves and a robe, and after taking photos of Dad and me with Ali, the aide left with the autographed items. Ali and I took seats next to each other. On a table at his side was a stack of Nation of Islam pamphlets that he autographed while we talked. Across the room, on as large a television screen as I'd seen up to that time, a game show was playing, sound muted.

My father sat on a couch opposite Ali and me, content to watch. Ali ignored him to the point of rudeness, never looking his way. For several more minutes, it was the same, Ali failing to acknowledge Dad's presence. Suddenly, Ali looked up as if he only now realized that somebody besides the two of us was in the room. He seemed unhappy about the discovery. Ali eyed Dad coldly and asked in an accusatory tone, "How old are you, anyway?"

"Eighty-three," Mook replied.

Ali softened like butter left out on a warm day. He murmured, "Eighty-three." He repeated the number several times, shaking his head in amazement, as if he was in the presence of Methuselah. "Eighty-three," he kept marveling. "My goodness, that's wonderful.... Imagine.... Eighty-three.... God bless you .... Eighty-three-years old...."

A pause and then: "Still getting any?"

It had been a setup. Usually an effective counterpuncher, Dad could only mumble feebly something about his wife taking pity on him on Christmas and his birthday.

The story on sportsmanship was scuttled, which was just as well because I never got Ali to engage on the subject. He was more interested in clowning. He showed Mook and me card tricks and performed his well-known illusion in which he lifted his heels in a way that made him appear to be levitating. Nor was he through with the japeries. When his wife, Lonnie, appeared, he introduced us and said, pointing to my father, "See that man there?" *Ninety-three* years old!"

My father had been bested in a different way the time he took eight-year-old David to dinner at a Benton Harbor restaurant, Bill Knapp's. For dessert grandfather and grandson both ordered vanilla ice cream. When the ice cream arrived, seeing that David's serving was bigger than his own, Mook pointed to his dish and told the waitress, "Tell the kitchen that if they can't give me more ice cream than this, they can shove it."

The waitress left with Dad's ice cream. Minutes went by and there was no sign of her. Finally, he caught her eye and motioned her over.

"Say, dearie, where's my ice cream?"

"They shoved it."

Dad loved recounting that story. As was the case with Muhammad Ali, he was the butt of a joke rather than the teller of one, but funny was funny.

He also found humor with, and at the expense of, Herschel Rolnick, a slight, fidgety man part *schnook* and larger part *mensch*. Herschel had eked out a living selling used batteries and later worked as a bagger at Meijer Supermarket. Dad was Don Quixote to Herschel's Sancho Panza, but this was a Don Quixote who tilted not at windmills but at Herschel. Long ago a wife breezed in and out of Herschel's life, and my father didn't let him forget it. "Herschel, you were married for one year," Dad said. "Why has it taken you 40 years to recover?" Herschel had idiosyncrasies. He bought long-sleeved shirts and cut off the sleeves. "Wouldn't it be easier just to buy short-sleeved shirts?" Dad inquired of him. At breakfast, Herschel politely told waitresses, "I'll have half a cup of coffee, please." Mook suggested, "Why not just order a cup of coffee and drink half of it? They're going to charge for a full cup anyway. Besides, I'm buying."

Many times, my father said, "There's only one Herschel," meaning that Herschel was an odd duck but too bad there weren't more like him.

Herschel was the rare friend who called my father Milton, not Mook. To repay Dad for picking up most of the checks at meals they had together, Herschel kept saying that he wanted to broil him a steak. It finally happened in Herschel's apartment above the Holly's restaurant in St. Joseph. Too nervous to eat anything himself, Herschel toiled at the stove while Dad read the newspaper. Serving the steak, Herschel hovered as his guest began to eat.

"How's the steak, Milton?" Herschel asked.

"If I survive, I'll let you know," replied Milton.

My father said it was lucky he'd finished reading the newspaper because that's what Herschel used for a placemat.

Herschel later moved to a St. Joseph apartment building where he became buddies with another divorced man living nearby, a retired factory worker, Joe Marcus. They were a mismatched pair — Herschel undersized and meek, Joe muscular and outgoing. In his salad days, Joe tooled around the Twin Cities shirtless in a Cadillac convertible with tattoos of naked women on his arms. When he acquired a family, he returned to the tattoo parlor and had bathing suits put on the women.

Joe had a mustachioed, tough-guy mien that drew the notice of Chicago casting directors, who put him in movies and TV shows, usually as a mobster in crowd scenes. This made him a minor celebrity in the Twin Cities. In the Coen brothers film *The Hudsucker Proxy*, Joe had a rare speaking line. Portraying a businessman named Sears Braithwaite, he shook hands with the actor Tim Robbins, who was playing a certain Norville Barnes. "Glad to meet you, Mr. Barnes," Joe said flawlessly.

In support of his postulation about widows being on the hunt for their next husbands, Mook could point to Joe's mother, Fannie Marcus, who was married five times. Joe's daughter Sheila described for me her grandmother's modus operandi. After each husband died, Sheila said, if Fannie got word of an eligible Jewish man in Chicago, "she'd have my father drive her to meet him. If the man could cook and vacuum, she'd marry him."

As a boy, I bicycled past Mrs. Marcus's house on Western Avenue and saw the names of all five husbands listed on her mailbox. Some people thought this was her way of paying homage to them, but Pop said, "She wants to be sure she'll get all their Social Security and pension checks."

After Mom's death, Dad began spending time at Dunkin' Donuts in St. Joseph, joined there, variously, by Uncle Abe, Aunt Rose and his handyman friend Ken Peterson. Other regulars included Bob Hynd, the former Benton Harbor High School head football coach I'd gotten to know when I was senior class president and he was our class advisor, and the Rev. Donald Adkins, pastor of the Second Baptist Church and father of David Adkins, a Benton Harbor High basketball standout later known as the comedian Sinbad. I don't know if Sinbad ever joined his father at Dunkin' Donuts as I did mine, but the place was laugh-filled without need of a professional comic.

With a man of the cloth in the mix, conversation at the

donut shop inevitably turned to religion. Mook had material to contribute. He said the custom of breaking glass at Jewish weddings had been abandoned because "they're afraid it'll cause the brides to miscarry." He reported that the synagogue had hired a rabbi's assistant. "The rabbi doesn't do anything, and the assistant helps him," he said.

Those jokes were harmless enough, but another Mook told mortified Uncle Abe.

"You know, when I go to the synagogue, I don't have to lock my car."

And why, somebody bit, is that?

"Because all the thieves are inside."

Abe urgently took Dad aside and asked how he could have said such a thing in front of the *goyim*.

Mook shared Abe's concern about how Jews were perceived in the Gentile world. When he saw *Goodbye, Columbus*, the movie adapted from the Philip Roth novella of the same name, he objected to a scene in which a gruff Jewish businessman played by Jack Klugman tells the youth dating his daughter, "In the real world, you need a little *gonif* in you. You know what that means, *gonif*?"

The younger man, played by Richard Benjamin, answers correctly, "Thief."

Mook complained, "People shouldn't hear Jews talk that way about themselves."

He also blanched at some of the business practices of his fellow poker player Sam Unger, owner of Unger's Family Clothiers on West Main Street. Unger periodically displayed a sign in the store's window reading GOING OUT FOR BUSINESS, in which "for" was written small enough to be mistaken for "of." Another sign trumpeted UNGER'S DECLARES WAR ON PRICES. One of Dad's workers excitedly told him

"Unger's has declared war on prices!" When the worker showed up in shoes bought at Unger's that were falling apart after a single wearing, Mook told him, "Looks like Unger's declared war on you."

Unger's Family Clothiers sold cheap jewelry in addition to shoes and clothes. Arriving at the store for a lunch date with Unger, Dad waited while Sam finished up with a customer, a Black man eyeing a wristwatch. Unger quoted a price of $25, and the man put two dollars down to lay it away. Leaving the store with my father, Sam said with a satisfied chuckle, "I'm buying lunch. That watch cost me 75 cents, and the *shvartzer* won't come back. Then I'll sell it to another *shvartzer* for 25 dollars."

"I didn't like that, and I told Sam I didn't like it," my father said. "For all the good Jews do for Negroes, that's why a lot of them don't like us."

How, then, could he have told the donut shop crowd the joke about thieves in the synagogue? His reply to Abe: "They laughed, didn't they?"

> *The wife and I were in California during an earthquake, staying at her sister Edna's house in Torrance. It was the middle of the night, and the house was shaking something awful from the earthquake. Edna had this fat maid...I don't remember her name. We'll call her Bessie. Frieda woke up and said, "What's Bessie doing vacuuming at this hour?" How do you like that?*

Chapter 20

"I Get No Complaints"

The Harbor Bag Company on Riford Street consisted of two conjoined buildings, one housing Dad's office and basement work area with the huge printing press and other equipment, the other building filled floor to ceiling with baled bags. When fire broke out overnight on May 7, 1990, it consumed the first structure, but the one with the bags was spared. Or so Benton Harbor fire chief David Lincoln assured my father. After Lincoln's men reeled up their hoses, embers smoldered unseen for two days, then reignited, burning the second building to the ground. Adding insult to inferno, the city ordered my father to clean up the debris from the fire at his expense.

Destroyed was a fortune in bags and my father's place of business. The blaze had been set intentionally. The target was the building next door, PR&D Casting Company. Two men were responsible, a 21-year-old former PR&D employee who'd been sacked for missing work, and a friend helping him wreak vengeance. They poured gasoline on the wrong building and set it aflame. There was ineptness in the execution but aptness in the timing: the conflagration occurred during Michigan Arson Awareness Week.

The two men went to prison. Sentencing the former PR&D employee to five to 12 years, Circuit Court Judge Zoe S. Burkholz gave him a tongue-lashing. "This fire completely put Milton Kirshenbaum out of business," she said. "His livelihood has been destroyed. The city of Benton Harbor is trying to come back. Businesses are not attracted to cities where residents torch buildings because employees are fired due to absenteeism."

But Milton Kirshenbaum wasn't completely out of business. Well into his 80s, he equated retirement with death and was determined to carry on. With enough bags stored at other locations to serve his few remaining customers, all he needed to keep going were places to park his trucks and himself. These were provided by his nephew Ben, who, after his ouster from the United Container startup with Cousin Ted was thriving with his own carton company. Mook had given Ben a helping hand when he started his business, and his nephew was returning the favor, making his Kirsh Cartons building on West Main Street the Harbor Bag Company's new home. Mook thought it a shame that Ben never knew his grandfather, the Chicago pool hall proprietor Ben Adler. "You were named after a good man," he told Benjamin Adler Kirshenbaum. "I think you take after him."

In one respect my father was better off than he had been before the fire. On Riford Street he no longer had full-time employees, and on some days, he was alone in a desolate part of a crime-ridden city. At Kirsh Cartons, he was in the company of Ben, two secretaries and a dozen warehouse workers. The secretaries were white and the workmen Black, and all called Dad "Uncle Milt." Ben set Mook up in a corner of his office with a desk, and over the desk he posted the photo of his uncle with Muhammad Ali from Pop's and my visit to Berrien Springs. The photo drew as much attention from visitors as the Marilyn Monroe calendar once did in Dad's Riford Street office.

My father showed up at Kirsh Cartons most days for an hour or two. Sometimes Ben pulled up a chair and listened to his uncle tell once-upon-a-time stories. "The reason old people talk about the past is they have no future," Dad liked to say. Ben shared with me a crude joke that Mook mixed in with the cracker barrel nostalgia. I'd heard Pop make off-color remarks, but the color of this one was three shades beyond scarlet, and I wondered why he considered it suitable for his nephew's ears and not mine. Perhaps because he and Ben were businessmen, the ground rules were different for them. I was fine with that. For me, father-son was better than man-to-man any day.

The time Dad spent at Kirsh Cartons and Dunkin' Donuts kept his days full, but his nights were empty. He took to quoting the words of a sainted Albanian nun. "Mother Teresa says that mankind's most crippling disease is loneliness, and I think she's right," he said. I phoned him frequently in the evenings to make sure he was all right. "Other than you, the only calls I get are wrong numbers," he said. His mail, he told me, consisted largely of solicitations from the environmental and other charitable causes to which Mom had donated. Her giving had been more indiscriminate than he realized. "I think she even contributed to Save the Chipmunks in Tennessee," he joked.

One day he offhandedly said, "To tell you the truth, I don't miss her." Although there was much about my mother that I didn't miss either — the hysterics, the bragging, the public scenes — I couldn't have said it as baldly as he did.

My father now was succumbing to the crabbiness that can afflict the elderly as the ticking clock grows louder. His telling the kitchen at Bill Knapp's to shove it had been good for a laugh, but now he complained in all seriousness about having to pay extra in restaurants for the baked potato when it used to come with the rib-eye. When he told a waitress, "This apple pie isn't worth a damn. It used to be good here. What's going on?" it sounded as if he'd suffered a personal betrayal.

He groused that restaurant servers weren't friendly enough — unless they were too friendly. He thought the overly friendly ones were only angling for bigger tips. He once tipped as if he was Diamond Jim Brady, but now, when 15% was the accepted rate for gratuities, he left 11 or 12%, and he rounded down when the standard edged toward 20%. Anti-tipping movements have cropped up at times in the U.S., fueled by the belief that tipping is a way for restaurants to underpay their help and is demeaning to both tipper and tippee. My father disliked tipping simply because he thought he was being taken advantage of.

Occasionally after Uncle Dave died, Mook took his sister Rose to dinner at Tosi's, a popular Italian restaurant in Stevensville where it was impossible not to run into a friend, an enemy or a full menu of both. Aunt Rose was a fixture at Tosi's — she was partial to the fried zucchini — and was friendly with the waitresses, and once, when Dad left a tip she considered insufficient, she tossed a few coins of her own on the table. He took offense. "Here I treat her to dinner, and she insults me like that," he said.

On top of his objections to having to scratch a waitperson's itchy palm, he was unhappy about how costly meals had become, never mind the tip. "I remember when you could get a steak for three dollars, and it was *good*," he said. He didn't need to add that it came with the baked potato.

When he was in his 80s, Mook underwent hip replacement surgery in South Bend performed by Dr. David Bankoff, an orthopedist and longtime Notre Dame football team doctor. The operation alleviated the pain he'd been experiencing, but he took to sometimes using a cane. At Kirsh Cartons, the sound of his tapping cane announced his arrival. "Here comes Uncle Milt," Ben's secretaries and workmen chorused. When he didn't bother with the cane, he steadied himself by grabbing chairs, a table or, unnervingly, lampshades and drapes.

Driving past our old house at 1530 Miami Road, he noticed a woman standing outside. His curiosity piqued, he stopped and hellos were exchanged. The woman said she was an antique collector and was there on business. My father told her the house used to be his. We'll call the woman Marion Roberts. Marion processed Dad's having owned this outstanding house and the Mercedes 300 SE he was driving, and the hook was baited. Susan and I were barely aware of Marion's existence when Dad called to say they were engaged. "She wanted a ring," he explained. It was my mother's diamond ring she wanted and now she had it. Next thing we knew, a wedding date was set. Marion had it all arranged. The knot was to be tied before a justice of the peace in La Porte, Indiana, a few days before Susan and I were planning to visit. By the time we arrived, I'd have a stepmother I'd never met.

One of my responsibilities as assistant managing editor at *Sports Illustrated* was to oversee investigations. To root out chicanery in the sports world, I was abetted by a rigorous senior editor, Sandy Padwe, who would become a professor and acting dean of Columbia Journalism School, and, reporting to Sandy, a team of dogged reporters including Armen Keteyian,

Jill Lieber, Craig Neff, Sonja Steptoe and Bob Sullivan. For added investigative firepower, a non-journalist, Martin Dardis, had been brought aboard. A decorated World War II Army artilleryman, Marty had been a New York state trooper and chief investigator in Miami for Dade County State Attorney and future U.S. Attorney General Janet Reno. While working in Florida, Marty helped Woodward and Bernstein crack the Watergate case by tracking down the Nixon campaign's laundered money in Mexico. He was portrayed in the movie *All the President's Men* by Ned Beatty.

Barrel-chested and gravel-voiced, Marty wrung information out of skittish sources by playing it tough or oozing charm, whichever worked best. He had contacts with police and prosecutors across the country and told of having battled "the linguini and lobster sauce crowd." After dinner together one night on Seventh Avenue in New York, Marty and I exited the restaurant and heard a police siren in the distance. "Ah, they're playing my song," he said.

I was friendly enough with Marty to ask him to check out Marion Roberts as a personal favor. The assignment was up his alley, and he pounced. He got back to me the very next day and told me that it wasn't just antiques that Marion collected but also elderly men of means. "Tell your father to run, don't walk," Marty said.

I passed along Marty's warning to Dad, who took it under advisement, which is to say, he seemingly ignored it. Susan and I considered moving up our visit, but Marion was outracing us. The day before the scheduled wedding, she took my father to her lawyer's office in Berrien Springs to sign what she and the lawyer called a prenuptial agreement.

Dad looked over the document and balked. It basically had two provisions. One was that if he died, Marion would inherit everything. This didn't much concern him. He'd be in the ground, and it wouldn't matter where his money went. Joel and I would get nothing, but he'd been overly generous with us all our lives, and we'd have no cause to object.

It was the other provision that stopped him cold. It held that if the marriage ended, Marion would receive fifty percent of his assets. "You mean you could divorce me the day after the wedding, and you'd get half of everything I have?!" he asked. Marion said she was hurt that he didn't trust her, and the lawyer offered assurances that everything was on the up and up. But Mook said he wanted to show the document to his own lawyer. Perhaps Marty's warning had registered with him after all. He wasn't running but he wasn't walking either.

Al Butzbaugh's law office in St. Joseph was a block from the Berrien County Court House. I was friends with Al and his wife, Tiffany. Al, who was soon to become president of the Michigan Bar Association, was gentlemanly and soft-spoken except when he was in his 50-yard-line seat in the Big House in Ann Arbor yelling his head off for the Michigan football team. He told my father and then called to tell me that the "pre-nuptial" agreement was one-sided and unenforceable but could be costly to fight should that become necessary. He said Mook had reason to file an ethics complaint with the state bar about the Berrien Springs lawyer, but that sounded to Dad too much like suing somebody, and he didn't do it. What he did do was break it off with Marion Roberts.

He next became involved with — real name — Arlene Federighi, a widow he remembered as the *beautifulblonde* who years before worked at the Department of Motor Vehicles license counter. When somebody mentioned that Arlene was available, he phoned her and got right to the point. "Are you still good looking?" he asked.

Arlene was a firecracker. "Why not tell me how *you* look?" she replied.

"I get no complaints," Pop said.

Mook and Arlene were off to the races. She didn't move in with him, but they watched television together, dined out and called on friends. Arlene teased him about his clothes — he now was sporting a bright red cap and high school windbreaker of mine too small for him that he found in a closet— but she didn't try to change him. At Tosi's she occasionally sweetened his tips but was careful he didn't catch her.

For the first time in his life, my father, in his early 90s, had a regular doctor, Abraham Koshy, an Indian-born cardiologist who shared a practice in St. Joseph with his internist wife, Betty. Arlene was taking him to his appointments. She called to tell me that Dad had developed a heart condition and that Dr. Koshy said he shouldn't be driving. He was ignoring the doctor's advice, she said, and still driving both car and truck. She said he was talking about going to the Cleveland Clinic for a second opinion but was dragging his feet.

By now Mook either was the oldest truck driver in America or was vying for the title. One day he was stopped in his truck by a Michigan state trooper who found that it didn't have a fire extinguisher as required by law. Checking Dad's driver's license, the officer did a double take. "Whoa... nineteen-oh-six... That makes you...."

"Ninety-two," Dad said.

"Well, I think I need to show you some respect."

No ticket was issued.

Dad now was spending more time with Uncle Abe, whose wife, Lucille, had died. One day Abe was telling proudly of a 100,000-square-foot warehouse his South Shore Development Company had acquired. He repeated the 100,000 figure one too many times to suit Mook, who cracked, "Abe, all you're going to need is six feet." When Abe died a few days later, Dad rued, "I shouldn't have said that."

As the world shrank around him, Pop clung to what remained of his bag business. On a visit to Benton Harbor, I went with him for lunch at a coffee shop where he'd been friendly with the hostess. A couple of times he'd given the woman burlap for free to use to control weeds in her flowerbeds, for which she'd been grateful, but now he was hounding her to *buy* bags for which she had no need. He approached her, and I saw her turn away with an eyeroll. It angered me to see my father disrespected by this woman, and it pained me seeing him demean himself trying to stay relevant.

The years had caught up with Abe, and they were gaining on my father. His skin took on a pallor, and his brown eyes were rheumy. He was napping more ("I don't get tired, I *stay* tired") and showing up less often at Kirsh Cartons. Visiting Susan and me in New York, he complained during a snowstorm of having cabin fever in our apartment. I was away, and Susan helped him climb over a snowbank to get to Joe Jr.'s, the coffee shop across from our building. She could recognize him through Joe Jr.'s window by his red cap, and when she saw him stand, ready to leave, she went over and walked him back.

When Dad was in Benton Harbor, I got a call from Arlene, who said he had fallen, hit his head and suffered a subdural hematoma that had to be relieved with a burr hole trephination — the drilling of a hole in the skull to remove blood buildup against the brain. A few years after he asked what a headache felt like, he had his answer.

A strategy had to be devised to keep him from driving. Every year since Mother died, he had spent Thanksgiving in the Berkshires with Susan and me, and we suggested that this year he come out earlier than usual. I proposed that I'd fly to Benton Harbor, and we'd go by car to Stockbridge together — and, by the way, I'd love the chance to drive his Mercedes. He said yes to it all. A solution had been found for now. What would happen after Thanksgiving, no idea.

We took the northern route to Massachusetts through Canada. The October weather was crisp, and we were in no hurry. We stayed one night in Hamilton, Ontario, and detoured to see Niagara Falls, which greeted us in all its thundering majesty. On the drive, the conversation turned yet again to how he and Grandpa had had no love for each other. I may have sensed that this was my last chance because the words came out almost without my realizing it.

"Dad, I've always wondered something," I bravely began. "You going to prison — was that one of the reasons Grandpa and you didn't get along?"

I held my breath. The question hung in the air for only an instant.

"I suppose that didn't help," he said.

His answer was so nonchalant that I thought he might have assumed we'd talked about his troubles in South Haven before. More likely, he no longer cared one way or another.

Emboldened, I ran with it.

"Something else. With all the accusations Mom threw in your face, she never once mentioned what happened in South Haven. Is it possible she didn't know?"

"If she'd known, maybe she wouldn't have married me," he said.

This exchange may sound pat, invented by me to tie up loose ends in my story, but if I'd invented anything, I assure you that I would have done better than have Dad give me non-answer answers. From his first reply, I still didn't know how his burglary and imprisonment and the death of Ethel Shapiro Esrig had affected his fraught relationship with Mendel, and the "if" in his second answer didn't tell me what Mom knew or didn't know about his lawbreaking. But I'd gotten across to him that I was aware of this dark chapter of his life, and he could tell that I loved him no matter what.

Not that he should have had any doubt about that.

My father always had been strong for me, and in a not uncommon parent-child role reversal, it was my turn to be strong for him. I was in the driver's seat, not just literally traveling through Canada but in every sense. After our arrival in the Berkshires, I suggested that he finally get the second opinion at the Cleveland Clinic he'd long been talking about. I was prepared to push him on this but I didn't have to. Here again he said yes.

On November 18, 1999, we drove the 50 miles from Stockbridge to Albany International Airport and flew to Cleveland. We spent the night at the Cleveland Marriott. At the hospital the next morning, a nurse helping him onto an examining table placed a pillow under his head and asked, "Are you comfortable, Mr. Kirshenbaum?"

No way was he going to miss a straight line like that. "I make a living," he replied, unburdening himself of what may be the hoariest of all Borscht Belt jokes.

The nurse laughed. At least it was new to her.

Dad was seen by a cardiologist, Dr. Mario J. Garcia. After tests, Dr. Garcia asked me how honest I wanted him to be. When I said my father was still driving, the doctor gave it to him straight. Mr. Kirshenbaum, Dr. Garcia said, had aortic stenosis. Installing a new valve was an option, but because of his age, there was a 20% chance he wouldn't survive the operation. If he did survive, the convalescence would be long and difficult. Without surgery, he had six to 12 months to live.

Mook said no to surgery. "I'm not afraid to die," he said. Then, narrowing his eyes, he looked hard at the doctor and added in a strong voice, "But I'm going to prove you wrong."

On the return flight to Albany, Mook was in a taking-stock mood. He talked about Mom. "Your mother and I didn't have much of a marriage," he said, "but she gave me three beautiful children." I thought of Roberta, gone three decades. I know Dad was thinking of her too. We remained silent for some time before resuming our conversation.[1]

In Stockbridge that night, Susan made up the couch in the living room so her father-in-law wouldn't have to climb the stairs to the bedroom. In the morning, he seemed to struggle eating his scrambled eggs. We thought he was just tired from the trip to Cleveland. We took him with us when we left to run errands. In the car he stared at the car's dashboard and asked what all the numbers were for. Something was wrong. We hurriedly drove to the Berkshire Medical Center in Pittsfield.

In the emergency room, a doctor held up a pocket comb and asked. "Do you know what this is?" Dad shook his head no.

The doctor showed him a set of keys. Again, no idea.

Ballpoint pen? A blank look.

Next the doctor took a quarter from his pocket. Mook brightened and said, "A quarter." Susan and I laughed in spite of ourselves.

My father had suffered a stroke. Could it have been caused

---

1. Roberta's date of death was July 12, 1968. Susan's and my son David's wife, Lisa Schwebke, was born on July 12, 1986. Perhaps numerologists can find meaning in the mirrored dates of the departure of one beloved woman in the family and the arrival of another.

by the shock of the news he'd received 24 hours earlier in Cleveland? He stayed in the hospital through Thanksgiving, then was transferred to Kimball Farms nursing home in nearby Lenox. Visiting him there, Susan showed him a photo of Joel's son, Joseph. "My little Benjie," he said, confusing Joseph with his nephew Ben. One night a nurse caught him wearing another patient's coat and struggling with a locked door, trying to leave the facility. "I have to gas up my truck," he told her.

Susan was at home in Stockbridge and I was at work in New York when a Kimball Farms nurse called and said my father had lost consciousness and been taken by ambulance back to the Berkshire Medical Center. I took a train up from Penn Station and met Susan at the hospital. Dad was in bed, breathing faintly. We spoke to him, hoping he could hear us. After spending two sleep-deprived days by his bedside, I felt a burning sensation on the left side of my forehead and itching in my left eye. I went downstairs to the hospital's emergency room. I had shingles.

When Joel arrived from San Francisco, having him with us was a great comfort. Joel, Susan and I maintained a vigil, taking turns holding Dad's hand as nurses came by to check on him. In his hospital bed, Mook didn't appear to be in pain. He was dying the same way he lived, unhurried and without complaint — one day at a time, sweet Jesus.

Joel was with him in the early hours of April 4, 2000. When he phoned, Susan and I joined him at the hospital. The three of us sat together as the sun came up on a sparkling Berkshires spring day. Dr. Garcia's estimate of six to 12 months had been overly optimistic. The end came four months after the visit to the Cleveland Clinic.

AFTER MOTHER DIED, Mook canceled his B'nai Shalom Synagogue membership. Uncle Abe's son David, now the synagogue president, phoned me. My cousin wanted to caution me that burial of non-members in Benton Harbor's Jewish cemetery cost $5,000. I called and told Dad, who said, "That was nice of David to let you know, but I can be buried in Hartford for $90." I knew he hadn't scouted the cemetery market in the rural Michigan town of Hartford but was only expressing his indifference to his place of burial. After talking it over with Joel, I began secretly paying the dues to maintain our father's membership.

"They keep sending me the Temple bulletin. Don't they know I dropped out?" Dad asked me.

I've never calculated whether it would have been more cost-effective to have waited and made a $5,000 outlay at the time of my father's death, but I believe that keeping him paid up with the synagogue was the right call. It meant that when Dad was laid to rest in the B'nai Sholom cemetery alongside Mom and Roberta and near the graves of Mendel, Gittel, his brothers and other relatives and friends, he would be there not as an outsider but as a member in good standing of the community in which he had lived most of his life. I'd like to think he would have forgiven me for paying his dues on the sly.

My father played it tough, but he had a tenderness uncommon among the Kirshenbaums. He was born into an emotionally buttoned-up clan. Some of my cousins say they never saw their parents show affection to each other. The same was true of our grandparents. Cousin Enid said that Mendel and Gittel had separate bedrooms at opposite ends of the farmhouse. "They weren't at war," Enid said. "They simply ignored each other." Mook, by contrast, was free with the hugs, the "I-love-yous" and the "dearies" and "sweeties." He could be cynical and hard-ass, but how could you make those labels stick when he also was sappy and warm-hearted?

At Twin City Bonders my father bailed out of jail a Notre Dame student who'd been arrested for stiffing a taxi driver. The student took a cab ride from South Bend to Benton Harbor, had the driver drop him off at the front door of the Vincent Hotel and went inside supposedly to get money for the fare only to sneak out a side door. Caught by police, the student told my father that if Notre Dame officials learned of his caper, he'd be expelled. Mook was friendly with the *News-Palladium's* editor, Bert Lindenfeld, and persuaded him to keep the arrest out of the paper, an action that as a journalist I can't condone but point to as an example of Pop's beneficence. For naught, it turned out. The *South Bend Tribune* had a Berrien County stringer who reported the incident, and the young man was expelled.

I was with Dad when Aunt Rose invited him to her home to listen to a tape recording she had of Grandma Kirshenbaum reminiscing. After a minute of hearing Grandma talking in Yiddish, Dad told Rose softly, "Turn it off." The disembodied voice of his deceased mother was too painful for him to bear.

Thoughts of my father come to mind unbidden. One night during our junior year in high school, Buddy Alberts and I got it in mind to check out the Research Pleasure Club, the African American hot spot in the Flats that featured the kind of music we and other friends listened to on WLAC, the Nashville clear-channel station we could pick up on our car radios at night in Benton Harbor if we parked in the right spot and if atmospheric conditions were favorable. WLAC played "race music" by performers like Chuck Berry, B.B. King, Big Mama Thornton and an important discovery of ours who had what sounded like two first names. In the dark of our cars, we sang along with Ray Charles *("Greenback, greenback dollar bill. Just a little piece of paper covered with chlorophyl...")* without yet knowing that he was singing in darkness too.

Buddy and I entered the Research Pleasure Club, two white teenagers hoping not to be carded. We were greeted by a joyous scene — bodies swirling on the dance floor, saxophone blaring, cloud of cigarette smoke, smells of beer and whiskey — when a hand grasped my shoulder. I turned and was relieved to see a familiar face. "Oh, hi, Jack," I said with my most ingratiating smile.

Jack Smith was one of Dad's truckdrivers. He was a large, handsome man who was usually friendly but who now commanded, "You get out of here or I'll tell Mook, and he'll give you hell for being where you don't belong."

I wasn't as worried about my usually permissive father as I was about the pain in my shoulder, which Jack was using as a fulcrum to slingshot me toward the door. If God has a voice, it must be the basso profundo with which Jack addressed me. Buddy and I hightailed it out of the Research Pleasure Club, but I'd had a revelation: God liked to have a good time, had a powerful grip and worked for Mook. That's as good a way as any to explain my father's importance to me.

Dad attended the funerals of too many friends to count, often as a pall bearer. He outlived rotund fishmonger Allen Denn, tough-guy Sammy Price, schlockmeister Sam Unger, lawman Erwin Kubath and every other man of his generation on both the Kirshenbaum and Goldberg sides of our family, including Uncle Jack, the writer of the pen-dipped-in-acid letter I received after my mother's funeral.[2]

---

2. Jack Netboy, 85, was fatally injured in a three-car collision in Hollywood, Florida. on February 29, 1996, while out celebrating his wife's birthday. Aunt

One friend who outlasted him was Herschel Rolnick. In 2016, home for a Benton Harbor High School reunion, I made it a point to see Herschel. I also drove through downtown Benton Harbor, which was showing signs of renewed life, with a couple of new restaurants and a budding arts district consisting of galleries in abandoned buildings and a small community theater on the way. For all that, the reunion was held not in Benton Harbor but in a VFW post in Stevensville, a location more sanitized and thought to be safer.

I sat with Herschel at a picnic table behind his St. Joseph apartment building. He was a spry 98 (he would die at 101), living alone and still driving his car. Because Benton Harbor's Jewish community had dwindled, the town no longer had a fulltime rabbi, and it frequently fell to Herschel, steeped in Jewish ritual, to conduct services at the B'nai Shalom synagogue.

Dad had teased Herschel about his eyeblink of a marriage, his scissored-off shirtsleeves and his half-cups of coffee, but the little man had a hide of steel. As we talked, Herschel said, "I miss your father. I miss his stories and his jokes. Nobody filled a room like he did." We spent an hour together. Herschel said several more times, "I miss your father." At one point he told me that his friend Milton hadn't died at 94, the age on his documents and his cemetery headstone and in the obituary that I wrote for the *Herald-Palladium*. "Your Aunt Rose said your father was older. She said he was 96 or 97."

Gere was 84, but it was only her 21st exact-date birthday observance because she was "a leapling," born on February 29, 1912. Jack, Gere and their daughters Francine and Madeleine were passengers in a car driven by Mom's cousin, the Camp Ojibwa nurse Sima Gebel. The others in the car survived. I learned of the accident in the *Miami Herald*. When I told Dad that Jack died, he said he was sorry to hear it.

I couldn't let that go unchallenged. "What, was Rose at his *bris?*" I asked.

Herschel laughed.

I gave him that one for old times' sake.

Epilogue

In September 2015, Susan and I visited Poland on what for me was a roots trip. I wanted to see Radziłów, the village where my father was born, and I arranged in advance for a guide to take us there. I'd been doing my homework. I knew of Poland's history of virulent antisemitism and had been reading of the horrors of July 1941, during World War II, when some 800 Jewish men, women and children in Radziłów were murdered, most of them herded into a barn that was set afire, others chased down and shot or axed to death. When the rampage was over, the once vibrant Jewish community of Radziłów was no more.

Similar atrocities against Jews occurred in the same days in nearby Polish towns and villages such as Jedwabne, Wilna and Szczuczyn. German forces had recently occupied the area, but it had been established through eyewitness testimony that the crimes were committed not by the Nazis but by the Jews' Polish neighbors.

None of this prepared me for the antisemitic harangue I was subjected to even before Susan and I stepped foot in

Poland. On LOT Polish Airlines Flight 7 from JFK to Warsaw, I was in an aisle seat with Susan next to me at the window. We hadn't yet taken off, and across the aisle from me, a wizened Polish man probably in his mid-60s was already drinking from a plastic cup. On his lap was a bottle of vodka of the size that when you see one gathering dust on the top shelf of a liquor store, you try to imagine how many Volga boatmen it would take to consume its contents. The man, traveling alone, was friendly and eager to talk. He told me he'd worked in the U.S. in a maintenance job but was retired because of a disability. He said he disliked America and was spending much of his time in his native Poland. From the little information I shared with him about Susan's and my itinerary, he knew I was Jewish. He said there had been many Jews in his hometown.

Once the flight began, he invited me to drink with him. I thanked him but declined.

"I don't like people who don't drink," he snapped.

"I drink but not on airplanes," I said.

I explained, truthfully, that on past flights to Europe, whether because of altitude, blood pressure or other issues, I'd become faint and clammy and for that reason had been instructed by doctors to refrain from drinking alcohol on such flights. The man eyed me disbelievingly and strained to see what I was reading. I was three-fourths of the way through *The Crime and the Silence* by Anna Bikont, a reporter for the progressive Warsaw newspaper *Gazeta Wyborcza* who brings exhaustive shoe-leather reporting to bear on the murderous events in 1941 in Jedwabne, Radziłów and other villages and conclusively finds Poles responsible for the massacres.

I was reading on a Kindle, but my prying neighbor was able to make out the book's subject enough to ask, "Why are you reading *that*?" From his tone, I sensed that I shouldn't answer.

As his vodka kicked in, he began a loud, sing-song-y tirade against Jews while repeatedly looking my way. His words were in both Polish and English. There were references in English to "drowning the Jews in the River Jordan" and a stream of other invective toward Jews. The other passengers in our cabin, almost all of whom appeared to be Polish, kept their heads down, seeming to ignore the man. An exception was a young woman seated next to him on his other side who asked to be moved. A stewardess took several minutes before finding an empty seat for the woman in another cabin on the crowded plane.

The man's ranting continued. Because much of it was directed at me, I complained to a stewardess. She spoke to him, and he quieted down only to soon start up again, as loudly as before. Once a different stewardess came by to talk to him without my asking. Another few moments of silence were followed by resumed hollering. By now the man had dispensed with the plastic cup and was drinking directly from the huge bottle. I no longer had to guess what his "disability" was.

Suddenly he leaned toward me and said, voice slurring, "I think I'm going to have to kill you."

I wasn't afraid of this pathetic, drunken man, but I thought that a death threat by one passenger against another was something the plane's captain would want to know about. But when I reported the threat to one of the stewardesses seated at the back of the plane, she gave me a helpless look and did nothing.

Eventually the shrieking ended. My neighbor had passed out. All was quiet, but I was too shaken to sleep. Susan didn't get much sleep either.

As the plane began its descent into Warsaw, a stewardess

passing through the aisles to check seatbelts took the bottle from the man's lap. It was empty.[1]

I'd experienced as ugly an introduction to Poland as could be imagined. I wondered if the reason that only one of the Polish passengers had reacted visibly to the man's outbursts was that they were so accustomed to condemnations of Jews that they were inured to them. But I was determined not to condemn Poles as a whole for one man's actions, which was made easier for me when an elderly Polish woman I hadn't noticed on the plane approached me in the baggage area at Warsaw Chopin Airport and said in English, "I felt sorry for you."

The rest of the trip was rewarding. Kraków, with its cobbled streets, horsedrawn carriages and rundown but intact ancient Jewish quarter of Kazimierz, lived up to its reputation as one of Europe's most charming cities, and Warsaw impressed with its vibrant street life and outstanding museums. One of them, the new POLIN Museum of the History of Polish Jews, differs from Holocaust museums in other world cities in that it focuses less on how Jews died than on how they lived, which at infrequent times in Poland's history had been peacefully. Susan and I also made sobering visits to Auschwitz and Treblinka, the most notorious of the many World War II death camps that Hitler placed on Polish soil.

Radziłów, a well-scrubbed village with rows of peaked-roof

---

1. After the trip I wrote LOT to complain about the Flight 7 crew's handling of the incident. An airline representative, Ewa Onacewicz, replied with an apology, writing, "According to our crew reports, the passenger in question had been requested to act so as his conduct would not disturb other passengers, and alcohol he had carried was confiscated." I didn't bother to advise Ms. Onacewicz that what was confiscated was an empty bottle and that the only way alcohol could have been taken from the man would have been to pump his stomach.

wooden houses, was quiet when we visited on a mid-week afternoon. On side streets, horse-drawn carts carried loads of hay. The only indication that Jews once lived here was the faded outline of a *mezuzah* that our excellent guide, Jakub Kuba Łysiak, pointed out to us on the padlocked doorway of a house. Could this be the house in which my father was born? Such are the thoughts one has on a roots trip when there's nothing to go on but one's imagination.

The site of the barn in which Radziłów's Jews were incinerated was a shrine of sorts, a fenced-off space demarking the barn's footprint. Within, a blame game was playing out. A stone monument bore an inscription claiming that the Jews had been murdered by *faszyści*, the Germans, while a makeshift cardboard sign leaning against a fence served as a corrective, clarifying that the victims' "Polish brothers" were responsible. Previous such signs had been destroyed, and this one was certain to be too, by Poles who refuse to acknowledge that their countrymen committed the abominations. Their denials are shared by Poland's right-wing Law and Justice party, which held power from 2015 to 2023 and seeks to protect the country's name by prioritizing the Polish people's own very real suffering through the rewriting of history.

In Radziłów's nearly empty main square, we spoke to a man probably in his early 70s who was keeping an eye on his running-free dog. The man wore a soiled jacket and a cap tilted back on his head and was coaxing every last bit of life from a cigarette that was little more than an ash. When he told us that his father had been present during the 1941 carnage, Jakub tried to question him. The man asked for money, and we left. He likely wouldn't have told us much even for pay. A conspiracy of silence exists in places like Radziłów, where many residents live in houses once owned by Jews and are suspicious of outsiders asking questions.

Poland's three million Jews were God-fearing but also godforsaken. They were wiped off the map, accounting for half the number of Jews killed in the Holocaust overall. None of the doomed Jews of Europe journeyed to far-off destinations with names like Philadelphia and Ellis Island on oceangoing ships such as *SS Merion* and *Kronprinzessin Cecille*. Their collective fate is a tragedy of history avoided by those who emigrated to America.

It's likely that I have Kirshenbaum relatives who died in Europe's 20th Century savagery. I have learned that on the Goldberg side of the family, an aunt of my mother, Rykla Gebel Stupnik, was murdered with her husband and two daughters by Poles in the city of Lomza early in World War II, their bodies thrown into a mass grave. It's inexplicable to me why I never heard Goldberg/Gebel family members speak of this tragedy.

Susan and I returned from Warsaw to New York on an incident-free LOT flight. I considered my roots trip a success. I'd seen where my father drew his first breath and came home filled with joy that it wasn't where he took his last.

Acknowledgments

My son and daughter-in-law, David Kirshenbaum and Lisa Schwebke, thought I needed a project to get me through the COVID-19 pandemic, and this book is the result of their urgings. Musical theater writer David contributed valuable editorial counsel, and Paramount Skydance senior graphic designer Lisa designed the book's covers and assisted with photos. I thank them for that and for the laughter and love that helped even more.

Gratitude to my friend of 60 years *New York Times* Pulitzer Prize-winner Ira Berkow for his insightful reading of two early drafts of the book and for keeping on my case to get the thing published already.

I'm grateful to my *Sports Illustrated* colleague and friend Peter Carry, who line-edited my pages with the attentiveness with which he improved countless stories in the magazine as its executive editor. If you've encountered mistakes in the text, they must have crept in post-Peter.

Thanks also to:

Anna Przybyszewska Drozd at the Institute for Jewish History in Warsaw for her research into my family's life in the Old Country; Dr. Richard M. Katz at Johns Hopkins Hospital for helping me obtain records of my sister Roberta's surgery; *The Sporting News* archivist Steve Gietschier, who unearthed the letter I wrote to that publication; the Benton Harbor *News-*

Palladium and successor *Herald-Palladium*, whose exhaustive coverage of hometown happenings made them essential resources; newspapers.com for sparing me untold hours in libraries spooling through microfilm; the Van Buren County Clerk office's Rachel Semrau and Western Michigan University Library's Lynn Houghton for records relating to my father's crime and imprisonment; publishing legend Michael Korda, who chanced to read my book and said it reminded him of Sidney Offit's *Memoir of the Bookie's Son*, which he assured me was a compliment; Alexander Wolff, author of the wonderful family memoir, *Endpapers*, for his encouragement and for the tip that chronology can be a memoirist's best friend; Jill Rauh of the Benton Harbor Public Library for the photograph of the Benton Harbor Fruit Market, and Judy Bass, Paul Golob, Kurt Reid and My Word Publishing's astonishingly patient Amanda Miller and Bryan Canter for helping me navigate the publishing world's choppy waters.

For their support I thank Cindy Brovsky, Bruce Conybeare, Craig Gartner, Deana Goldstein, Enid Goldstein, Ben Kirshenbaum, Kevin Leonard, Melissa Ludtke, Ivan Maisel, Gabrielle Schonder, Maggie Simmons, Art Tauder and Nancy Williams Watt.

Love and deepest thanks to my brother Joel, who confirmed many of my reminiscences and contributed rich ones of his own. Joel and I were in the trenches together. In many ways, my story is also his.

Above all, I thank my wife Susan, a blessing in my life in every way, for helping me iron out the wrinkles in my writing. Without complaint, Susan read several incarnations of the book, and when I hounded her with, "Does this brilliant sentence make sense?" or "What do you think of the amazing paragraph I've added here?" she didn't hesitate to tell me my changes weren't so brilliant or amazing. When I asked, "Do you remember the time...?" she invariably did, often better than I.

    I dedicate MIAMI ROAD to families. Everybody has one, and everybody has a story to tell about his, hers or theirs if so inclined. I'm happy I've given the telling of mine a whirl. I couldn't have done it if my father and other relatives — including those from whom I became estranged but love all the same — hadn't provided the material.

www.ingramcontent.com/pod-product-compliance
Lightning Source LLC
Chambersburg PA
CBHW031944080426
42735CB00007B/250